POINT!

Also by James B. Spencer:

HUP! Training Flushing Spaniels the American Way
Retriever Training Drills for Marking
Retriever Training Drills for Blind Retrieves
Retriever Training Tests
Training Retrievers for Marshes and Meadows

POINT!

Training
The All-Seasons Birddog

JAMES B. SPENCER

Alpine
PUBLICATIONS
Loveland, Colorado

POINT! Training the All-Seasons Birddog

ISBN 1-57779-059-6

Cover Photo: German Shorthaired Pointer, Westwind's Erick Bon Greif, MH, owned by James B. Spencer. Photo by Ray Taylor.
Text Photos: James B. Spencer unless otherwise indicated
Cover Design: Laura Newport

The information contained in this book is complete and accurate to the best of our knowledge. All recommendations are made without guarantee on the part of the author or Alpine Publications, Inc. The author and publisher disclaim any liability with the use of this information.

This book is available at special quantity discounts for breeders and for club promotions, premiums, or educational use. Write for details.

Printed in 1995 by Howell Book House
Reprinted by Alpine Publications, January 2004.

1 2 3 4 5 6 7 8 9 0

Printed in the United States of America.

To my wife Theresa, who has patiently endured almost fifty years
of my preoccupation with dogs!

Author Jim Spencer prepares to flush a bird. His German Shorthair, Erick, is pointing. *(Ray Taylor)*

CONTENTS

FOREWORD

Perhaps the best way I can express my opinion of this book is to say that I wish I had had it when I started training birddogs back in the 1940s. It would have kept me from making so many of the mistakes that all beginners make. What's more, Jim Spencer is one hell of a writer. This book is easy and enjoyable to read.

Part I will get the newcomer started on the right foot by helping him select the breed and individual dog that's right for him. Too many people fail as trainers because they started with the wrong breed, or the wrong dog within the right breed. Problem is, concise information about each of the many birddog breeds just hasn't been available in one book until now. At least I haven't read another book that brings out the unique character and working abilities of each of the 10 most popular breeds as completely and as briefly as this one does. The 10 chapters on breeds are informative for beginners and enjoyable even for experienced folks like me, who are fully committed to one breed. They are also a great reference for anyone interested in birddogs.

Part II explains what a person needs to know to train the birddog of his choice, regardless of breed, into a fine hunting dog. This training section covers *everything:* puppy training, yard breaking, bringing out the pointing instinct, developing ground pattern, staunching, steadying to wing and shot, honoring, retrieving, and force-breaking. Throughout Jim offers sound, time-tested training techniques, but he also includes approaches that have only become possible recently because of technological advances. Here I speak of remote bird-release traps, the electronic collar (used gently and judiciously), and even the Flexi-Lead as an occasional substitute for the checkcord. The combination of standard training techniques and modern technology, while useful for anyone, is especially good for those who live in urban areas where they don't have access to extensive training grounds with wild birds.

Further, Jim's approach to training is gentle and positive. No one will get in trouble with his wife or kids by training a dog as this book recommends. As I said, even where he recommends the electronic collar, he recommends gentle and judicious usage—and he offers alternative approaches for those who prefer to train without the collar.

In Part III, Jim explains the various ways people go about enjoying birddogs—hunting, of course, but also field trials, hunting tests, and other such formal off-season activities. Let's face it, hunting seasons are short and far apart. If a guy wants to get the most out of his birddog, he should participate in these off-season sports. And with so many to choose from, everyone should find one he likes.

Jim added three appendices that make this book a complete reference. The first contains an extensive glossary of birddog terms that will help the newcomer understand the "foreign language" we old hands have developed over the years. The second explains how to read birddog pedigrees—which fits in nicely with the first section of the book on selecting the right birddog. The third lists names and addresses of important contacts for birddog fanciers—registries, trial and test sponsors, national breed clubs, conservation organizations, birddog magazines, canine tattoo registries, and health clearance organizations.

As I said, I wish I had had such a volume back when I was starting out. And I hope everyone who buys one of our Gunsmoke Pointers will use this book.

I also recommend it to those hunters who have their dogs trained professionally, for it will help them understand how to keep the dog trained and how to deal with the little problems that come up now and then in the life of every birddog.

Herb Holmes,
Gunsmoke Kennels

Pro Bill Holmes, Herb Holmes's son, working a group of high-tailed FDSB Gunsmoke Pointers (and one English Setter). *(R.D. Horne)*

INTRODUCTION

This book is primarily for what I call the "ignored majority" of pointing breed *aficionados* (and *aficionadas*). Who belongs to this group? Every urban and suburban *pater familias* (and *mater familias*) whose lifestyle keeps him or her from following the procedures of training books that assume the reader has access to extensive training grounds with either an abundance of wild birds or a capacity for permanent quail call-back pens, plus all the backyard paraphernalia found around the homes of most professional trainers (force-breaking tables, exercising carousels, *Whoa* posts, etc.). These books—written by pros, clients of pros, and wealthy amateurs—may incite envy among the ignored majority, but don't offer them much useful training information.

Members of the ignored majority live in town—in houses, duplexes, condos, and apartments. They do not own, nor do they have access to, lush and extensive training grounds well-stocked with wild birds. They don't even have small places in the country where they can establish releasable coveys with call-back pens.

They also work for a living, doing the "hard 40" every week. They cannot spend their summers on the Canadian prairie and their winters in the deep South. Further, they have family responsibilities that prevent them from devoting every waking hour to turning promising puppies into bird-finding phenoms. Yet they love birddogs and want to train them properly, even given their limited time and facilities.

How do I know so much about these folks? I'm a charter member of the ignored majority. I live in town, in a single-family dwelling on a normal-sized lot. I've had to learn to scrounge for training grounds. I've had to learn how to train with portable equipment, for I can't leave anything (like a call-back pen) out there, lest some bovine or equine squatter stomp it into the turf. I've had to learn how to train mostly with pigeons, using gamebirds only occasionally. Pigeons prefer sitting on the courthouse roof; they don't willingly stay on the ground in cover. Making one sit tight and flush vigorously (like a quail) at just the right moment takes ingenuity, but it can be done. In this book I tell you how.

Please understand: I have nothing against pros and those wealthy amateurs who have pro-quality grounds and facilities. In some ways, I envy them. But I cannot train their way. That doesn't mean I cannot train another way. I can and I do. If you belong to the ignored majority, you can train my way, too. *What's more, as an amateur, you have a couple of advantages over the pros that you probably haven't recognized.*

First, you suffer no time (and economic) pressure from demanding clients. You aren't making your living at this. You keep your close kin in cider and sowbelly at your regular job; birddog training is just your hobby. You train only your own dog(s). You can train at whatever pace both you and your dog find comfortable. Every pro on earth envies you that one, believe me.

Second, and most important, you can develop greater rapport with your dog than a pro can with any of his. Your dog will bond with you more strongly than any dog can bond with a pro. You spend more total time with your dog—per day, per week, per year—than the pro can with any of the dogs in his string. The pro may spend more time training each one, but you will spend more total time with your dog. He's your buddy, your pet, as well as your birddog. He may even live in the house with you. In any positive training program—like mine—*rapport is everything.* The greater the rapport between you and your dog, the more he will want to please you; the more he wants to please you, the less pressure you will have to apply in training; the less pressure you have to apply, the more enjoyable training will be for both you and your dog.

When you stop to think about it, as a birddog trainer you have it pretty good—for an amateur without pro-quality grounds and facilities. In this book, I tell you how to maximize your advantages and minimize your disadvantages. After you've gotten into this program, you will no longer think in terms of advantages and disadvantages. You will just train your dog and enjoy it!

I have divided the book into three parts: "Acquiring Your Birddog," "Training Your Birddog," and "Enjoying Your Birddog." Although only the middle section discusses training procedures specifically, the entire book is about training. The first and third sections discuss important topics that are peripheral to training and—in my opinion—essential to it. Study all three to get the big picture.

Part I, "Acquiring Your Birddog," explains how you can get the right birddog *for you.* Most beginners who fail as trainers fail because they started with the wrong animal. Training is easy with the right dog. It's difficult to impossible with the wrong one. This section has a chapter on each of our 10 most popular breeds to help you evaluate your choices. It also has a chapter on how to get the right individual dog for you from whichever breed you prefer.

Part II, "Training Your Birddog," tells you how to train your dog so he will hunt your way—even if you are (like me) a city-bound amateur who already has a life.

Part III, "Enjoying Your Birddog," tells you how to enjoy your birddog year-round, not just during the hunting season. You can only hunt two or three months a year. If you do nothing with your birddog the rest of the year, you miss most of the enjoyment you should be getting from him. Others who have faced that same problem have solved it for you with a variety of what I call "dog games"—field trials, hunting tests, and working certificate tests. These may not be *exactly* like hunting, but they are close enough for most of us, *and they are a damned sight better than nothing*. In this section, I tell you what's available.

I have capped this book off with three appendices that should be helpful to all birddog fanciers, but especially to beginners. Appendix I contains an extensive glossary of birddog terms. Appendix II explains the meaning of all the hieroglyphics you will find in birddog pedigrees. Appendix III gives the names and addresses of a variety of important contacts, such as national breed clubs, registries, conservation organizations, commercial birddog magazines, and so forth.

Good luck, and—most of all—*enjoy!*

PART I

ACQUIRING YOUR BIRDDOG

Overview

The adage "you can't make a silk purse out of a sow's ear" applies to all canine activities, but probably more to birddog work than to any other. Birddogs come in more "makes and models" and with more "optional extras" than any other type of sporting dog. Why? Apparently because birddog fanciers have a wider range of expectations than do spaniel or retriever fanciers. But no one birddog can do everything any given person might want. Some excel at one thing, others at other things. Thus, it matters little how great a trainer you may be; if you do not start out with the right dog you will fail to develop the kind of dog you have in mind—and you will waste an irreplaceable year or two of your life in the process.

The term "right dog" has three dimensions: First, it should come from a breed known to operate in the manner the individual owner prefers—and, as indicated above, that varies widely; the dog must have inherited the proper instincts, which only come from proper breeding. Second, it should be properly bred from good working stock. Third, it should have a personality compatible with the boss.

If in your quest for an ideal birddog you miss any of these three dimensions, you will fail. If you select the breed that works as you wish and pick a pup that hasn't been properly bred, it won't develop as you hope. If you get a well-bred pup, one with all the proper instincts for its breed and that suits your personality perfectly, but it comes from a breed that doesn't work according to your preferences, you will not be satisfied with it. Even if you pick a well-bred pup from a breed that functions afield as you wish, you will fail if you and the dog develop a personality conflict that forces an early divorce.

Because of the importance of starting with the right dog (in all three dimensions), this section may well be the most important of the entire book for the person about to buy his first birddog. It may be almost as important for the person who is buying his second—or tenth—birddog, but whose experience has been entirely in one or two breeds. Perhaps a change would be refreshing, perhaps not.

DETERMINING YOUR EXPECTATIONS

Pointing dogs come in a variety of types, each suited to a different set of hunting situations and—more important—to a different set of human personalities and preferences. Chapter 1, "The Birddog's Job in America," explains the various possibilities.

The birddog function in which human preferences vary most is *hunting range*. Some want their birddogs way the hell out there, heading over the next hill, searching for distant birds. Others want theirs within spitting distance all the time. Most fall between those extremes, wanting their dogs hunting somewhere in the 50- to 400-yard range, but in sight most of the time. Regardless of preference, everyone seems to have strong feelings about what constitutes proper range—*and everyone is right!* As Kipling wrote, "There are three and fifty ways/Of composing tribal lays/ And every single one of them is right!"

The problem is, each birddog comes with a built-in natural range, a range the dog finds most comfortable. Although a dedicated and persistent trainer can modify that natural range somewhat, most will agree that it is a lot easier on both halves of the team if the dog's natural range coincides with the trainer's preference. Why fight nature when you can work with it? Some breeds produce a preponderance of wide-running dogs, other breeds specialize in close-working animals, and so on. You need to discover which breeds—or which lines within various breeds—produce the kind of range you like.

But range is not the only consideration. Some people want their dogs to perform functions not covered in the straight birddog's job description—functions like waterfowl retrieving, or even trailing fur like a hound. Some breeds take more readily to these chores than others. People who have such interests should stick to the breeds that will accept these tasks easily. They should also understand that such dogs will have neither as much *class* (animation) while hunting nor as much *style* (loftiness) on point. As in everything, we face trade-offs when we diversify functions.

Each person must also make decisions about features beyond range and non-traditional hunting functions. Different people have different preferences in canine energy levels, different tolerances for canine independence, different expectations of their dogs around home—even different preferences as to size, color, and coat texture.

Until you understand what is available, you cannot make an intelligent choice of a pointing breed. Chapters 2 through 11 present each of the 10 most popular breeds in sufficient detail to help you select the most appropriate breed for your situation.

WHY THESE 10 BREEDS?

I have included a chapter on each of these 10 breeds: Pointer, English Setter, Irish Setter, Gordon Setter, Brittany, German Shorthair, German Wirehair, Weimaraner, Vizsla, and Wirehaired Pointing Griffon. But I must admit I am not completely comfortable with my selections. You see, I can name 10 more pointing breeds Americans use that I have not included: Irish Red and White Setter, Large Munsterlander, Small Munsterlander, German Longhair, Wirehaired Vizsla, Cesky Fousek, Pudelpointer, Spinone, Braque D'Auvergne, and Braque Francais. What's more, that isn't the complete list of birddog breeds in America. I'm not sure anyone knows all of them. Every time I think I do, I read a magazine article about yet another breed we've imported. And another. And another.

Clearly, I cannot devote a chapter to each breed used in America—not even to each breed I know about—and still have room for the other two sections of this book ("Training Your Birddog" and "Enjoying Your Birddog"). So I had to make some difficult choices.

Choices require criteria. The criteria I used in selecting these breeds are: The breed must be recognized by both major birddog registries, the AKC (American Kennel Club) and the FDSB (Field Dog Stud Book); and it must have a sponsoring national breed club that will provide additional information to interested readers. Recognition by the major registries assures you that you can find a registerable dog, one that can participate in suitable off-season dog games (field trials, hunting tests, and working certificate tests). The support of a national breed club assures you of additional information, including breeder lists and club newsletters, as well as the opportunity to become acquainted with other people who share your taste in birddogs.

We classify birddog breeds in several ways. The most common is—strange as it may sound to beginners—by the length of their tails. Long-tailed breeds originated in the British Isles, tend toward specialization in traditional birddog functions, and have been in America almost from the beginning. Bobtailed breeds originated in continental Europe, are frequently called "continental breeds," tend to be more multi-purposed, and have been imported here more recently. In this section, I cover four long-tailed breeds (Pointer and three setters) and six bobtailed breeds (Brittany, German Shorthair, German Wirehair, Weimaraner, Vizsla, and Wirehaired Pointing Griffon).

We also classify birddog breeds by coat type. Shorthaired breeds excel in warmer climates; longhaired breeds withstand cold weather better, and wirehaired breeds suffer less in punishing cover and also in cold-water retrieving. Here I present four shorthaired breeds (Pointer, German Shorthair, Weimaraner, and Vizsla), four longhaired breeds (three setters and Brittany), and two wirehaired breeds (German Wirehaired and Wirehaired Pointing Griffon).

We also classify them by size. For those who prefer a dog of a particular size, I offer two relatively small breeds (Brittany and Vizsla), four large breeds (Gordon Setter, German Shorthair, German Wirehair, and Weimaraner), and four medium-sized breeds (Pointer, English Setter, Irish Setter, and Wirehaired Pointing Griffon).

The temperaments of these 10 breeds offer enough variety to satisfy every taste. Pointers and German Shorthairs are aloof and independent. English Setters, Irish Setters, Brittanys, Vizslas, and Wirehaired Pointing Griffons are affectionate and personable. Gordon Setters, German Wirehairs, and Weimaraners make good watchdogs.

This mix of breeds should allow you to find a breed that functions as you wish, a breed with a compatible personality.

AN OBJECTIVE ASSESSMENT

I have owned dogs of four of the included breeds. I have had frequent contact with most of the others through training buddies and off-season dog games. But even if I had owned dozens of each breed, it would not be fair for me to offer you my opinion only. I have my likes and dislikes, which probably differ from yours in significant ways.

To present as objective a view as possible of each breed, I have consulted three or four longtime breeders/owners/trainers of each—even for those breeds with which I have had extensive personal experience. Whenever possible, I consulted a professional trainer who specializes in the breed. My goal has been to present each breed fully and completely, as seen by people who genuinely like it, people (in many cases) who would have no other. I have tried to avoid judgmental words and comments. The features of a particular breed that I might like or dislike may affect you in exactly the opposite way, so I have tried to identify the characteristics of each breed without indicating whether it looks good or bad from my knothole. Without the help of the various breed experts I have consulted, such impartiality would not have been possible.

Because I am trying to help you become familiar with these breeds as hunting companions, I have limited the coverage of each to features of interest to hunters: physical description (size, coat, color, tail length); temperament; and the breed's hunting niche *in America.* I have not dwelt on breed origins and history, because you won't base your breed selection decision on such irrelevant factors. Besides, once you select a breed, you can find in other sources as much breed history as you care to read. Right now, you need to know what these breeds are like, both to live with and to hunt with.

THE RIGHT DOG FOR YOU

After you have decided how you want your birddog to operate afield and which breed you find most attractive, it still remains to find a properly bred individual within your chosen breed. That is as critical to success as deciding on functions and a breed. In Chapter 12, "Finding the Right Birddog for You," I explain how to go about it. You may be surprised at how strongly I recommend a started dog if this will be your first birddog. Don't make up your mind to get a pup until you have thought about this option awhile. It makes a lot of sense.

Good luck in getting the right birddog for *you!*

CHAPTER

1

The Birddog's Job in America:

A Niche Based on Tradition, Romance, and Modern Reality

A pointing dog must *find* and *point* birds, as Glen Hershberger's English Setter, Champ, demonstrates here, with great style and intensity.

To understand the birddog's job in this country, it helps to understand its place in the overall scheme of American dogdom. That scheme is delineated most clearly in the AKC classification system. The AKC is not the only registry in America. In fact, many would say that the FDSB has better credentials for pointing breeds. However, the AKC is our biggest and oldest all-breed registry that has activities for all breeds. Thus, its classification system best matches the different roles of various breeds in America. The AKC segregates its 137 (and increasing) breeds into seven groups: sporting, hound, herding, working, terrier, toy, and non-sporting. Sporting breeds hunt birds. Hounds hunt fur. Herding breeds handle livestock. Working breeds pull sleds, carts, and so forth. Terriers go to earth after vermin. Toys mostly live in someone's lap. The non-sporting group is a catch-all collection of breeds that don't fit in any of the other six.

The sporting group breeds come in three basic types: pointing dogs, flushing spaniels, and retrievers. Each type was developed to hunt specific birds in specific ways. Pointing breeds range out, find and point upland gamebirds, and hold them for the hunters. Flushing spaniels quarter within gun range, flush upland gamebirds, and retrieve those the hunter shoots. Retrievers sit quietly by the blind until the hunter has downed a bird, then retrieve it.

American sportsmen—being generalists at heart—have expanded beyond the original functions of each type extensively. Many require their pointing dogs to retrieve shot birds, sometimes even making waterfowl dogs out of them, and a few have required a little basic hound work (trailing and tracking fur). Some flushing spaniel owners use their dogs in their duckblinds. Some retriever folks expect their dogs to quarter and flush upland birds like a spaniel. A few—foolishly, methinks—expect them to point.

Thus, today we do not have clear lines between the three types of sporting dog, as we once had. That does not mean that we have a large collection of breeds that can do everything very well. Quite the contrary. Pointing dogs may retrieve, but they cannot mark and remember falls like retrievers, or even like spaniels. Spaniels may swim out and fetch up ducks in pleasant weather, but only the American Water Spaniel can withstand the rigors of late-season duck hunting like retrievers. And retrievers may quarter and flush in the uplands, but they can't do it as effectively as spaniels. Nor can the so-called pointing retrievers cover ground and pick up slight traces of scent like birddogs. Unfortunately, money-mad promoters of such multi-purpose dogs annually persuade thousands of neophytes that these animals (especially those of the speaker's breeding) can outdo all other breeds in every sporting dog specialty. This is utter nonsense, of course, but it sells lots of puppies.

When you hear such a sales pitch, remember this painfully apparent truth: Each type—and each breed—excels in the work it was developed to do; each may also learn to do passable (but not outstanding) work in a few other functions; but no type, no breed, no line, no individual dog stands out above all others in every form of bird hunting.

THE GREAT AMERICAN ROMANCE

Our birddogs need not be all-around whiz kids to hold their place in our hunting world. American upland bird hunters have carried on a mad, passionate love affair with pointing dogs since Colonial days. For an indication of the enduring ardor of that affair, consider the generally accepted name for pointing dogs in America: *birddog*. Flushing spaniels and retrievers also hunt birds, but we reserve the name *birddog* for pointing breeds, just as Southerners reserve the name *bird* for quail. Although Southerners hunt grouse, pheasants, and other avians, when they speak of "birds," they mean quail. That little colloquialism testifies, colorfully, to the reverence bobwhites enjoy in the deep South. Similarly, when American upland hunters say "birddogs," they mean dogs that point. And the term carries a similar but more widespread reverence. Our affair with pointing breeds—birddogs—continues today, and promises to go on indefinitely into the future.

Granted, American hunting conditions are becoming less and less birddog-friendly. Every year America converts more land from rural to urban uses. Even in rural areas, more and more land is posted. As the number of family farms diminishes more and more of this posted land belongs to nonresident owners, which makes it difficult for hunters to contact them for permission to hunt. The growing number of shooting preserves, on which hunters pay to hunt planted birds, indicates how difficult it has become to find decent hunting on wild birds. But even on these shooting preserves, where the entrepreneurs furnish dogs as well as land and birds, resident pointing dogs outnumber spaniels and retrievers probably two or three to one. When a sportsman pays to shoot birds, he expects to see those birds pointed. For many, no other kind of dog work adds as much to the enjoyment of a hunt.

Granted, also, our upland gamebirds no longer sit as nicely for a pointing dog as they did 20 or 30 years ago. Even bobwhite quail, although still the most ideal bird for pointing dogs, run more today than they did when I first hunted them. Pheasants have always had long legs and itchy feet. Grouse sprint more now than ever before. Chukkars run uphill and fly down. From a purely practical point of view, most will admit that flushing dogs are more effective than pointing dogs on avian track stars. A flusher puts the bird in the air with a fly-or-die charge, whereas a birddog stands there politely while the bird scoots through the cover. Even if the dog relocates—and relocates and relocates—he may never pin the bird down long enough for the boss to catch up and flush it.

In spite of these difficulties, pointing dog numbers increase every year. True, they no longer dominate the AKC sporting breed registration numbers, as they did until well after World War II. Retrievers have passed them up. However, we have more pointing *breeds* than retriever or spaniel breeds. The AKC recognizes 10 pointing breeds, 6 retrievers, and 7 spaniels. If we add in all non-AKC breeds (pointing, spaniel, retriever) currently operating in this country, pointing breeds would easily outnumber retriever and spaniel breeds combined. And we import new birddog breeds quite regularly, mostly from Europe's seemingly inexhaustible supply.

Why this continued growth in spite of diminishing areas of opportunity? Pointing dog numbers—breeds and dogs—continue to grow for the same reasons that fly fishing continues to grow in America: *romance* and *tradition.*

Romance: Why do so many fishermen prefer catching one fish on a tiny floating fly laid out with a delicate fly rod over limiting out with spinning or bait-casting tackle? The sheer artistry of the experience, from the initial backcast through creeling the fish. Similarly, many hunters prefer shooting one bird over a class birddog to limiting out over a flushing dog, whether spaniel or retriever. A pointing dog floats through the cover, turning this way and that. Just watching his easy, athletic movement is rewarding. Then he hits bird scent and slams into a stylish point. The hunter walks in, flushes the bird, and shoots it. The dog prances out and retrieves it. This is a visual experience that lingers for years.

Tradition: American sportsmen have favored birddogs since Colonial days. Most of us first learned about them from our fathers and grandfathers. They, in turn, learned about them from their fathers and grandfathers. Shooting over a pointing dog somehow puts a person in touch with his ancestors. Besides, these fiercely independent, active, impatient animals mirror the American character and personality so much that we find them quite comfortable. We identify with them.

Are pointing dogs the most effective, the most productive, upland bird hunters? Who cares? We don't hunt to feed ourselves and our families (a nicety of modern life for which lousy shots like me are grateful). No, we hunt for recreation, to refresh our souls in these stressful days. So the most effective, the most productive dog is the one that best refreshes the soul of its owner. For many, that is a pointing dog. No one needs any more justification for his breed selection than that.

THE BIRDDOG'S TWO ESSENTIAL FUNCTIONS

People use pointing breeds for many jobs afield. And people being what they are (gregarious, cogitative, opinionated, articulate), they disagree strongly—often loudly—about what these dogs should and should not do. However, all agree on two functions: *finding* and *pointing* birds.

Clearly, to merit the name, *a pointing dog must point birds.* The pointing instinct, so strongly developed in these breeds, derives from the basic canine instinct to hesitate and prepare before pouncing. However, in the better pointing dogs, it has been raised to an art form, a *style.* When a birddog fancier speaks of style, he usually means the dog's manner of pointing.

Preferences in style are purely a matter of taste. No style is more effective—in the sense of adding birds to the gamebag—than any other, but some are more enjoyable to watch. Over the years, American tastes in pointing style have changed considerably. Most really old pictures show the dogs pointing with level or slightly elevated tails, with their necks stretching forward, and with a low head. Even today, some prefer this style. But most have come to prefer a style in which the dog is "high on both ends." The tail should be high—a 12 o'clock tail thrills most purists—and the head should also be held aloft. The entire body should appear elevated.

Of course, no point is considered stylish unless it is intense. A dog that flags (waves its tail slightly), looks around, or shows any other softness on point has poor style, no matter where its head and tail happen to be.

The dog points to indicate the presence of gamebirds. The basically trained birddog (called *staunch on point* or simply *staunch*) remains in place and on point until the hunter walks in and flushes the birds. The fully trained birddog (called *broke, steady to wing and shot,* or simply *steady*) remains in place after the flush until released by the hunter either to retrieve or to resume hunting. Staunchness and steadiness are not part of the pointing instinct. They require training. But without a strong pointing instinct, all the training in the world won't make much of a dog.

The second essential function follows necessarily from the first. Clearly, before he can point, *a pointing dog must find birds.* He can't do that walking at heel, so he must move out ahead of the hunter to search for birds.

One look at a birddog tells you he is built to run. These dogs are taller, slimmer, and rangier than spaniels or retrievers. They are full of nervous energy, always dancing around, ready to go. I call Erick (my Shorthair) "my whirling dervish," because when I put a checkcord on him he spins and spins, then runs around and around me, then spins some more. Pointing dogs are independent, curious about the world around them, and more focused on their jobs than their owners. Everything in their nature, both physical and mental, inclines them to be runners and hunters.

But just how far should a birddog range out ahead? Ay, there's the rub. This question stirs more controversy among enthusiasts than any other. So different are the views and so intense the feelings about effective range that I call this the "Great American Range War."

Some, mostly those who hunt atop horses, feel their dogs will find more birds hunting the horizon, half a mile or more ahead. Today this group consists mostly of field trialers. However, some areas of the country and some birds lend themselves to this type of dog: quail hunting in the deep South; chicken hunting on the Canadian prairie; any wide-open place that has birds that sit tight for a pointing dog. With staunch dogs—those that hold the birds until the hunters ride up, dismount, load their guns, and prepare to flush—the wider the range and the faster the pace, the more birds they can find.

At the other extreme, some insist that their dogs stay within the effective range of an open-bored shotgun, about 15 to 25 yards. These folks mostly hunt tough cover and/or spooky birds that won't sit long for the best-trained dog. Grouse hunters especially prefer close-working dogs. So do some pheasant hunters. They keep their dogs within flushing dog range, where a birddog has no functional advantage over a spaniel or retriever. These hunters choose pointing dogs only for esthetic reasons. They enjoy watching them point more than they would a spaniel or retriever flush. *De gustibus non disputandum est* (there is no disputing tastes).

Most pointing dog *aficionados* fall between these two extremes, preferring a medium-ranging dog. Even so, they have a variety of comfort zones. Some feel 100 to 150 yards is far enough, regardless. Others don't panic until their dogs get beyond a quarter of a mile. Folks who prefer medium-ranging dogs hunt every bird that flies, in every type of cover and terrain situation. They argue that by getting out some distance ahead, their dogs find more birds, even if they do cause an occasional wild flush or runaway. They also prefer dogs that adjust their ranges to hunting conditions, staying in close in tight cover and moving out wider only as cover and visibility allow. These hunters want their dogs in sight at least most of the time, feeling that watching their dogs work is the most enjoyable part of the hunt.

The discussions among the various schools of thought on range tend to be as calm and rational as those stimulated by differences on religion or politics. As I said, it's the Great American Range War. In My Frequently Disputed and Often Erroneous Opinion (MFDOEO), none of the combatants is right and none is wrong. To each his own. Every fancier should hunt with a dog whose range he finds comfortable.

The Great American Range War explains, in part at least, why we have so many pointing breeds in America. Through most of this century, we have imported one close-working breed after another from Europe. If a specific breed becomes popular, certain breeders Americanize it to broaden its appeal. They adjust its pointing style to our tastes and increase its range out to the medium distances favored by most Americans. Generally they make these changes through selective breeding within the breed itself. However, rumors persist that some of them, at least in some breeds, speed up the process with surreptitious crosses to other American or Americanized breeds.

Once most of the stock in the breed has been Americanized, those who prefer close-working dogs look for another breed to import. They find one, too, for Europe seems to have an endless supply. But guess what? If we like the new import, breeders Americanize it, just like all its predecessors. Thus, we have more pointing breeds in this country than most of us can name, and we import new ones regularly.

This Americanization process doesn't explain all of our imports. Sometimes a group will import a breed with specific features and/or talents not available in other breeds in this country: various coats, waterfowl retrieving, trailing fur, and so forth.

THE BIRDDOG'S OPTIONAL FUNCTIONS

Most pointing dogs in America do more than just find and point birds. A large percentage retrieve at least the birds shot over their points. Many learn to find downed birds they haven't seen in a *hunt dead* fashion—sniffing around in a small area until they find the bird. Some also do *non-slip* retrieving of doves and/or waterfowl—retrieving in which the dog sits quietly at heel or beside a blind between birds. A few do hound work, like trailing fur and/or tracking wounded big-game animals.

Some enthusiasts tout dogs that do all or most of these things as all-around hunting dogs. The more inspired call such a breed "the one dog for all gamebirds and animals." True only for those who substantially lower their overall performance expectations. No dog that does it all does everything well. Each of these optional functions has some negative impact on the dog's performance in finding and pointing birds. Let me explain; then you make your own decisions.

Retrieving comes in three basic types: fetching up the birds shot over the dog's point; finding downed birds in a "hunt dead"; and non-slip retrieving, as in dove or waterfowl hunting. Even the first type can take a little out of a "broke" dog. The dog that knows it will be sent to retrieve has more incentive to break when the bird falls than has the nonretrieving dog. Keeping a dog that retrieves steady to wing and shot requires more *pressure* (a popular euphemism for *corrections*). That pressure can adversely affect the dog's class and style. Thus, some purists do not allow their pointing dogs to retrieve. A few take retrievers or spaniels along for that chore. However, for most—especially for those who don't fully steady their dogs anyhow—retrieving shot birds after a point is just part of the dog's job.

Most of us also like a dog that can do a basic "hunt dead," too. You know: Your dog is off on a cast when a bird pops up right in front of you. You shoot it and it falls into some nasty cover. You have a much better chance of adding that bird to your bag if your dog will hunt out that patch of cover on command and find the bird for you. True, this does encourage pottering around, but only if it's done too much and too early in the dog's career. Besides, it's really handy.

Non-slip retrieving, at least when it involves long periods of tightly controlled inactivity between birds, can stress a birddog's high-strung nervous system. Further, retrieving doves on land in hot weather can overheat the dog, while retrieving waterfowl in cold water and heavy seas can bring on arthritis. However, retrieving doves from a pond in nice weather, especially for short periods in the morning and evening, shouldn't harm the most delicate canine system. Ditto for early season ducks, except that a mostly white dog may spook birds.

Hound work encourages nose-to-ground hunting. In finding birds, the dog should hunt high-headed so he can search for body scent, not foot scent. The dog with his nose down will crowd birds into flight because he can't pick up their scent in time to point from a safe distance. Most people who use their birddogs as hounds insist that they stay quite close when hunting birds. If you are at all uncertain about it, I recommend that you not expect your dog to trail and track fur.

In the end, you will have to decide which optional functions you want your pointing dog to perform. That decision should affect your breed choice, for some breeds handle different optional jobs better than others. Here are a couple of examples: The wirehaired breeds adapt to foul-weather duck retrieving better than the other breeds, and the German breeds have a more natural inclination for hound work. You will get a better feel for these differences as you read the breed chapters that follow.

Most birddog fanciers expect their dog to retrieve, as Ray Taylor's German Shorthair, Arkie, is doing here.

CHAPTER 2

The Pointer:

Flagship and Fountainhead

A 9-month-old Pointer puppy on point. Notice the high tail, which is highly desired in FDSB Pointer circles. *(Barbara J. Constant)*

Every birddog fancier has strong feelings, at one extreme or the other, about the Pointer. His admirers see him as a bird-finding wizard; his detractors, as an incorrigible outlaw. Either way, this sleek and light-footed animal is the ultimate athlete among birddogs—in fact, among all sporting breeds. Of English origin and often called "English Pointer," the breed has become in the last 100 years or so *the* all-American birddog.

American Pointers are split, totally and irreconcilably, into two types: field-breds and show-breds. So dissimilar that they should be separate breeds, the two don't even share a common registry. The popular, animated, and classy field-breds hunt and win major American Field–type field trials and are registered with the FDSB. The rare, laid-back, and statuesque show-breds prance and pose at dog shows (although a few exhibit field ability, too) and are registered with the AKC.

The Pointer was among the first batch of breeds recognized by both the AKC and the FDSB when these two registries were founded (AKC in 1884 and FDSB in 1900). To this day, the AKC emblem carries the likeness of a Pointer.

An old breed and probably the first to stand its game, the Pointer started its career afield long before the introduction of wingshooting. Falconers used them to locate gamebirds for their birds of prey. Coursers used them to locate hare before turning their (high-speed/low-endurance) sighthounds loose. Historians have found written records of Pointers being so used back into the early seventeenth century.

Like most old breeds, its origins are more inferred than known. Most educated guesses include the Greyhound, the Foxhound, the Bloodhound, and various other progenitors. No one knows for sure whether the breed started in continental Europe and spread to England, started in England and spread to Europe, or started independently in England and Europe.

Regardless, the Pointer has played a significant role in the development of other breeds. Reliable histories of most birddog breeds, although tentative about precise origins, generally postulate an infusion of Pointer blood somewhere along the line.

Further, many claim that the Pointer continues to influence other breeds today—mostly through surreptitious crosses. For example, whenever an established pointing breed has recovered after being in trouble, with only a few remaining working specimens, rumors abound that breeders turned to the Pointer to rejuvenate their stock. Similarly, whenever American breeders have dramatically improved the range and style of a newly imported breed, rumors persist about Pointer crosses.

True or not, such rumors testify eloquently about the esteem the Pointer has earned as a birddog. Think about it: Every time another pointing breed, or even one strain, shows significant improvements in the field, observers "blame" the Pointer.

PHYSICAL DESCRIPTION

Field-bred Pointers, which make up about 90 to 95 percent of the breed's population, come in various sizes, usually from about 21 to about 26 inches at the withers and from 35 to 70 pounds. A few are smaller and a few are larger, but that is the typical range. Their short, sleek coats are mostly white with markings of liver, black, yellow ("lemon"), or orange. They have short backs, well-sprung ribs, businesslike heads, and high-set tails. They are active, nervous animals with tremendous endurance. Everything about them indicates athletic ability. They mature, both physically and mentally, more quickly than any other pointing breed.

Show-bred Pointers vary in size, too, but are more standardized than the field-breds. Taller and more willowy than the field-breds, males stand from 24 to 29 inches at the withers and weigh 55 to 80 pounds. Although they share the same short, sleek coat and the same colors, they are more apt to be heavily marked with the darker color. They have sloping backs, low-set tails, deep but narrow chests, and slab-sided heads with heavy flews. They move gracefully at a dog-show gait, but cannot approach the grace and elegance of the field-breds at higher speeds. They mature, both physically and mentally, much more slowly than do the field-breds.

The AKC Pointer is taller with a more finely chiselled head. Typically it points with a lower tail, too, although it can still be stylish and intent, as Ch. Kinnike Justin, JH, owned by Erica Bandes, shows here. *(Jim Basham)*

TEMPERAMENT

To understand the temperament of the field-bred Pointer, you should keep in mind its historic role in the American birddog world. Since the early 1900s, it has been our top winner in American Field–type trials. Breeders have made the Pointer the premier all age stake dog. It is the featured attraction in the world of Southern plantation trial grounds, Tennessee Walking horses, and professional trainers. To earn its keep in that world, a dog must reach out as far and as fast as necessary to get to the birds first without worrying about where the boss happens to be. Most all age Pointers run so wide that their handlers need mounted scouts to help keep track of their dogs.

Granted, not all American Field trials are big-running, all age affairs. They also offer "shooting dog" stakes for dogs of more modest range. But even in these stakes, the handlers ride horses and the dogs run to prodigious distances. And Pointers dominate these shooting dog stakes, too.

Life is simple for field trial dogs. Winners get bred and losers get . . . ah . . . lost. So most field-bred Pointer litters come from forebears that have distinguished themselves in field trials, either all age or shooting dog types. True, some breeders specialize in foot-hunting Pointers. True also, even in the best-bred field trial litters, some of the pups will hunt quite close. So you can find a Pointer that will hunt at whatever range you prefer—if you look hard enough.

However, it will not be a lap dog. Although there are exceptions, a *typical* Pointer won't show the boss much affection, or even attention. Field-breds have one mission in life: to find birds. People as such make little impression on them. The Pointer's favorite person is whoever happens to be taking it afield at the moment, even if it happens to be a total stranger.

Pointers will bark when strangers approach their owner's property, but they are not territorial. They get along well with other dogs; in fact, they pay little attention to them.

Because the Pointer is so aloof, he can be a real challenge to the trainer. Getting the dog's attention is difficult, and keeping it is sometimes impossible. Furthermore, when the boss has his attention, the unpredictable beast can turn strangely soft and sensitive—or stubborn and pig-headed. Thus, a good trainer must alternate severity and gentleness appropriately if he is to establish and maintain control without cowing the dog.

Other than training, field-bred Pointers don't require much human attention. They can live as comfortably in a kennel as in the home, perhaps not noticing the difference.

They mature earlier than dogs of any other pointing breed. Many can be steadied to wing and shot long before their first birthdays. However, they don't retain training as well as the slower-maturing breeds. They need either year-round work or periodic retraining.

Those who work them year-round should be careful during hot weather. Because of their intensity, these dogs will run and hunt until they drop dead. So it's up to the owner to limit how long they run in hot weather.

The show-breds, although slightly more people-oriented, are also aloof and independent. They enjoy living in the house but do adjust to kennel life, at least on a part-time basis. They are also territorial around home.

"Mine are very protective," said Erica Bandes of Bethlehem, Connecticut, who has for many years bred, shown, and field-trialed show-bred Pointers. "But they have little loyalty. If I were to put one in someone else's home and come back an hour later, it would probably look at me as if to ask, "Who are you?"

Show-bred Pointers have less desire to find birds, but can be acceptable hunters. They mature much more slowly, more like the other pointing breeds, and normally should not be steadied until two years old or older. "Mine don't mature until they are past two years, sometimes two-and-a-half or three years," said Erica Bandes. "But when they're ready for steadying, they get through it very quickly. One of mine was completely steadied in 48 hours. And they retain it quite well. They don't need retraining every year like some dogs do."

HUNTING NICHE

A person wanting a close-ranging field-bred Pointer, especially a first-time buyer, should look at started dogs, not just-weaned pups. A pup, no matter the breeding, may grow up to run wider than such a person likes, leaving him with three bad options: accept the greater range, fight with his dog continuously, or get another dog. Better to buy an older dog with a known and comfortable range.

Because of their field trial backgrounds, field-bred Pointers have the widest ranges of all pointing breeds. All age stake dogs run consistently at distances of one-half to one mile ahead of their handlers. Even shooting stake dogs hang out there a quarter of a mile or more.

Some big-running dogs adapt their range to their situation. They run big when the boss climbs upon a horse, and they stay in closer when he walks carrying a shotgun. Such a dog has learned from experience that when the owner rides a horse, the run will be short, but when the owner walks, it may be an all-day affair. The dog learns to pace himself. However, field-bred Pointers have unbelievable endurance, so they won't adapt as much as other breeds.

Not all field-breds run big. Many pups from all age parents never get out more than 100 yards. Trouble is, you can't tell which these are until they mature. That's why I recommend started dogs to first-time buyers.

"I've had a couple of field trial dogs," said Fred Rowan, longtime Pointer fancier of Atlanta, Georgia, "but mostly I'm a hunter, a foot hunter, so I want a closer-working dog. I've had good success in getting what I want by buying started dogs. It's impossible to peg the range on a puppy."

The better field-bred Pointers have class to spare in every movement. They seem to float through the cover, even when going at breakneck speed. They turn gracefully and when they hit bird scent, their sudden stops can be electrifying. They point very stylishly, with 11 or 12 o'clock tails, head held high, muscles twitching, and eyes popping out with excitement. It is this class and style that has made the Pointer our top fieldtrial dog. It is this class and style that makes it popular with so many hunters.

One other reason for the breed's sustained popularity among both trialers and hunters: They have outstanding noses, probably the best of all sporting breeds. Because this breed covers so much ground so quickly, serious breeders have always stressed the importance of nose. Speed and range do more harm than good if the dog can't pick up the slightest whiff of bird scent as he sails through the cover.

"I won't breed two dogs," said Herb Holmes, breeder of Gunsmoke Pointers for over 35 years, "unless both of them have shown me that they are outstanding bird-finders."

Show-breds tend to hunt closer. They point with a level tail. Quite frankly, so few show-breds see action in the field that it's difficult to say much about their potential there. However, the new AKC noncompetitive hunting tests should bring out more of them. Let's hope so.

Field-breds have less natural retrieving talent than most other pointing breeds. American Field trials don't require retrieving, so those who want their hunting dogs to retrieve may well have to force-break them. Jigger, a field-bred I had years ago, didn't retrieve naturally. He would pick up a dead bird, shake it to make sure it was dead, drop it, and take off looking for another covey. Even after I force-broke him, he did only a minimal job of retrieving.

Show-breds seem to have more natural retrieving instinct. Although AKC field trials don't require retrieving for this breed, many of the trials do include retrieving (because other breeds require it). The new AKC hunting tests require retrieving for all breeds, so future generations of show-bred Pointers may exhibit even more inclination to retrieve.

"The ones I have run in hunting tests," said Erica Bandes, "have retrieved naturally. I have also run several of mine in AKC field trials where retrieving was required, and they did it just fine. I've never force-broken my dogs."

Of all pointing breeds, the Pointer is least comfortable in water. However, they will swim if encouraged early, and they will retrieve the odd bird that falls in or across water. However, they have no place in the duck blind. They have too little coat, too little body fat, and too much energy to sit quietly for long.

CHAPTER

3

The English Setter:

Calendar-Art Birddog

Glen Hershberger's FDSB English Setter, Sunrise, on a stylish point (high on both ends).

As a child back in the 1930s, I learned that these are birddogs. Much later I learned that they are also English Setters. On one wall of the barber shop to which my folks sent me (where, as I recall, a haircut cost two bits) hung a large illustrated calendar. One November, the picture-of-the-month was a country scene featuring a pair of dogs standing stiffly near a split-rail fence against a background of scattered corn shocks. Both dogs had long, silky coats that were mostly white with irregular markings, one of black, the other of orange. Both had elevated tails, cocked front paws, and hypnotized expressions in their eyes. Who hasn't seen such a picture?

"What kind of dogs are those?" I asked, dumb city kid that I was. My canine knowledge didn't extend beyond Scrappy, our feisty Boston Terrier.

"Them's birddogs, son, setting birds," answered the barber with a finality that discouraged further inquiry. He probably knew little more than that about them. During the Depression few folks had the time and money for the recreational pursuits we take for granted now.

I asked no more questions, even though I had no idea why such noble dogs would pay attention to anything as trivial as birds (which to me meant robins and sparrows). Silent, I stared at those two dogs, doing whatever they were doing and doing it so beautifully. I hardly noticed the occasional sting when the barber's not-too-sharp clippers plucked rather than snipped. "Wow," I thought, "them birddogs sure are pretty." To this day, when I hear someone say "birddogs," I conjure up a pair of staunch English Setters near a split-rail fence against a background of corn shocks.

This is an old breed. Documents from the 1500s describe the English Setter plying its trade for falconers and netters. Even today, an occasional throwback will lie down on point, which was what netters trained and bred them to do centuries ago. The very first dog registered with the fledgling AKC back in 1884 was the English Setter Adonis, AKC registration number 1. The breed was among the initial breeds recognized by the FDSB when it was founded in 1900.

"I had one outstanding trial dog," said Glen Hershberger of Newton, Kansas, who has bred, hunted, and run English Setters in American Field field trials for many years, "that started lying down on point. That is severely penalized in trials, so I retired her. I just couldn't cure it. It was in her genes."

This is also a breed that is split—four ways. The major split is between the English Setters registered with the AKC and those registered with the FDSB. A further minor split exists in each of these.

Most AKC English Setters are the large, heavy-coated, mellow "show type." However, a few AKC lines—those bred for AKC field trial competition—are small, light-coated, and athletic. These resemble the FDSB field trial dogs, and a few are dual registered (AKC and FDSB).

"I think the split within the AKC breed," said Bill Miller of Raymond, Nebraska, who has trained professionally for over 20 years, "goes all the way back to the Laverack and Llewellin strains."

Most FDSB English Setters are small, light-coated, big-running dogs bred for competition in the trials conducted by American Field. However, a few FDSB lines—mostly grouse and woodcock dogs that do not run in field trials—are large, heavy-coated dogs more like the AKC show-breds.

An example of an AKC English Setter, M.A. Samuelson's FC Heathrow's Robin Hood. *(Bill Miller)*

Confusing as they are, these overlapping splits benefit those who fancy the English Setter. No matter what kind of birddog a person wants, from a tight-working grouse dog to a horseback field trial animal, he can find it within this one breed. Of course, he has to know which breeders to approach.

PHYSICAL DESCRIPTION

The gorgeous and serene AKC show type and the FDSB grouse type resemble each other. Both are large dogs, with the males standing about 25 inches and weighing about 65 to 70 pounds. (The females run slightly smaller.) They have long and flat coats, fully plumed tails, and long feathering on the legs and underside. They have square muzzles, long and low-set ears, a sloping back, and a low-set tail.

The athletic and energetic field type, whether FDSB or AKC, is smaller, with males standing about 22 inches and weighing about 45 pounds. Their coats are shorter and thinner than those of the show/grouse types, and may be a bit curly. The tail is set on quite high (to facilitate a high-tailed point), the back is level, the hind legs are less angulated, the ears are shorter and set on high, and the muzzle is more wedge shaped.

Colors and markings vary. Most AKC show types are *belton*—blue (really black) belton, orange belton, or lemon belton—in which white is evenly and heavily ticked with the other color. Some are tricolored (blue belton with tan points). Other colors—solid white, the various colors as large spots on a white background, and *roan* (a belton in which the darker color predominates)—occur, but are not looked on kindly in the show ring. The FDSB dogs (both types) and the AKC field-type dogs may be solid white, belton, spotted, roan, or any mixture of these (in white and black, white and orange, white and lemon, or tricolor).

TEMPERAMENT

In addition to being our calendar-art dog, the English Setter may also be our premier fireside birddog. Surely you've seen paintings of a person relaxed by the fireplace after a day afield. Wearing a robe and seated in an easy chair, he holds a book in one hand and pets an English Setter with the other. The dog sits beside him, looking up adoringly, ignoring the drink and snack on the tray beside his muzzle (a sure clue that this is a painting rather than a photograph).

The temperament of the English Setter—either type—makes it an ideal fireside companion. The breed is affectionate, gentle, and eager to please. Even the high-energy field type mellows quickly when allowed to share the boss's quarters on a regular basis. Sure, the dog sheds long white hairs and his swishing tail can launch bric-a-brac in all directions. But for so much canine charm, you can do a little extra vacuuming, and you can put your knickknacks up higher.

The English Setter gets along well with both people and other dogs. It makes a poor watchdog: too friendly. Sure, it will bark when a stranger approaches, but it is not territorial enough to protect its turf.

"The English Setter with a correct temperament," said M.A. Samuelson of San Jose, California, who breeds, shows, and field-trials AKC show-type dogs, "likes other dogs, likes people, and is good with children. If a burglar breaks down the door, an English Setter should lead him down the hall and show him what he's looking for."

Although an ideal house dog, the English Setter can adapt to kennel life, too, as long as it gets daily human companionship—and exercise.

"I shift mine in and out of the house," said Bill Miller. "They adjust to kennel life just fine. They enjoy the company of the other dogs there."

The breed matures more slowly (by far) than the Pointer, but a bit faster than the other setter breeds.

"They are a 'medium' maturing dog," said Bill Miller. "I usually steady them after they're out of the derby—when they're two years old."

"You can start breaking one," said Glen Hershberger, "at about one year, but you have to go slowly and not use much pressure. If you do it right, by the time the dog is two, you will have a broke dog that still has plenty of style."

The English Setter neither needs nor will respond well to harsh training methods. This is a soft, eager-to-please breed. When mature enough to accept each level of training, these dogs enjoy being trained, try to learn, and pick things up easily.

"I wouldn't call them 'soft'," said Bill Miller. "When it comes to hitting nasty cover, they're as tough as a dog gets. But they are sensitive around people."

"The breed has some 'make-me' dogs," said M.A. Samuelson, "and most of them are a little independent, but they want to please and try to figure out what you want them to do. But they can't take much pressure."

They retrain what they learn quite well, requiring only a light brush-up after a long layoff. "They learn quickly and retain well," said Bill Miller. "To a pro that is not all good. If an owner teaches the dog the wrong things, they learn it so well it takes some undoing to change things."

HUNTING NICHE

Whatever you want in range you can get in an English Setter—if you know where to look.

The little FDSB field trial dog can really pick 'em up and lay 'em down. These are horseback dogs. Sure, by American Field–field trial standards, only a few display all age range—which is way the hell out there, folks. But most have shooting dog range, which still requires a horse.

"The pace is so fast in American Field trials," said Glen Hershberger, "that you have to have a horse to keep up—and you have to have a lot of dog to compete. Not many English Setters can keep up with the Pointers, but a few can."

Many of these big-running trial dogs learn to adjust their range for hunting. When the boss climbs aboard his horse, the dog scoots. But when the boss picks up a shotgun and starts walking, the dog shuts down and hunts reasonably close. Why do they do this? Easy. When a horse enters the picture, the dog knows he will run only 30 minutes to an hour. But when the shotgun comes into play, he realizes it may be an all-day foray. In short, the experienced dog paces himself.

"English Setters," said Glen Hershberger, "have great endurance. We breed for that. Of course, we have to keep our dogs in shape, too. But in general, these dogs have lots of endurance, whether trialing or hunting."

The FDSB grouse dog hunts close, usually within gun range, which is appropriate for its mission in life. This also suits many hunters all over the country, those who prefer close-working dogs under all circumstances.

Many self-proclaimed experts say—no, they preach—that AKC show-breds are useless as hunters. Not true, as their success in the new AKC hunting test program has proved.

"Once, when show people first became interested in hunting tests," said Bill Miller, "I put on a field demonstration at the national specialty show [of the English Setter Association of America]. Afterwards, I evaluated field potential in 43 show dogs. I got a point out of each of them within 10 minutes. They still have the right instincts."

The range of AKC English Setters, both show and field types, varies from very close to medium. In AKC trials, all age dogs have a range approximating that of shooting dogs in American Field trials, and gun dogs have a more restricted range, which is more suited to a walking hunter.

"The AKC show and field types have equal ground speed," said Bill Miller. "The little field-breds remind me of a Corvette stuck in second gear. Real busy looking. The long-legged show-breds don't look like they're going anyplace, but some of my Pointers can't keep up with them. They can really stretch out and cover ground. You can adjust range by where you train the dog. If objectives are some distance apart, the dog learns to run bigger, and vice versa."

"We've done a lot of work stretching our show types out," said M.A. Samuelson, "and some of them can run at AKC all age range. But most hunt more close in than that."

Pointing style varies considerably, too. The FDSB field trial dog points *high on both ends*, that is, with both its head and tail high. So does the AKC field type. The other types (AKC show and FDSB grouse type) point with a lower tail, and perhaps with the head lower and extended forward.

"Our AKC breed standard says the tail should be an extension of the backline," said M.A. Samuelson, "so we prefer a lower tail on point. We are more interested in intensity than in specific pointing poses."

"Show people see a 12 o'clock tail as a fault," said Bill Miller. "The little field-bred usually has a high tail. But tail position has been misused for years. Intensity matters more."

The English Setter may or may not retrieve naturally. Those that don't can be force-broken. In fact, many owners feel the force-broke dog makes a better retriever, even if it started life as a natural retriever.

"Since dogs don't retrieve in American Field trials," said Glen Hershberger, "breeders haven't worried much about it. So the instinct has lessened in many dogs. Since I'm a hunter first, I want my dogs to retrieve. In my opinion, force-breaking is the only way to go."

Although not a duck dog, especially in nasty weather, the English Setter takes easily to water and will retrieve birds that fall in or across a pond or stream.

"They're not the greatest water dogs in the world, but they adapt to it if you expose them to it," said Bill Miller. "I've had some of mine retrieve ducks—in mild weather."

"I had one that retrieved ducks for me," said Glen Hershberger, "but not when it was cold. He was too smart for that."

CHAPTER 4

The Irish Setter:

The Comeback Kid

This is Jeannie Wagner's 7-month-old AKC field-bred Irish Setter, Karrycourt's Pandora, pointing staunchly. *(Jeannie Wagner)*

Tall, clean of line, lush of coat, the Irish Setter stands with lofty elegance and moves with freewheeling grace. But, as befits a dog from the land of shamrocks, saints and scholars, he cannot long hide the leprechaun within. Thus fanciers describe him as mischievous, impish, and unpredictable more often than as stately, statuesque, and stunning (all of which he certainly is).

Fanciers treasure their dogs as priceless. The late Horace Lytle, in his 1942 book *Gun Dogs Afield,* devoted a chapter to his famous Irish Setter, Smada Byrd (born in 1921). At the peak of her field trial career, a wealthy man tried repeatedly to buy her. With each attempt he increased the price until it reached an amount many times the appraised value of any trial dog. Mr. Lytle, tiring of the man's persistence, told him he didn't have enough money to buy Smada Byrd, that no one had. The man, aware that Mr. Lytle was not wealthy, responded, "Do you realize how much you're turning down? That dog might die tomorrow, and then where will you be?"

"If she dies tomorrow, she'll die *mine,*" Mr. Lytle answered, and walked off. Smada Byrd did die *his*—many, many years later, after a full life of hunting, trialing, and living with the Lytles. Mr. Lytle never regretted refusing to sell her.

Around 1800 the Irish Setter emerged from the centuries-old confusion of setters that plied their trade in the British Isles. Although its exact ancestry is unknown, the breed carries the blood of the other setters plus that of other breeds, especially land spaniels. People in Ireland call it the "Red Setter" to distinguish it from their similar Red and White Setter. Having arrived here early in the nineteenth century, the breed was among the original group recognized by the AKC in 1884 and by the FDSB in 1900.

Today in America, it is split three ways. First, the FDSB version differs substantially from that of the AKC. Second, the AKC show type differs significantly from the field type. The show type is large, substantial, and heavily coated. The field type is smaller, more lightly boned, and more thinly coated.

The FDSB dog is small, fleet-footed, and athletic. It may be more orange than mahogany, and it may sport a lot of white here and there. Although registered as an "Irish Setter," this FDSB dog is more often called the "Red Setter," for several reasons: to identify it with the original Irish breed; to distinguish it from the AKC show type; and to honor its distinct origin.

Back in the early 1950s, a few fanciers who wanted to bring the breed back to field trial respectability formed the National Red Setter Field Trial Association (NRSFTA). To improve the breed's range and pointing style, they obtained FDSB permission to cross their dogs with English Setters and then, after breeding true for three generations, to register the resulting animals as Irish Setters. This program succeeded so well that Red Setters today hold their own with English Setters and Pointers in big-time American Field trials.

"W.E. (Ned) LaGrande started the movement," said Don Beauchamp of Cheney, Kansas, who has been breeding, hunting, and field-trialing FDSB Red Setters for over 20 years. "He wanted to bring the breed back from oblivion and make it again competitive in American Field trials against the top Pointers and English Setters."

PHYSICAL DESCRIPTION

The AKC show-type male stands about 27 inches at the withers and weighs about 70 pounds. The females are smaller. The muzzle is square, but not as deep as that of the English Setter show type. The ears are low-set and long. The back slopes from the shoulders to the rump. The tail is set on low and carried straight back. The coat is rather long, showing plenty of feathering on the legs, stomach, and tail. The color is a deep mahogany red. Although the AKC standard allows a little white on the head, feet, and chest, most show winners are solid-colored dogs.

The AKC field type varies in size, from little bitty rascals of about 21 inches, all the way up to show-sized animals. The muzzle is more wedge-shaped. The ears are shorter and may be set on a bit higher than the show type. The back is usually level rather than sloped, and the tail is set on high and is carried a bit high. Although the color is the same deep mahogany as that of the show type, the field type often exhibits a little white here and there.

"The major differences between the two AKC types," said Jeannie Wagner of Wellington, Ohio, who has been breeding, showing, field-trialing, and hunt-testing AKC Irish Setters for over 20 years, "are size and the amount of coat. Field types are smaller and have less coat."

"The Irish Setter Club of America," said Robin Johnston of Crooked River Ranch, Oregon, who has been showing, field-trialing, and hunt-testing AKC Irish Setters for about 20 years, "limits entries in the annual futurity field trial to dogs without disqualifying faults. That discourages excessive white, improper color, and so forth in our field-type dogs. But we have no disqualification for size."

The FDSB Red Setter is usually quite small, averaging about 22 inches at the withers and weighing 40 to 45 pounds. The muzzle is wedge-shaped. The ears are short and set on quite high. The topline is level, and the tail is set on quite high and carried up. The coat is shorter and thinner than that of the AKC show type. It may be any color from light orange to deep mahogany and may flash white spots and streaks on the head, neck, chest, and feet.

"You often hear Red Setter people say, and they're only half-kidding," said Don Beauchamp, "that a lot of white probably indicates a pretty good birddog."

Don Beauchamp's FDSB Red Setter, Matlock, on an exceptionally stylish point. *(Don Beauchamp)*

TEMPERAMENT

The Irish Setter character mirrors that of the Irish people: affectionate, devoted to family, proud, courageous, energetic, curious, impish, and refreshingly unpredictable.

"The temperament is typical of Ireland," said Jeannie Wagner. "The dogs are very loving, jolly. Very active dogs. They're owner-oriented, preferring to work for their owners. They love kids."

"An Irish Setter is a fun dog, a happy dog," said Robin Johnston, "and easy to train. They have fantastic memories."

"One reason I like the Red Setter," said Don Beauchamp, "is that it can be a companion and pet as well as a hunting dog and a field trial dog. They're active and quick in the field, but relaxed and easy to live with in the home. They want to please."

In training, the breed may seem alternately soft and tough. Although soft when focused on the trainer, the dog—especially when young, curious, and full of himself—finds the world too full of wonders to allow him to focus long on anything. Distracted from the trainer, he may appear tougher than he is. The perceptive trainer regains the dog's attention by whatever means necessary, and then lightens up again. The foolish trainer turns the training session into a battle of wills that first mystifies, then intimidates, the happy-go-lucky Irisher. An aging Setter may develop a mind of his own, requiring an occasional heart-to-heart talk with the boss; but again, the wise trainer lightens up after making his point.

"They don't handle severe corrections well," said Jeannie Wagner. "Most of them can be steadied to wing and shot without the electronic collar, for example. But they do like to play mind games with you if you let them."

"Some of them are pretty tough," said Don Beauchamp, "but most of them have some softness in them."

The Irish Setter is friendly with people and other dogs. Although not a watchdog, he will bark when strangers approach. He prefers life in the house with the family, but can adapt to kennel life, too, if given sufficient attention and exercise.

The maturity rates vary among the three types of Irish Setters. The fiery little Red Setter matures quite early, often being ready for steadying to wing and shot at 15 to 18 months. The AKC field type matures a bit slower, being ready at 18 to 24 months. The show type takes until 24 to 30 months.

"We have derby dog Red Setters that are completely broke," said Don Beauchamp. "They are winning all age stakes against Pointers and setters. I have broke some of my dogs by 18 months, which is a young derby. The really nice thing about this breed is that they retain their training so well. Once broke, they stay broke."

"Once mature," said Jeannie Wagner, "an Irish Setter learns quickly and retains training quite well. That means you have to teach them right initially and insist on obedience every time. If they learn they can get away with something sometimes, they can be a handful."

"Sometimes," said Robin Johnston, "after feeling I have failed to get something across to one of my dogs, I will put him up and not go back to that lesson for a few days. Usually, when I try it again, the dog remembers what I wanted and does it. That still amazes me about the breed."

HUNTING NICHE

According to the sporting press, the Irish Setter, as a hunter, has taken more 8- and 10-counts than the worst boxer in history—but keeps getting off the canvas for another round.

As far back as I can remember, I have read and reread two somewhat wistful opinions about the Irish Setter as a hunter: first, that this once wonderful gun dog is now worthless afield as a result of show breeding; second, that some mysterious someone in some mysterious someplace is trying to bring the breed back to respectability afield.

The first is nonsense. Show breeding can split a breed, but cannot ruin it. As long as field breeders persevere, the breed will have field dogs. Although field breeders have deserted the Irish Setter in droves through much of this century, a few have continued to breed capable field Irish Setters. Further, the success of show types in the new AKC hunting tests has demonstrated that their hunting instincts may have lain dormant for decades, but they haven't atrophied.

The second usually reflects a vague awareness of the activities of the few field breeders. Since the early 1950s, it may also refer to the efforts of the National Red Setter Field Trial Association.

Contrary to both opinions, the hunting Irish Setter has never gone down for the count, and is today taking on all comers in three weight classes, as defined by range, pointing style, and endurance.

Many Red Setters run big enough for American Field shooting dog stakes and a few can hold their own in American Field open stakes. They point with a high tail, ideally at 12 o'clock. The best Red Setters have the endurance to maintain the breakneck pace and range required for a three-hour heat in all age horseback trials. When the boss picks up a shotgun and starts walking, many of these same dogs will shut down and hunt all day at a more comfortable range.

"We now have all the range and nose we need in our Red Setters," said Don Beauchamp. "Now we are working hard on stamina and endurance. Our Red Setters may not be quite up to Pointer standards there, but we're getting closer all the time. The smart ones shorten up when we take them hunting, but they're still a lot of dog."

Most AKC field-type Irish Setters run wide enough for AKC gun dog stakes, and many of them wide enough for AKC all age stakes. They point with a high tail, usually from 10 to 12 o'clock. They have the endurance to race from objective to objective for an hour in AKC horseback field trials. In hunting, many of them shut down and work all day at a moderate range.

"Our national field trials run for an hour," said Robin Johnston. "An hour is a long time for a dog to run at field trial speed. Hunting for two or three hours can't compare with a one-hour field trial heat."

Most AKC show types hunt quite close, but a few reach out to AKC field trial range. They point with a lower tail, usually from 9 to 10 o'clock. Although they lack the stamina of their smaller kin, they can hunt all day within gun range.

"They work for their owners," said Jeannie Wagner. "They are not self-hunters. They have plenty of endurance, but in hot weather they tire more quickly than dogs with lighter colored coats, of course."

In all three types, some dogs retrieve naturally and some don't. Most Irish Setters, regardless of type, take well to water, although they are not late-season duck dogs.

"I've had some that were natural retrievers," said Jeannie Wagner. "Others couldn't care less about it, but will point dead. I did force-break one. All of my dogs love water—sometimes too much."

"Some retrieve naturally and some don't," said Don Beauchamp. "Most of them like water, if introduced to it young. They have soft mouths."

"Most of mine have some natural retrieving instinct," said Robin Johnston, "but some of them don't want to bring the bird back. I force-break all of mine. They are good water retrievers, as long as it's not too cold."

CHAPTER 5

The Gordon Setter:

The Clydesdale Setter

Barbara Morris's NFC/FC Belmor's Knight Train on point. *(Jim Basham)*

The large, rugged black and tan setter from Scotland derives its name from Alexander, the fourth Duke of Gordon, who bred them in the late 18th century. He did not originate the breed, as its name might indicate. Historians have found written references to black and tan setting dogs dating from about 1620.

First imported into America in the early 1800s, the Gordon was recognized by the AKC in 1884 and by the FDSB in 1900. The breed initially earned respect in this country as a close-working grouse and woodcock dog. Over the years, it has distinguished itself in hunting other birds, especially those best handled by dogs of restricted range with vacuum-cleaner noses—birds such as pheasants, chukkars, and Midwestern quail. Some Gordons have also made their mark in field trials; even more are distinguishing themselves in the AKC's new noncompetitive hunting tests.

The breed is split into two types, one for show and the other for field. Most breeders register their stock with the AKC. Some dual-register with both the AKC and the FDSB. But unlike the other long-tailed pointing breeds (Pointer, English Setter, Irish Setter), the Gordon has no separate FDSB breed. Even so, rumors persist that some field trialers have surreptitiously followed the Red Setter fancy's lead by introducing English Setter blood into their field-bred Gordons to get more range and a higher tail. Some claim such crosses still take place.

The term *show-bred* can mislead the uninitiated. Although it does indicate breeding intended to produce show-ring winners, it doesn't necessarily imply a lack of field ability. Many breeders and owners of show-breds also hunt their dogs.

"Many show-breds," said pro trainer Jim Basham of Nova, Ohio, "are outstanding shooting dogs. Good foot-hunting range, staunch on point, natural backers and retrievers, these dogs work to the gun very well."

The success of some show-breds in AKC hunting tests prove that even the most gorgeous Gordons can do a day's work afield when asked. And the breed has its share of dual champions.

"Those of us who breed dual dogs," said Susan DeSilver of Northford, Connecticut, who has been breeding and exhibiting Gordons to dual championships for many years, "will settle for nothing less than competing successfully with the best in both worlds—shows and field trials."

PHYSICAL DESCRIPTION

The elegant show-breds are imposing animals, carrying more heft and muscle than the other setter breeds. Males stand 26-plus inches at the

Susan DeSilver's DC/AFC Gordon Hill Hangfire is a true dual-purpose Gordon. *(Jim Basham)*

withers and weigh 70-plus pounds. (Females, of course, run a little smaller.) They have gorgeous heads, with low-set ears, deep stops, and square muzzles. The luxurious coat—long and straight, with plenty of feathering on the ears, tail, legs, and belly—is black and tan. That means the coat is mostly black, with tan points at specific places, namely on the feet, over each eye, and on the muzzle, throat, chest, upper thighs, and rump. The AKC show standard allows a white spot on the chest.

"The traditional Gordon Setter," said long-time breeder and amateur trainer Frank Lallas of Brighton, Colorado, "is a dog of considerable substance. The Scots first bred them to hunt on the moors, where the underbrush can be quite punishing. That's why the Gordon has so much bone and muscle."

The field-breds run much smaller, with males standing about 22 inches and weighing about 45 pounds. They may have high-set ears and snipey muzzles. Their coats are shorter and sparser, and may even be a bit curly. Although black and tan, the tan spots may not be so precisely placed, and "misplaced" white spots are common. Some attribute such mismarkings to surreptitious cross-breeding with English Setters. The tail-set is quite high for field-breds, to achieve a high tail on point.

"The field-breds," said Frank Lallas, "are smaller and more active. They're bred to compete in field trials against the bigger-running dogs in other breeds."

The show-bred Gordon matures more slowly, both physically and mentally, than the English Setter. "Most of my dogs," said Susan DeSilver, "have done their big winning in the show ring after their third birthdays. Before then, they just aren't physically mature."

Mental maturity is similarly slow. Most Gordons are not ready for breaking until after their second birthdays, and a few remain puppies past three.

"It doesn't bother me at all," said Susan DeSilver, "to wait until a dog is two-and-a-half or even three years old before steadying—if that's what his individual maturity rate requires."

The field-breds mature earlier, but still not as early as the English Setter. "I have one field-bred right now," said Jim Basham, "that is just 15 months old and is already steady. That's unusual. Most of them aren't ready until about two years."

TEMPERAMENT

As you might expect of a dog developed in the clannish world of Scotland, the Gordon is one dog to his family and quite another to everyone else. With those he knows and loves he is gentle, affectionate, eager to please, and at times playful. To the rest of the world he is aloof, independent, and undemonstrative.

He is a one-family dog rather than a one-man dog. As such, he needs to spend most of his life in close contact with the members of his family. Although he can adapt to kennel life for short periods, he will not develop properly if left there most of his life. He will not bond properly with people, and will therefore be all but impossible to train. Living in the house, he will attach himself to each family member, try to please each of them, and will learn more about them than they will about him.

"This breed," said Susan DeSilver, "needs to have a lot of jobs—pet, family protector, hunting companion, and so on. You can't leave them in the kennel all the time and expect them to develop their full potential. They need to be with people."

Like most one-family breeds, the Gordon is territorial about the home, yard, and possessions of his chosen humans. Thus, he is the best watchdog among the several breeds that originated in the British Isles (the Pointer and the various setters). Although he may not rival some of the German pointing breeds in this capacity, the Gordon is a big, strong, athletic dog. As such, he "ain't nothing to mess with." Even so, he is not aggressive toward people, unless they seem to threaten his family or their possessions. He mostly ignores nonthreatening strangers.

"All birddogs like being with people," said Frank Lallas, "but the Gordon really adopts the entire family, wants to be with them all the time. He is also very protective of the family, very territorial, but he is not mean toward people who are accepted by the family."

The Gordon gets along with other dogs quite well, at least as long as the other dogs want to get along, too.

"They're not wimpy dogs," said Frank Lallas, "but they aren't aggressive either."

When trained by someone with whom he is bonded, the Gordon can be very soft and sensitive.

"They like to be trained," said Jim Basham. "They like to be shown, but they resent being yelled at. They want to please, so all a trainer has to do is show them how."

"They're soft dogs," said Frank Lallas. "I've had an electronic collar for 20 years, but I don't use it on my Gordons. They respond better to more positive training."

However, when a stranger attempts to train him, the Gordon can be tough, stubborn, and devious. This doesn't mean that a pro cannot train the breed. It just means that, to succeed, the pro must spend considerable time, especially at first, bonding with the dog. It also means that the owner must allow the pro the time to do this before expecting noticeable improvements in performance.

"Occasionally," said pro Jim Basham, "I get one that doesn't take to training because of homesickness. Most of them, however, adjust to me just fine, especially after they figure out that I'm the guy who puts them into birds. They'll sacrifice their home for a while if it means getting into lots of birds."

Because the Gordon matures slowly, the trainer should wait on nature before starting each phase of training. Whenever the dog appears confused, he is indicating he isn't yet ready for whatever the boss is trying to teach him. When he is ready, he will grasp it easily, and quickly—and he will retain it for life, with very few repetitions.

"They retain their training very nicely," said Jim Basham. "You don't have to go back each year and re-break them."

"They are thinkers," said Frank Lallas. "They develop a little slower than the other setters, but once they grasp a concept, they retain it."

This retention trait is not an unmixed blessing, for the dog remembers the wrong things he learns, too. Therefore, it behooves the trainer to get it right the first time with this breed.

HUNTING NICHE

Americans first imported the breed as a big, cover-busting, close-working birddog, especially for grouse and woodcock hunting. Most hunting Gordons still fall in that category. However, during the past 100-plus years, Yankee ingenuity developed specialized lines that expanded the breed's role to include more ambitious ranges. Today American breeders offer strains that run big and strains that run medium-wide, as well as the more traditional strains that stay in close.

"The classic Gordon Setter," said Jim Basham, "hunts quite close, like from 20 to 60 yards ahead of the owner. But we also have some strains that do nicely in horseback field trials."

Many dogs from the wide and medium strains learn to adapt their ranges to the boss's needs at the moment. When the boss climbs on a horse (which means a short run in a field trial), the dog kicks in all his afterburners and holds nothing back. When the boss slings his old smokepole over his shoulder and starts walking (which means an all-day hunt), the dog shuts down to a more comfortable pace at a more moderate range. This takes experience, of course, for no dog is born with this savvy.

"I won an American Field National Championship," said Jim Basham, "with as nice a horseback Gordon as you'll ever find. A dog called Casey Jones. But get off the horse, pick up a shotgun, and you can shoot birds over that dog just fine."

"A Gordon should adapt his range to the cover," said Frank Lallas. "If cover is scattered and the country open, he should range out farther. In dense cover, he should stay in closer. My Gordons are capable of adjusting to conditions wherever I put them down."

Endurance varies from dog to dog, strain to strain, but overall, the Gordon is a physically tough dog, one that can put in an honest day's work when properly conditioned. Of course, the black coat limits its endurance in hot weather.

"Overall, endurance in the breed is very good," said Jim Basham. "Once in a while I find one that doesn't have much bottom—my term for endurance—but, in general, this breed has plenty of bottom."

"I hunt mine from sunup to sundown, sometimes every day for a week," said Frank Lallas. "They're sore—just like I'm sore—but they hold up."

Some who have never shot over a Gordon worry that they wouldn't be able to see a black dog out in the field. Actually, black is second in visibility only to white. Thus, Gordons show up against fall foliage better than dogs of most other pointing breeds covered in this book, better in fact than any except Pointers, English Setters, and Brittanys.

Pointing style varies, most markedly between the ponderous show-breds and the flashy field-breds. The field-breds stand their game according to field trial standards, that is, high on both ends—with 11 to 12 o'clock tails and heads held aloft.

"One problem I have noted with the high-tailed field-breds," said Susan DeSilver, "is flagging. In striving for that magic 12 o'clock tail, some breeders have let flagging slip into their stock. One cannot help but wonder if this hasn't been caused by surreptitious cross-breeding with other breeds known for 12 o'clock tails. If true, that is really a pity, for heaven only knows what other genetic time bombs these crosses may have brought into our breed."

The show-breds typically point lower on both ends. Many point with both head and tail level. Some have tails as high as 10 or 11 o'clock. Both show-breds and field-breds seem to have keen olfactory organs.

"One thing I must say about the Gordon," said Frank Lallas, "is they have outstanding noses. I have English Setters, too, and I've had Irish Setters in the past. When it comes to finding birds, my Gordons outdo the other breeds every time."

Some Gordons retrieve naturally, but others require force-breaking before they will fetch shot birds for the boss. Field trials have not encouraged retrieving. FDSB field trials do not include retrieving. It is optional in AKC trials. The Gordon Setter is one of the several breeds that need not retrieve to earn their AKC field trial championships. However, most AKC trials include retrieving in certain areas of the country, even though it's not required. The new AKC noncompetitive hunting tests require retrieving in the upper two levels, so perhaps in a few years more dogs will retrieve naturally—because breeders will breed for it again.

"Some of my Gordons retrieve naturally," said Frank Lallas, "and others don't. Either way, I force-break them—for reliability."

Most Gordons that will retrieve will retrieve from water when asked. Of course, they do not have the body-build or coat for serious, foul-weather ducking. Still, an occasional up land bird does fall in or across water, so swimming is handy.

CHAPTER 6

The Brittany:

The All-American from France

DC The Acremaker, owned by Dave Blais, on point. *(Rob Green)*

In recent years, this apartment-sized birddog has become the most popular AKC pointing breed. It seems to be closing fast on the FDSB Pointer for the number-one spot among all pointing breeds in this country. And for good reasons.

Developed in France in the nineteenth century, the Brit was first imported to the USA early in the twentieth century. The AKC recognized the breed in 1934, FDSB in 1935, as the "Brittany Spaniel," which remains the breed name in France and other countries to this day. In 1982, at the request of the American Brittany Club, both the AKC and the FDSB shortened the name to Brittany to clarify the breed's function as a pointing dog, not a flushing spaniel.

Originally the Brit was a very soft, close-working upland pointer/retriever. American breeders have customized it to our tastes and traditions through years of selective breeding. Still a friendly, eager-to-please little bugger, the Brittany today can cover quite a bit of ground and can also take serious training, as long as the overall thrust is positive.

The Brittany makes a nice combination of family pet and hunting companion, whether the family lives in a high-rise apartment or on an acreage. The dog is small, its coat is relatively short, its tail is short, and the Brit loves people and has a pleasing personality. Although not territorial, it will bark at the approach of a stranger, so does an adequate job as a watchdog. True, it would be more inclined to help a burglar than drive him off, but few burglars know that.

In 1957 Michigan voters selected the Brittany as their official state dog. If all states were to hold such elections, this breed would carry more than some of our presidents.

The Brittany has never split into two types. In fact, AKC statistics through 1992 indicate that the Brittany has more dual champions (266) than any other pointing breed and more than all other pointing breeds combined (258).

"The American Brittany Club really promotes the dual-dog concept," said Velma Tiedeman of Omaha, Nebraska, who was for many years secretary of that club, "even though it is so hard to both show and field-trial a dog simultaneously. You see, the shows and trials are on the same weekends. Most people complete one title and then start working on the other."

The typical Brittany has plenty of energy in the field, but settles down nicely around the house.

PHYSICAL DESCRIPTION

Our smallest birddog, the Brit stands 17 1/2 to 20 1/2 inches and weighs in at 30 to 40 pounds. It is lighter and leggier than the field-bred English Springer Spaniel, which some say it resembles.

The Brit has a light but protective coat that may be flat or wavy, but isn't very long. The ears, the backs of the legs, and the belly carry a little feathering. The colors may be orange and white (any combination), liver and white (any combination), or tricolored (liver and white with orange accents here and there). The American show standard disqualifies a dog with any black in its coat. The standard in France and most other countries allows black and white. Those who favor black and white in this country call their dogs French Brittanys.

The American standard requires a tail no longer than four inches. Some Brittanys are born tailless. Those not so born usually have their tails docked shortly after birth.

TEMPERAMENT

Perhaps the Brit's most significant personality trait is its love for people, and its need for attention and affection, especially from members of its family. No breed wants to please more than this one. No breed tries harder to understand what its owner wants. Thus, training a Brit can be a joy—for those who use a light touch.

"This is a tremendous little dog," said longtime hunter/trialer Francis Clasen of Goddard, Kansas. "They're even-tempered and they love attention. They make terrific pets and family dogs."

"Most Brittanys are really tuned in to people," said Rob Green of Granbury, Texas, who trains all pointing breeds professionally and breeds Brittanys.

"They are very anxious to please," said Rob's wife and fellow pro trainer, Bunny.

"We train over 100 Brits a year," Rob went on, "and we see everything from dogs afraid of their shadow to dogs so tough they would run through a tank, but the norm for Brits is to be the family hunting companion. Over the years Americans have bred a lot of independence into the Brittany, and that has helped their hunting ability substantially. But they still have a very high desire to please. They are easily trainable. I guess I would characterize the breed as a '90s kind of birddog, well suited for our more highly sensitized modern society."

"Definitely *not* a macho dog for the macho hunter," Bunny added. "Today's more gentle training techniques work beautifully with the Brittany."

Overall, then, this is a soft breed, one that responds to gentle training techniques. True, some breeders have developed lines that are atypically tough. But most Brits respond best to considerate, thoughtful training, rather than rough stuff.

"With most Brittanys, the trainer has to be careful that he doesn't overdo corrections," Velma Tiedeman said. "If he makes too many mistakes of that type, he'll ruin what could have been a good working dog."

"They're still a bit soft," said Francis Clasen. "We have bred a lot of that out of them, but they are probably a soft breed for the most part."

Although it can adapt to kennel life, either part-time or full-time, the Brittany makes a wonderful house pet. If anything, living in the house (at least part-time) will make the dog a better hunter, for it will learn more thoroughly what the boss is like, what pleases and displeases him.

"Many of the dogs we get in for training are house pets," Rob Green said, "but they adapt to life in the kennel very quickly. After they learn that this is the place they get to hunt birds every day, they really look forward to coming back and living in a kennel again."

The Brittany matures earlier than some breeds, more slowly than others. Call its maturity rate "average."

"They don't mature like a Pointer," Francis Clasen said. "But they learn quickly because they want to please so much."

"The bitches mature quite a bit earlier than the dogs," Velma Tiedeman said.

"We like to get pups in at about six months for some initial training," Rob Green said. "While they are here for that, we assess when each dog will be ready to finish up—steady to wing and shot, backing and retrieving—and we find most dogs are ready between 12 and 15 months of age. Not all, of course, but most."

"We've finished some Brits as early as 8 months," Bunny Green added.

HUNTING NICHE

With the breed's current popularity, any hunter who wants a pointing dog can find a Brit that can do the job he has in mind. Some breeders specialize in extremely close-working dogs. Others have developed strains that can hang out there on the horizon almost like the widest-running Pointers and English Setters. Most breeders produce stock that falls somewhere in the middle—which is what most hunters want.

"Some of our all age trial dogs range out to a half mile or more," Francis Clasen said, "but most Brittanys stay within foot-handling distance. Today they range wider than they did 30 years ago, when most of them wouldn't get out of gun range. That's due to a lot of selective breeding for a lot of years."

"By selecting a pup from the right litter, a guy can get whatever range he wants," Rob Green said. "True, we can push a dog out some or pull it in some, but each dog has a natural range. Today, you can get whatever range you want in a Brittany."

Pro Rob Green walks in to flush ahead of Art Lopez's Cindy, on point. *(Bunny Green)*

The Brit, regardless of range, retains its strong desire to please and its attachment to the boss, so controlling one requires little effort. The Brit retains its training well, too, so it requires less touch-up work between seasons.

"The Brittany's a smart little dog," Francis Clasen said. "Once they get something, it stays with them. Maybe because they want to please so much. I've seen a Brit go through a tune-up after a two-year layoff, and it only took about a half hour to get him back where he was before his layoff."

"I would give the Brittany higher marks for retention than a lot of other breeds," Rob Green said. "We spend every August, September, and October reconditioning dogs we have previously trained. The Brittanys definitely tune up quicker than the other breeds."

The Brit tends to retrieve naturally, even though AKC field trials for the breed no longer require retrieving.

"We no longer have a retrieving requirement in our AKC field trials," Velma Tiedeman said. "But if you plan to run hunting tests or hunt your dog, you must have it retrieve. Most of them do this naturally."

"You can't go bird hunting if your dog won't retrieve," Francis Clasen said. "All of my Brittanys retrieve naturally. Way back when field trials required retrieving, my trial dogs were force-trained, just to make them better, more reliable retrievers, but they all retrieved naturally."

"Most Brittanys retrieve naturally," Rob Green said. "What's more, thorough training in the command 'Here!' will cure most retrieving problems. Most retrieving problems involve poor return or refusal to return with the bird. I quit force-breaking about five years ago. Bunny's never done it. I don't enjoy it. The dogs don't enjoy it. Besides, you can't make a good retriever out of a dog that has no natural retrieving instinct no matter how thoroughly you force-break him. So why bother?"

The Brit will retrieve from water, too, if properly introduced.

"Our local club used to have water-retrieving fun trials during the summer months," Francis Clasen said. "No big deal, but just a chance to prove our dogs in the water. A few dogs didn't like it, but most of them really loved swimming out to and back with the bird."

"We work our dogs in water because, in hunting, a bird might fall in a pond," Rob Green said. "We don't do any duck hunting, but we have never had a problem getting a Brit to retrieve birds from water."

The Brittany has plenty of endurance, as long as it is in proper condition. Like most dogs, it will adapt its pace to the length of time you usually hunt it at a stretch.

"Physically, they're a pretty tough little dog," Francis Clasen said. "They'll hunt all day if you want them to. Of course, they'll slow their pace down accordingly. But they'll keep hunting for you."

CHAPTER 7

The German Shorthaired Pointer:

Our Workaday Birddog

The author's Shorthair, Westwind's Erick Von Greif, during a training session. *(Doug Meierhoff)*

Germans developed the sturdy, short-coated, liver-and-white Deutsch Kurzhaar *(Doytch Kurts-har)* in the nineteenth century as a versatile breed, that is, a dog to do everything: track big game, trail rabbits, point upland birds, and retrieve waterfowl. Americans began importing the breed early in the twentieth century, but the FDSB didn't recognize it until 1927, and the AKC delayed until 1930.

For American tastes, the German-type dog was too hound-like, too ponderous, too slow. Early breeders in this country "customized" it, and today's Yankee-ized Shorthair stands tall and sleek, moves with light-footed grace, and hunts high-headed (as we perceive an upland pointing dog should). Historians disagree on how the early breeders made these changes. A few insist they did it solely with selective breeding. Most concede that they must have surreptitiously infused Pointer blood into their Shorthair lines. Those of this latter opinion differ on the extent of such crosses, on how long they continued, even on whether they continue today. But regardless of how they modified the breed, they succeeded so completely that the Shorthair became the standard against which we have judged other continental pointing breeds that followed it into this country.

"For me," longtime breeder/trainer/trialer/hunter John Radke of Goddard, Kansas, told me, "the Shorthair is our most versatile breed. It finds birds, points them, retrieves them, and even fetches up ducks, hitting the water as big as Labs. Of course, the Shorthair isn't built for real cold water retrieving."

The Shorthair is so popular in this country, so widely bred, that anyone attracted to the breed can find one that suits his hunting preferences. Most Shorthairs hunt a moderate range, one that is comfortable for the walking hunter. However, the person who wants a dog that quarters within gun range can find such an animal in this breed. Ditto for the horseback hunter who wants his dog to hunt the farthest horizon ahead of him.

The breed has never split into separate types for show and field. Of course, some lines do better in one activity or the other, but two distinct types have not emerged. Over the years, the Shorthair breed has produced a remarkable string of dual champions.

"I personally have seen a Shorthair run a hunting test in the morning and then take Best of Breed in a dog show the same afternoon," said Rick Paine of Arcade, New York, who trains gun dogs professionally and runs his Shorthairs in various field events.

PHYSICAL DESCRIPTION

Males stand 23 to 25 inches at the withers and weigh 55 to 70 pounds. Females are a bit smaller. The short coat may be any combination of liver

A dual-purpose Shorthair, Charles Williams DC/AFC Lyans Holy Smoke, on point. *(Charles Williams)*

and white. Most are heavily ticked, giving a salt-and-pepper impression. Solid liver Shorthairs have gained popularity in recent years, and you occasionally see one that is almost all white, with liver mostly on its head. The tail should be docked to about one-third its original length.

Of moderate bone and muscle, the Shorthair is stockier than a Pointer of the same height, more lithe than a comparable Weimaraner or German Wirehair. Although it doesn't float across the scenery as effortlessly as the Pointer or English Setter, it moves more lightly than the Weimie or Wirehair.

The Shorthair has a high energy level, so needs a high-energy owner and plenty of exercise.

TEMPERAMENT

Temperaments vary, of course, as they do in every breed. However, the typical Shorthair exhibits greater stability than typical dogs of most birddog breeds. It adjusts to whatever life offers it. For example, the Shorthair adjusts well to either life in the house or in the kennel—or any combination of the two.

"They adjust quite well to kennel life," said Buck Irwin of Englewood, Colorado, who has been training, showing, trialing, hunt-testing, and hunting Shorthairs since the late 1960s. "But they also adapt quite well to life in the house."

"The Shorthair personality really comes out in the house," Rick Paine said. "But they adapt easily to living in a kennel. We have seven Shorthairs in the house when we are home, but when we go to work, we put them in their runs. They're perfectly content to stay there."

"Of the 20-some dogs I've had," John Radke said, "none has lived entirely in the house. I bring them in, of course, and they settle right down. But they adjust to kennel life quite easily when I put them back out there."

Typically German, the Shorthair respects authority from its trainer. It gets along with other family members and will handle for anyone who knows how, but it bonds totally with a firm trainer.

"A Shorthair seems to become more attached to the person who trains it," John Radke said. "It responds to other family members, but it bonds mostly with the person who has established initial control." However, the Shorthair is neither a one-man nor one-family dog. It will hunt with anyone toting a shotgun.

"Dogs I train for others adapt quickly to me when their owners bring them in," Rick Paine said, "and then adapt back to their owners when I finish them."

The typical Shorthair is neither soft and compliant nor tough and self-willed. It wants to hunt, wants to get the job done, but will comply with the known wishes of its owner. The owner need only use reasonable methods for communicating his wishes—and do it with sufficient repetitiveness and consistency—and the dog will respond. When the dog needs correction, it will accept it without sulking. The dog seems to say, "OK, boss, if it's *that* big a deal for you, I'll do it your way." The Shorthair has more of a desire to get along and get on with the work than a desire to please.

"They want to learn," Rick Paine said. "They aren't so tough that you pull your hair out with them, nor are they so soft they won't accept corrections."

"I switched to Shorthairs in 1971," John Radke said, "partially because they are a little tougher than Pointers. They stand up to serious training better, especially when you start breaking them to wing and shot. I've steadied at least 20 of them, and never ran across one I couldn't break successfully, that is, retaining its boldness and style."

"I see myself as a very positive trainer," Buck Irwin said. "I try to show the dog what I want and then get him to do it because he wants to do it *for* me. I don't use a lot of force. But, even so, I've had Brittany people tell me that if I trained a Brit the way I train Shorthairs, I'd ruin the dog. They can't take as much pressure as a Shorthair."

However, a pat on the shoulder and a quiet word of praise will help reinforce training, too. With my background in Goldens, English Springers, and other soft breeds, I tend to lay on the praise and encouragement. Erick, my Shorthair-in-residence, sometimes looks at me as if to say, "OK already, so you like what I am doing. But could we just get on with things?"

Like most German breeds, the Shorthair is territorial and protective around home and in the car. But it will relax and accept a stranger (human or canine) if a family member tells it to.

"My Shorthairs patrol my property, and another dog probably hadn't better come on it," John Radke said. "They are also very protective when strangers come around. Especially the bitches."

"They will protect their owner's home and family from intruders," Rick Paine said, "but when told to relax and accept a stranger in the house, they do. Very stable temperaments."

The breed matures faster than some breeds, slower than others.

"I prefer to let a youngster develop his desire before starting serious training," Rick Paine said. "I usually don't start steadying a Shorthair to wing and shot until it is at least 18 months of age."

"I never put the clamps on a Shorthair—like in enforcing 'Whoa'—until it is a year old," John Radke said. "I steady to wing and shot only after the dog is 2."

"Shorthairs mature more slowly than Brittanys," Buck Irwin said. "But the longer I train, the earlier I start steadying. The last one I trained was steady at 6 months and went on to become the number-one Gun Dog Shorthair in the country. But I did it by never letting her chase as a puppy, not by putting a lot of pressure on her."

Although Shorthairs learn quickly, they need occasional reminders that the boss still insists on compliance.

"Most Shorthairs get the picture on steadying to wing and shot in two or three sessions," John Radke said. "After that, they will test you more than, say, a Pointer, so you need to convince them you are still in charge. But you never need to start over completely, even after a layoff."

"They retain their training quite well," Rick Paine said. "That doesn't mean they won't 'sucker' an over-indulgent owner."

In other words, like most dogs, the typical Shorthair reads its owner better than its owner reads the dog.

HUNTING NICHE

As our workaday dog, the Shorthair fits nicely into any hunting situation in which it makes sense to use a pointing dog. Some lines hunt very close; others stay out there with the big-running Pointers and English Setters. Most hunt at a moderate range that most walking hunters find comfortable.

"Most Shorthairs hunt at a comfortable foot-handling range," Rick Paine said. "They adapt to the cover, going wider in more open country, shutting down more in the grouse woods."

"Range in field trial Shorthairs has increased significantly in the past 20 years," John Radke said. "Dogs that were winning the all age stakes back then would be running in the gun dog stakes today. Today's AKC all age Shorthairs range as far as American Field Shooting Dog Pointers. I'm sure this is due partially to infusion of Pointer blood. However, the foot-hunter who wants a dog with a more comfortable range can still find one in the Shorthair breed."

"Range depends a lot on breeding," Buck Irwin said. "Sure, you can modify it a little in or out, but the dog tends to hunt at whatever its natural range is. So getting a dog from the right line is important in getting the range you want. On the average, I suppose, the typical Shorthair hunts closer than a Pointer but farther out than a Weimaraner or Gordon Setter."

The Shorthair has as good a nose as any continental pointing breed. It busts cover quite well. Most Shorthairs retrieve naturally.

"I find them to be natural retrievers," Rick Paine said. "Even so, for formal events that require retrieving, I put them through what I call modified force-breaking to insure reliability."

"I've never had a Shorthair I had to force-break," John Radke said. "But I've had a few that would probably have required force-breaking if I had field-trialed them."

"All of mine have retrieved naturally," said Buck Irwin. "I had one that stopped retrieving after a few months, and I thought I was going to have to force-break him. But I just kept working with him, and his natural retrieve came back."

Most Shorthairs will retrieve from water, especially if started early. The breed should not be used for cold water duck hunting, but it can retrieve upland birds that fall in or across water in most weather conditions. Dove hunting? Sure, but the typical Shorthair doesn't like to sit still very long.

"When I started field trialing, a Shorthair had to pass a water test to earn its field championship title," John Radke said. "I still introduce all of mine to water, and they love it. Good exercise for them during the summer, too. Where I hunt in western Kansas, we flush an occasional duck from the tail-water pits. These are too deep to wade, so I depend on my Shorthairs to retrieve these ducks for me. I've never had one hesitate to jump in."

"We built a pond just for the dogs," Rick Paine said, "and they love it. Oh, sure, I wouldn't expect a Shorthair to retrieve diving ducks in the Niagara River in January, but they do love retrieving from water under normal conditions."

Shorthairs have good endurance, but like any breed, if you hunt them too long at a stretch, they will adapt their pace and range accordingly. Some owners like this, others don't.

"I've seen very few Shorthairs that would hunt a half day straight without letting down noticeably," John Radke said. "But if you rest them about every hour, they will continue making the kind of moves I like to see hunting dogs make—popping and firing from objective to objective, showing great intensity, you know. That's why I always take two dogs hunting and rotate them."

"Endurance is important even in field trials," Buck Irwin said. If your dog 'dies' toward the end of his half-hour or hour heat, that's what the judges will remember. But endurance depends on conditioning more than anything else. You have to keep your dog in shape if you want it to keep going. You can be less demanding when hunting, but your dog still needs to be in shape."

"I've done a lot of guiding on shooting preserves," Rick Paine said, "and we hunt the dogs all day there. Not if it's really hot or if the terrain is unusually rocky, but under normal conditions they will go all day at a reasonable pace."

CHAPTER 8

The German Wirehaired Pointer:

The Americanized Deutsch Drahthaar

Silke Alberts's multi-purpose Wirehair, DC/AFC Lutz Zur Cadenburg, CD TD. *(Silke Albert)*

This big, rough-and-tumble breed has a short, wiry coat (any combination of liver and white), and a tail docked to about one-third its full length. German sportsmen custom-built this breed from a variety of other breeds in the nineteenth century.

In America, the breed suffers a strange split, but not into show and field types, as is usually the case. No, the German Wirehaired Pointer has a German counterpart that also plies its trade in America. Those who favor the German breed call their dogs Deutsch Drahthaar (pronounced *doytch draht-har*). They register their dogs in Germany and conduct German versatility tests under the sponsorship of the German parent club, Verein Deutsch Drahthaar (VDD).

How did the breed split in this curious way? Although it was recognized by the FDSB (as the Deutsch Drahthaar) in 1928, the AKC didn't recognize it until 1959. Before recognizing the breed, the AKC insisted on translating the name into English. Thus, the breed became the German Wirehaired Pointer in this country, just as the Deutsch Kurzhaar (*kurts-har*) had earlier become the German Shorthaired Pointer. Good idea, too, for as Phil Harris once sang, "Talk American, big A-A-A, so's I can understand."

Some Americans preferred to stay with VDD and German registration. Thus the split in this breed. Since Deutsch Drahthaars are purely "versatiles," with their own German-style tests, I will limit the discussion here to the AKC German Wirehaired Pointer.

PHYSICAL DESCRIPTION

"This is the Jeep of the pointing breeds," said longtime breeder/trainer Bernee Brawn of New Hope, Pennsylvania. Pretty good metaphor, too, even if it slights the Wirehair's amphibious inclinations. (I know, I know, we had amphibious Jeeps during WWII, but few remember them.)

Standing the same 22 to 26 inches at the withers as its Shorthaired countryman, the Wirehair carries a tad more muscle. If the two were footballers, the Shorthair would play tailback, the Wirehair fullback. If they were baseballers, the Shorthair would play shortstop, the Wirehair third base. If basketballers, the Shorthair would play forward, the Wirehair center. You get the idea.

The Wirehair has a double coat, which comes in various combinations of liver and white. The wiry outer coat turns brambles and sheds water. Except for the whiskers and eyebrows, it is surprisingly short (about an inch and a half)—long enough to protect the dog from the nastiest cover, but too short to collect junk afield. Beneath the wiry outercoat lies an insulating (wooly) undercoat.

Conscientious breeders struggle to maintain proper coat. And it ain't all that easy. The breed was developed in the nineteenth century from several other breeds, each with a distinctively different coat: the Wirehaired Pointing Griffon, with its longer, softer outercoat; the Pudelpointer, with its shorter outercoat; the German Shorthair; and the almost extinct Stichelhaar. ("What's a *stichel*?" I asked German-born breeder Silke Albers of Vallejo, California. "Porcupines have stichels," she answered.)

Throwbacks still occur, even in the most royally bred litters. Since the Wirehair matures slowly, breeders may not know how well they have done until the litter is fully grown. Thus, breeding properly coated Wirehairs requires knowledge, perseverance, a touch of luck, and copious humility.

But a proper coat is worth the effort. It may not be bullet-proof, but it is briar-proof, bramble-proof, and burr-proof. Those who use their Wirehairs in water say it is also a shake-dry coat.

Surprisingly, this coat requires negligible grooming. "With an ideal coat," Silke Albers said, "you don't have to do any grooming beyond stripping it out once a year."

Some Wirehairs are almost all white, like Bernee Brawn's Ch. Dunkee's Justa Topflite, JH. *(Bernee Brawn)*

TEMPERAMENT

American breeders can take pride in the improvements they have made in the Wirehair's temperament. They have brought German sharpness under control. Sharpness (aggressiveness), which is prized in Germany where the dog is expected to dissuade poachers, creates more problems than it solves in this country.

Other German breeds have gone through a similar attitude adjustment in America. For example, the early Weimaraners (of which I had several) were nothing for a stranger to mess with. Today's Weimaraners have stable temperaments. So do today's Americanized Wirehairs.

"The Wirehairs I had in the early days," said professional trainer Walter Furesz of Dryden, Michigan, "were marvelous hunters. Did everything I wanted afield. Trouble was, they were aggressive toward people. I dreaded running across another hunter. Not too practical in this country. The Wirehairs I have these days give me no such concerns."

"Temperament," said breeder/trainer Barb Hein of Ortonville, Michigan, "has improved tremendously in the past 15 years or so."

The breed remains territorial and protective. A typical Wirehair, being rough-and-tumble in body and mind, can and will defend its clan and castle from hostile intruders. But when faced with a nonthreatening stranger, the dog exhibits aloofness rather than aggression.

Among its own people, the Wirehair is anything but aloof. It prefers to live in the house, where all the family action goes on. Within the family, it sees itself as a lapdog.

Like most protective breeds, the Wirehair bonds with one family member. That person should train it. Actually, the dog will probably bond with the person who assumes the training role.

"I train our Wirehairs," said Bernee Braun, "and my husband mostly feeds them cookies. When I tell them to do something, they do it. When my husband gives a command, they ignore him—or beg for a cookie."

Without bonding, a Wirehair will not respond to training. Do what you wish, but the dog just won't care. "A Wirehair has to like you before you can train him," Bernee Brawn said. "Otherwise, the dog will just thumb his nose at you."

"Once you gain a Wirehair's confidence," Walter Furesz said, "it will do anything you ask, anything you can get across to it. But we have a saying that 'Wirehairs think too much.' Sometimes they are too smart for their owners."

"They are very intelligent," Barb Hein said, "and they don't always use their intelligence to cooperate with you. They have their own ideas about how things should be done. They take a little more patience."

Wirehairs mature slowly, so the initial training takes longer than it would with, say, a Shorthair. However, a Wirehair retains its training better and requires less frequent refreshers.

"I maintain," Walter Furesz said, "that a Wirehair is a puppy until it is about two years old. You have to step lightly with them."

"But once they understand something," Barb Hein said, "it stays with them."

In temperament, the Wirehair males and females have reversed roles. The females are tougher, more independent, more difficult to train. The males are more affectionate, more sensitive, more responsive. Those who buy their first Wirehairs after having had some other breed should consider getting the opposite sex.

"Females," Walter Furesz said, "are more hard-headed, stronger-willed than males. In most breeds, it's the other way around."

"Males are easier to train," Bernee Brawn said. "They will do what you tell them. Bitches have to think about it awhile first."

HUNTING NICHE

With its Jeep-like anatomy and mental toughness, the Wirehair can handle the nastiest cover situations. And the breed has plenty of stamina to go all day.

"I've hunted a Wirehair for six straight hours," Bernee Brawn said. "I took an occasional break, but the dog never tired, really."

The dog's range is close to moderate. True, a few run wider, but not many. Regardless of range, the typical Wirehair maintains contact with the boss.

"The Wirehair is a foot-hunting dog all the way," Walter Furesz said. "The dog wants to know where you are all the time."

"I have found Shorthairs much more independent," Bernee Brawn said. "A Wirehair wants to maintain contact with you. He may run big in trials—mine really cut a rug then—but when I sling a shotgun over my shoulder, they relax and stay close. Even when running in a trial my Wirehairs look over their shoulder often, to make sure I'm where they think I am. If not, they come looking for me."

Wirehairs have a tendency to quarter rather than run edges. Of course, like all good dogs, they will go where the birds are, regardless of what pattern that requires.

Their noses equal those of the other bobtailed pointing breeds. They have a strong pointing instinct. However, since they mature slowly, they should be staunched up a bit later than, say, Shorthairs. Most Wirehairs retrieve naturally, and they love water.

"We have a lot of water in Michigan," Walter Furesz said. "Pointing birds is only half the job. I expect my dogs to retrieve them, too, even when they fall in a pond."

Wirehairs can do light to moderate duty in the duck marshes. However, the dedicated waterfowler (who hunts in cold, miserable conditions) should still consider one of the retriever breeds.

Wirehairs will trail fur if encouraged to do so. But too much of this, especially early in life, can make the dog hunt with its nose on the ground.

"The VDD has a test in which their Drahthaars must track deer blood," Bernee Brawn said. "Really impressive, but deer hunting with dogs is illegal here. When I run NAVHDA [North American Versatile Hunting Dog Association] tests, I choose a bird for the tracking."

"A dog that has been trained to track and trail," Walter Furesz said, "seldom excels in bird work. It hunts with its nose to the ground, so it bumps too many birds. It just can't pick up air scent soon enough to point before the bird flushes. About all you can do is teach it to stop-to-flush and keep it within gun range. But you can't make a real birddog out of one that runs with its nose to the ground."

Walter went on, "A man once brought me a dog he was going to run in a VDD test. He wanted me to get it ready for the birdwork. It tracked and trailed impressively, but hunted with its nose to the ground. I had an awful time with it. But the owner said all he needed was a flash-point."

Then Walter added a thought shared by many American birddog fanciers. "Personally, I feel that the guy who wants to hunt rabbits should get a Beagle."

Silke Albers, who has run her dogs in VDD and KDK tests in Germany, told me, "I have seen more than one dog running high-headed hunting for birds when it hit rabbit scent, then stick its nose to the ground and trail the rabbit until producing it. Amazing." (**Note:** KDK, or Klubbe Deutsch Kurzhaar, is the German organization that sponsors the Deutsch Kurzhaar breed.) Perhaps these dogs were well-trained in birdwork before being introduced to tracking and trailing.

CHAPTER 9

The Weimaraner:

The Great Survivor

Charles Williams's Weimaraner, Mick, on point. *(Charles Williams)*

Ah, yes, now we come to the often repeated story of the "Gray Ghost." I remember a comedian who used this line: "If you've heard this one before, don't stop me, for I want to hear it again myself!" Well, even if you've read the Weimaraner story a thousand times, don't stop me, for I want to read it again myself. Frankly, it contains several good lessons for both of us.

The Weimaraner—pronounced *WYmarHONor* in this country—or "Weimie" (*WYmee*), was developed by Grand Duke Karl August of Weimar, Germany, in the early years of the nineteenth century. The Grand Duke aspired to turn Weimar into a reborn Athens. On the whole, he did a passable job, too, not only because he was a man of vision, but also because he was a consummate opportunist. For example, he kept Weimar intact through the Napoleonic Wars by supporting the French when they initially advanced eastward, and opposing them when they later retreated to the west. Interesting character, the Grand Duke.

Now, what would nineteenth century Athens be without legendary hunting dogs? Inadequate, that's what, or at least the Grand Duke felt so. Thus, he developed his breed of gray dogs, initially to hunt big game. Only later, when big game became scarce, did the Germans introduce the Weimaraner to birds.

Quite early, breed fanciers formed the Weimaraner Club of Germany to protect rather than promote the breed. They did a good job, too, until 1929 when American sportsman Howard Knight joined the club and began importing Weimaraners to this country. He and his friends formed the Weimaraner Club of America in 1941, initially to protect the breed, but later to promote it in the most unconscionable ways. For example, they hired journalist Jack Denton Scott to publicize the Weimaraner nationally, which he did very successfully, especially after WWII.

Mr. Scott and his numerous imitators created the "Wonder Dog" myth, which first lifted the breed to great heights of popularity and then plunged it almost into oblivion in America. Gullible Americans, weary of wartime restrictions and anxious for recreations like hunting, believed Mr. Scott's press-release journalism. They accepted as fact the description of the Weimaraner as the one dog that could do anything better than any breed, everything better than all breeds combined. Many paid outrageous prices for Weimaraners.

The AKC recognized the breed in 1943, the FDSB in 1944. Soon after WWII, fast-buck breeders were crawling out of their holes everywhere to hawk Weimaraners. Many made fortunes from the breed. But of course, the dogs couldn't perform up to their Wonder Dog billing. What breed could? Gullible Americans realized they had been had. Demand (and prices) fell to near zero. The fickle press reversed its attitude. The very publications that had created the Wonder Dog image (without investigating their own claims) began ridiculing the Weimaraner as totally useless afield (still without investigation).

The party was over. The breed was in shambles. To the few serious Weimaraner fanciers, it must have looked like the party site on the morning after a world-class New Year's Eve bash. First, they had to get the drunks (fast-buck operators) up and out—which wasn't difficult in most cases. Then they had to clean up the mess these "guests" had left. It took years, but they succeeded admirably.

Today in America, the Weimaraner holds its own as a working birddog with the other continental breeds. Although it is no Wonder Dog—never was—it is an honest hunting companion for those who like its appearance and personality.

In other words, it has survived the worst disaster that ever befell a breed in this country. That's why I call it the Great Survivor, rather than the Gray Ghost (as so many do).

Like the other continentals, the breed has not split into distinct field and show types. Granted, some lines excel at field work while others excel at conformation, but the breed shows no clear split.

PHYSICAL DESCRIPTION

The Weimaraner is a big, muscular animal with a short, sleek, gray coat. The males stand 25 to 27 inches tall and weigh 60 to 80 pounds, give or take a little. The females run somewhat smaller. Although they have a lithe appearance, they are solidly built, with plenty of bone and muscle. The nose is light colored, and so are the eyes. The light eyes give a variety of expressions to the Weimaraner face, from forlorn puzzlement to shocked outrage to blazing determination.

The preferred tail-dock leaves about one-third of the tail on the dog. Esthetically, that balances the dog's overall appearance nicely—at least for me. The few I see with very short tails seem to lack overall symmetry—again, at least for me.

New-born puppies have stripes like chipmunks, which disappear within a few days. Mature coats come in various shades of gray, appearing to me more beige or taupe than pure gray. As in many self-colored breeds, the Weimaraner breed standard allows a small patch of white on the chest, but the smaller the better. White anywhere else constitutes a major no-no.

Germans accept two coat variations that Americans do not: longhairs and blues. Some Americans like each of these and have imported them, so they are available here. However, the AKC breed standard (per the wishes of the Weimaraner Club of America) accepts only the short gray coat. Both longhairs and blues are disqualified.

TEMPERAMENT

The Weimaraner is a personal dog. It bonds strongly with its human family, and especially with one person. As such, it develops most fully if it lives in the house rather than in a kennel. Granted, like most breeds, it can adapt to kennel life, provided the family gives it plenty of attention on a daily basis.

Having a Weimaraner around the house can be wonderful—at least most of the time. You will never want for attention, and they delight in learning any parlor tricks you care to teach them.

For example, while housebreaking Misty many years ago, I taught her to ring a bell when she wanted to go out. Very helpful, I thought. However, as she matured, she learned to control me with that stupid bell. When the kids were out playing and she wanted to join them, she rang the bell—and looked at me with full Weimaraner indignation until I obeyed. When she was bored and wanted to go out back to retrieve a dummy, she rang the bell—and dared me to ignore her. I have never taught another dog this trick.

Weimaraners can be destructive when left home alone. They want to be with people. I have heard of some who have jumped through windows to get out when the family was gone. I have also heard of at least one that, weary of being outside alone, jumped through a window to get in where the family was.

The breed is territorial. No stranger will get into a car guarded by a Weimaraner. Ditto for a house or fenced yard. However, when the owner shows his approval of an "intruder," the dog settles down and accepts that person—with a little reserve at first, but then whole-heartedly.

"The Weimaraner is the most territorial of the sporting breeds," said Dick Wilbur, long-time breeder/trainer of Lubbock, Texas. "It may well be one of the most territorial of all breeds."

The Weimaraner protects its people, too—"with total disregard for its own safety," according to Dick Wilbur. But it can exercise unbelievable judgment regarding the amount of force a given situation requires. When my oldest daughter was two, I had a hunting buddy over for Sunday dinner one time. I left him momentarily alone in the living room with my daughter and Misty while I went into the kitchen to help my wife in some way. Next thing I knew, my buddy was calling to me to come and convince Misty to let loose of him! I went back into the living room and, sure enough, Misty had a firm grip on his arm. She wasn't biting him, but she wasn't letting loose either. He explained that when my daughter had approached a dirty ashtray, he had reached for her. But before he touched her, Misty grabbed his arm and wouldn't let loose. She didn't hurt him, and she looked at him quite apologetically all the time. I told her to release him. She did—and waggled all over as she snuggled up to him, seeming to say, "No hard feelings, but I have a job to do around here."

Weimaraners mature more slowly than, say, German Shorthairs. "Male Weimies especially," Dick Wilbur said, "mature slowly. It may take until they are two and a half or three years old. But once they mature, they retain their training very well. They don't need a two-week refresher at the start of every year.

"I let mine break to retrieve during hunting season," Dick went on, "but steadying them back up in the spring for field trials only takes about five minutes. I show them, and they seem to say, 'Oh, we're gonna play by those rules again, huh? OK, boss, let's go.'"

To train a Weimaraner, you need to take a very personal approach. The dog wants to please you—assuming it has accepted you as one of its people, preferably as its main person—and you should use that desire in all your training. That means showing the dog what it can do that will please you, praising successes consistently, and showing displeasure at mistakes rather than punishing them (at least most of the time).

"Fun, that's the key to this breed," said Charles Williams, long-time breeder/trainer of Brighton, Colorado.

Dick Wilbur's FC/AFC Zach's Grau Geist Gruppe B on an intense point. *(Dick Wilbur)*

HUNTING NICHE

The typical Weimie works quite close in, as most modern upland hunters prefer. Granted, some lines run as wide as all age Pointers in field trials, but even those dogs typically shorten up to a more moderate range when the boss gets off his horse and starts walking.

"Most Weimaraners," Dick Wilbur said, "hunt within 20 to 50 yards of the hunter. Of course, it depends on the cover and terrain and where the objectives are at any point in time. I have two trial dogs that will stay out a mile or more when I run them from a horse. But when I hunt them on foot, they stay quite close."

"If you train them right," Charles Williams said, "they'll range however you want them to. Some of mine will stay out there with Pointers when I run them in trials from a horse, but they hunt at a much more moderate range when I foot-hunt them."

The breed has a good nose and points as stylishly as most continentals do. And they tend to retrieve naturally.

"I start them retrieving when they are 4 or 5 weeks old," Charles Williams said. "You know, in the house, with a sock or something soft. By the time they go to their new owners, they are retrieving quite well."

Dick Wilbur agreed. "I've never had one that didn't retrieve naturally, but I always start mine quite young."

Although not suited for serious duck hunting, the Weimaraner usually takes to water easily, especially if introduced quite young. This is one of only two pointing breeds that must pass a water retrieving test to become an AKC Field Champion or Amateur Field Champion. (The other breed is the German Wirehaired Pointer.)

"I don't do water work very much," Charles Williams said. "I don't have time, what with AKC trials and hunting tests, American Field trials, NSTRA [National Shoot-To-Retrieve Association] trials, and an occasional state pheasant championship trial. But I've never had a problem getting one to retrieve from water when I wanted him to."

CHAPTER 10

The Vizsla:

The Glamorous Hungarian

Pro Hank Rozanek's DC Rebel Rouser ET demonstrates that pheasants might be anywhere, even hidden in a plowed field. *(Hank Rozanek)*

The Gabor girls were not the only beautiful post-WWII immigrants from Hungary. About that time, concerned Hungarian breeders began smuggling a few Vizslas (*VISH-la*) through tight Russian security and out of their native land, where the breed had been a closely protected national treasure for many centuries.

Some say the Vizsla goes all the way back to the fourth century. Perhaps, but no one can deny that it existed as long ago as the fourteenth century. In 1375 a group of Carmelite Friars, under the direction of Hungarian King Lajos (Louis) the Great, wrote the *Illustrated Chronicle,* which includes information about the breed. From then until the present, Hungarian literature offers a reasonably complete history of the breed. Initially used in falconry, the sleek, short-haired, rusty gold pointer adapted readily to the shotgun when that became the preferred tool of Hungarian bird hunters.

The Hungarian nobility controlled the breed through all those centuries, for they alone had the time and money for sport hunting. They guarded the Vizsla jealously, refusing to export the breed. True, a few (dogs and owners) found themselves on foreign soil from time to time when international squabbles redrew national boundaries. Some historians speculate that such dislocated Vizslas were part of the foundation stock for the Weimaraner. In spite of these occasional losses, the Hungarian nobility adamantly refused to export the breed until fear of Russian annihilation of the breed changed their minds.

By the early 1950s Vizslas began arriving in the United States. Thus, perhaps the oldest pointing dog on earth became one of the newest arrivals here, where every pointing breed seems to find a niche in our varied uplands. The FDSB recognized it in 1954 and the AKC in 1960.

The breed has remained one. That doesn't mean every Vizsla excels both at dog shows and field trials. The breed does have separate lines that specialize in each area; however, the show lines produce plenty of competent hunters, and the field trial lines have plenty of dogs that conform to the physical standard of the breed.

PHYSICAL DESCRIPTION

Physically attractive, as one would expect of a dog from the land of the Gabors, the Vizsla stands about 23 inches at the withers and weighs about 50 pounds. Their short, self-colored coat shimmers and shines with its lush, golden-rust color. The nose and eyes are brown. Serious Vizsla breeders accept a bit of white on the chest and feet, but the less the better.

Smaller and lighter-boned than the German Shorthair, the Weimaraner, and most other continental pointing breeds, the Vizsla has a racy appearance. The longer tail-bob contributes to this impression. The Vizsla carries about two-thirds of its original tail. With their rangy bodies and longer tails, Vizslas seem to move effortlessly, with a grace that is pleasing to watch.

TEMPERAMENT

The Vizsla forms a strong attachment to its people and demands more human attention than most breeds. Although it can adapt to kennel life as long as it receives enough human contact, it does better in the home.

"They really prefer to be in the home and a member of the family," said Nancy Staley, owner/trainer of Minneapolis, Minnesota.

"I keep mine in my kennels most of the time," said professional trainer Hank Rozanek of Schuyler, Nebraska. "They still demand plenty of personal attention. When I bring a Pointer in, he just curls up and goes to sleep somewhere. Not my Vizslas. They want to be with me—all the time."

Vizslas are friendly with both people and other dogs, but they are territorial. They will protect their turf from unauthorized intrusions. However, when the boss indicates acceptance of a visitor, the dog will make up immediately.

"They're supposed to protect a guy's property," Hank Rozanek said. "But as soon as you tell them to stop, they settle down. Then they'll try to crawl into a complete stranger's lap."

The breed tends to be "soft," responding best to gentle training techniques. They don't require—nor will they accept—much pressure. A typical Vizsla wants to please so much that the trainer need only let the animal know how to do that. Mostly that means leading it through the work and praising success. When the dog does need correction, it will usually respond to a harsh word. If over-corrected, it will become sulky and stubborn.

The breed matures rather slowly and may not be ready for serious training (like steadying to wing and shot) until after the second birthday.

"Most trainers around here," Nancy Staley said, "let their dogs chase birds until they're about two years old. Then they steady them as gently as they can."

"Some dogs from straight field trial breedings mature early," Hank Rozanek said. "But most lines develop more slowly.

HUNTING NICHE

Where does the Vizsla fit into the American hunting scene? Years ago Chauncey Smith, longtime Vizsla breeder and trainer of Clarksville, Virginia, described the breed to me as "a walking gentleman's shooting

Lakeside Tizzie Whiz-Bang, MH honors the point of her littermate, Sundance Selle, MH UD VC. Both dogs belong to Nancy Staley. *(Nancy Staley)*

dog." Some today would modify that somewhat to eliminate the blatant maleness of the word *gentleman.* But, at whatever risk, I'll stick with "a walking gentleman's shooting dog." No gender-free equivalent is so pithy, so descriptive.

As a breed for walking hunters, the Vizsla must hunt within a restricted range. Few of us anymore have wide open spaces in which to hunt. We hunt small parcels of land surrounded by other parcels on which we do not have permission to go. A dog that pushes onto that adjacent land too often is no pleasure to hunt with.

"They're a close-working dog," Hank Rozanek said. "Their range varies, of course, but only about one or two percent really reach out the way Pointers do. Most Vizslas are not independent. They want to know where you are."

"Mine stay in close," Nancy Staley said, "which is where I want them."

The Vizsla's outstanding nose complements his restricted range. It can pick up and follow the slightest trace of scent wafting up from scattered birds. So the breed works close in and has an excellent nose. But that doesn't exhaust the meaning of "walking gentleman's shooting dog." Let's proceed.

The word "gentleman," as used here, does not refer to how one dresses for dinner or whether one has a domestic staff. No, it means a person who forms a close bond with his dog, a person who brings out the best in the breed. The Vizsla, with its intense desire to please, needs a close attachment to its owner. And since it is a soft dog, only a *gentle* man (or *gentle* woman) will bring out a Vizsla's full potential.

"Most people who own Vizslas," Nancy Staley said, "can't separate the hunting aspects from the family pet aspects. The two just blend together somehow."

The rough-and-tumble trainer won't get much out of this breed. Neither will the impatient. The quick-tempered will get least of all. Even the reasonably gentle trainer who consistently neglects to praise his dog's successes adequately will have some problems. The Vizsla wants to be a respected colleague at home and afield. The only way a person can confer that status on the dog is through frequent appreciation—which means petting and praising.

So much for "gentleman." But the expression "a walking gentleman's shooting dog" has still more meaning.

The term "shooting dog" means two things: the dog finds and points birds for its owner to shoot, and it retrieves birds that fall to the gun. Such a dog completely complements the gun.

The Vizsla has a strong pointing instinct, and it develops early. The dog enjoys pointing, especially after he understands that pleases the boss.

"My first Vizsla pointed the first quail it ever scented," Nancy Staley said. "So have most other Vizslas I have trained or helped train. What's more, most of them seem to back another dog's point naturally, too."

The Vizsla may or may not retrieve naturally. Those that don't can be force-broken rather easily.

"All of my personal Vizslas retrieve naturally," said Hank Rozanek. "I've had to force-break a few of my customers' dogs. Either way, they usually have soft mouths. I have noticed some lessening of natural retrieving in the breed over the years since it has been de-emphasized in AKC field trials."

"Mine retrieve naturally as puppies," said Nancy Staley. "One four-month-old dragged a dead pheasant back to me by the wing. Later that may disappear as the pup develops more interest in hunting and pointing. So I force-break mine to get a more reliable retrieve."

"Funny thing," Hank Rozanek said, "you can't tell a force-broke dog from a natural retriever. Most likely, the force-broke dog will do a better job of retrieving. That's not true of pointing. The dog that has to be taught to point will never show much intensity and style."

Most Vizslas take easily to water, especially if introduced while quite young. Although not suitable for fetching ducks from cold water or heavy seas, a Vizsla can retrieve early season ducks, doves, and any upland birds that fall in or across water.

So there you have the Vizsla, the "walking gentleman's shooting dog." And now that so many women are hunting and field-training their own dogs, the Vizsla is also a marvelous "walking gentlewoman's shooting dog." Some say that women train this breed more effectively than do men. Why? Well, probably, after centuries of pampering the fragile male ego, women find training a soft dog a walk in the park.

CHAPTER 11

The Wirehaired Pointing Griffon:

The French Dog with a German Accent, or Vice Versa

Denny Smith's Ch. Drummen Von Herrenhausen on a tight point. *(Denny Smith)*

Although imported into this country before the other continental pointing breeds (according to AKC records), this smallish, rough-coated jack-of-all-trades has never achieved much popularity here. That may seem strange to anyone who properly assesses both modern American hunting conditions and the WPG's many talents: a close-working upland hunter/pointer/retriever, a waterproof ducker, and an affectionate family pet. Perhaps its dingy-colored, unkempt coat puts potential admirers off. For sure, its dedicated supporters, preferring quality to quantity, refuse to promote the breed.

Eduard Karel Korthals began developing the breed in his native Holland in 1874 from dogs he acquired in several European countries. Restless, he moved first to Germany, then to France, continuing his breeding program in both countries. Today we think of the breed as French for three reasons: Korthals completed his work in France; the breed's name, Griffon (pronounced Grif-FON), is French; and today most active breeders live in France.

According to the AKC's *The Complete Dog Book,* the AKC registered its first Wirehaired Pointing Griffon in 1887. The dog's name was Zollette; its AKC registration number was 6773. After Zolette's name and number, this AKC book carries the following parenthetical note: (Russian Setter). Intrigued, I inquired at the AKC library about what that note might mean. After checking, the librarian told me that no one at AKC has any information about it. So it remains a mystery. If Zollette was indeed a Griffon, she lived a lonely life in America. Other Griffs didn't start landing here until around 1900, when Louis Thebaud (of Brittany fame) began importing them. The FDSB registered its first Griffon in 1910.

Today the breed suffers (or enjoys, depending on your point of view) an unusual split. Two national breed clubs sponsor their own version of the breed. Those clubs are the Wirehaired Pointing Griffon Club of America (WPGCA) and the American Wirehaired Pointing Griffon Association (AWPGA).

WPGCA, which was founded in 1951, maintains its own registry and sponsors its own field testing program (of the versatile type, patterned after European models). They oversee their own breeding program, with strict controls aimed at maintaining the versatile talents of the breed. To improve those talents, since the mid-1980s they have permitted planned crosses with the Cesky Fousek, a Czechoslovakian wirehaired pointing breed.

"The WPGCA breeding program's goal," said Joan Bailey of Beaverton, Oregon, longtime secretary of WPGCA, "is to produce mentally stable dogs, physically sound, that are easy to train and make good family dogs."

The AWPGA, which was founded in 1989, is an AKC member club. They register their dogs with AKC, which forbids crosses with other breeds. They participate in AKC show and field activities. Many also participate in NAVHDA tests.

"Some of us who disagree with the Fousek cross," said Denny Smith of Eugene, Oregon, corresponding secretary of AWPGA, "formed a separate club and went through the process with AKC to become the parent club of the breed. We want to maintain a dual-purpose Griffon, one that both shows and works afield. We show our dogs and we field-test them, too, mostly in NAVHDA but also in AKC hunting tests."

PHYSICAL DESCRIPTION

The Griffon is smaller than the German continental breeds, but larger than the Brittany. Male Griffs stand 21½ to 23½ inches at the withers and weigh 40 to 55 pounds. Females are proportionately smaller. The Griffon is powerfully built, or, as dog folks say, has plenty of substance.

The coat identifies the breed. Standing next to the sleek German Wirehair, the Griff looks shaggy. The Griff's wiry outercoat is longer and its wooly, insulating undercoat is heavier. This ample double coat protects the dog from both icy water and nasty cover, but it picks up a few burrs. The color may be anything from solid liver to solid off-white. Most Griffs are steely gray and liver-ticked.

"Coats vary," said Denny Smith. "At one extreme, some dogs have mostly undercoat with too little outercoat. Such a coat is wooly, so it soaks up water and fills with burrs. At the other extreme, some dogs have mostly outercoat, with almost no undercoat. Such a coat doesn't adequately insulate the dog against severe weather and water conditions. The proper coat lies between those two extremes, a coat with a dense wiry outercoat—about two and a half inches long—plus an abundant undercoat. That's what we aim for when we breed."

The tail is docked long, with one-half to two-thirds remaining. Such a tail creates fewer problems around the house and still allows the dog to communicate with the boss afield with appropriate tail actions.

The Griffon has an interesting facial expression, which Joan Bailey explains this way: "His unique expression is due to the round, dark eyes with their canopy of eyebrows, and his well-pronounced moustache."

TEMPERAMENT

As you might guess from its German/French background, the Griffon has a temperament that falls somewhere between those of the German breeds and the Brittany. Like the Germans, the Griff can be territorial and protective, making it a reasonably good watchdog.

"They're everybody's buddy," said Denny Smith, "until somebody comes to the house when the family isn't home."

Like the Brit, the Griffon is anxious to please, responsive, affectionate, friendly. It adapts well to kennel life, but prefers to live in the house with the family. Indoors, it may not be in someone's lap all the time, but neither will it spend all its time lying off by itself. It will insist on a reasonable amount of attention, and it does like physical contact. Although an active dog, the Griff has a lower energy level than the German breeds.

"They are a people-oriented breed," said Denny Smith. "When they want attention, they will make pests of themselves. They are clownish around the house. Very, very happy dogs."

Although not a soft breed, the Griffon wants so much to please that it requires fewer and less intense corrections than the German breeds.

"I wouldn't call them soft," said professional birddog trainer Tod Peterson of Rockford, Iowa, who owns and breeds Griffons. "They are what I call mild-mannered, and they have a strong desire to please. They try to figure out what you want, and do it."

"Most well-bred Griffons are quite intelligent," said Joan Bailey, "so this, coupled with their cooperative nature, makes them easy to train, or produces dogs that almost train themselves."

The Griff matures earlier than most German breeds, earlier than the typical Brittany. "In this breed," said Tod Peterson, "the males mature earlier than the females. Last year I had two males steady to wing and shot and backing at nine and a half months old—with no force. They both finished their AKC Senior Hunter hunter test titles at nine months. One of them passed his first Master/Hunter test at nine and a half months and went on to finish with five passes in seven tests."

"Most Griffons mature at a medium to fast rate," said Joan Bailey, "meaning by 12 months you can hunt them, with some modifications. However, since 1989, with the injection of the Cesky Fousek, we have found that some of our dogs are slower to mature. We do not want to breed for this slow maturation and will eventually breed away from this, back to the more normal rate most hunters desire."

HUNTING NICHE

The Griffon hunts at a close-to-moderate range, depending on the conditions it faces: cover, terrain, type of birds, speed of its handler. Of course, a dog so anxious to please will work at whatever range the boss prefers. Some Griffs move rather slowly, while others cover their ground with great animation. They have better-than-average noses and point quite intensely.

"They are a fairly close dog," said Denny Smith, "but they are meticulous hunters, hitting all the good cover."

"Most Griffs hunt close," said Tod Peterson. "Some are plodders, but others hunt with pizzazz, which we strive to produce in our

Pro Tod Peterson hunting in the snow with a pair of Griffons, Von Baxter Jakes Gunner and Von Baileys Axel Gunner. *(Courtesy of Tod Peterson)*

breedings. Even the stylish ones adapt well to conditions. I have a female that stays at the edge of gun range—50 yards or so—in front of me when hunting pheasants around here, but moves on out to 100 yards or more when we hunt quail in southern Iowa. She handles running pheasants cleverly. She loops ahead of the bird, sometimes going 200 yards, to trap it between us."

"The dog will be pretty much what you want," said Joan Bailey. "In the short wheat stubble of Montana, where you are hunting Hungarian partridge, pheasants, and sharptails, the Griffon covers the ground well in front of you, *but always for the gun*. If you move from the stubble field to the edge of thick ditches, the dog is going to hunt closer to you. If you are hunting the ditches of Nebraska or Iowa, or the fence rows there, on the uncultivated set-asides with thick, high grass, the dog is going to be close."

Griffons have outstanding endurance. "I hunt mine all day on chukkars here in Oregon," said Denny Smith. "They can stand that uphill-downhill hunting better than I can. They don't give out—I do."

Most Griffs retrieve naturally, and they are outstanding at trailing crippled birds, both on land and in water. "Nearly every well-bred Griffon," said Joan Bailey, "has the tendency to retrieve items to his master. This can be easily cultivated by fun retrieving and positive reinforcement and can be finished off with modified force retrieving if the owner is looking for that polished performance."

"I have a six-week-old litter right now," said Tod Peterson, "and every pup is retrieving to me in the kitchen already. I don't force-break my own Griffs, but if a client requests it, I force-break his—with a very, very mild procedure."

"They are very tender-mouthed, and they are excellent tracking dogs," said Denny Smith. "I've never lost a downed bird when shooting over one of my Griffs. They track ducks on water, like most continental breeds."

Griffons make good waterfowl retrievers, too. They love water and can endure late season cold water and winds. Those with proper coats are so well protected that their skins remain dry even after a lengthy swim. They are calm enough to sit quietly in or beside the blind or in a boat for the long periods that frequently transpire between flights of waterfowl.

"A well-bred Griffon, with sound temperament," said Joan Bailey, "loves water and is at home in the marsh. Dogs with the proper protective coat have a longer endurance for sitting in a blind than those with a soft coat. Well-bred Griffons are excellent at tracking and retrieving wounded ducks. They enjoy retrieving geese, too."

"My male Griffon," said Tod Peterson, "loves to swim in the river just for fun. Sometimes during the summer he paddles around out there for an hour or more. Even after that, his skin is dry. His coat is so waterproof that I have difficulty giving him a bath. Late last year, when it was so cold that ice kept forming on our decoy spread, three of us limited out on both ducks and geese from a boat. My male Griff stayed in the boat with us and retrieved every bird all day. I sometimes jump-shoot ducks from my little pumpkin boat. I put my Griff in the front, and he stays right there until I tell him otherwise. Very patient dogs."

CHAPTER 12

Finding the Right Birddog for You:

Following Your Informed Heart

Bob Wilbanks, editor of *Gun Dog* magazine, says hunting just wouldn't be hunting without his Shorthair, Freddie. Everyone should have a dog he likes that much.

The first rule of successful dog acquisition is *Stay away from litters of puppies until you have done three things:*

1. Selected a breed.
2. Decided whether to get a trained dog or a puppy.
3. Selected a source (trainer for a trained dog or breeder for a puppy).

If you ignore this rule, you will probably buy a puppy from the first litter you visit. That all but dashes your chance of getting an ideal dog for your particular situation. It also transfers control of the process from you to the most appealing of a bunch of squirmy young canines.

SELECTING YOUR BREED

First, select the best breed *for you.* That will not necessarily be the one experts tout as perfect for your type of hunting. At best, such experts have personal experience with only three or four pointing breeds. At worst, they are parroting what they have read or heard from other experts, who in turn may have been repeating what they had picked up from still other experts, and so on.

Which is the best breed for you? Once you understand your options, let your heart rule your head. Go with your gut. As you read the preceding chapters on the 10 most popular pointing breeds, one or two appealed to you more than the others. If just one stood out, go with it. If two finished neck-and-neck, read the two chapters again, and maybe a winner will emerge. If not, get acquainted with people who have adults (not puppies) of each breed. To find them, ask the secretary of the local field trial or hunting test club, the local kennel club, or the local obedience trial club. If none of these folks can help you, contact the secretaries of the two national breed clubs (see Appendix III, "Important Contacts").

Ideally, you should talk to owners who actually hunt with their dogs. If no local owners hunt, talk to distant hunters by phone. Ask them about the breed's hunting strengths and weaknesses, its level of trainability, and what it's like to live with.

After investigating both breeds, you will probably like one better than the other. Good. That's your breed, end of discussion. Breed selection should be based on an emotional process, not on a pseudo-intellectual analysis. Shooting one bird over a dog you love will please you more than limiting out with one to which you are indifferent.

CONSIDER A TRAINED DOG

Few first-time buyers consider a trained dog. Too bad, for they would benefit more from such an animal than a person adding a second dog or replacing one that has died.

This picture should tell you why you shouldn't look at puppies until you've picked a breed and a breeder—and considered buying a trained dog. *(Frank Lallas)*

Trained dogs come in two types: fully trained and started. Neither is well defined. But a fully trained dog should hunt enthusiastically, respond to basic control commands (*Whoa, Come-in, Turn*), and be staunch on point. It may or may not be steady to wing and shot, may or may not retrieve, and may or may not like water. A started dog should hunt enthusiastically, show a strong pointing instinct, and respond reasonably well to basic control commands. It may or may not be staunch on point, may or may not retrieve, and may or may not like water.

In the above discussion, I deliberately omitted range so I could discuss and stress it here. Every pointing dog buyer has strong preferences about range—close, medium, or way-the-hell-out-there—and every pointing dog buyer should limit his selection of trained dogs to those whose range falls within his personal preferences. You know what range you like, so don't let any other canine virtue—pointing style, steadiness, retrieving prowess, or whatever—induce you to buy a dog whose range will make you uncomfortable afield.

In fact, *the chief advantage of a trained dog is its known range.* No one can predict with any certainty the range a puppy will develop as it matures, regardless of its breed or breeding.

So when you discuss trained dogs with a pro, make sure to convey your preferences in range. Then stick to your guns, at least for your first dog. Your preferences may—and probably will—change with experience. Typically, a beginner wants a very close-working dog, but over the years learns to appreciate dogs that cover a bit more ground. Even so, you should never buy a dog whose range is outside of your current comfort zone.

A trained dog removes the risk from the acquisition process. You know exactly what the dog can and cannot do before you spend any money. Besides, if you deal with a reputable source, you will receive (as part of the purchase) adequate instructions about how to handle the dog, how to keep up its training, plus a promise of whatever advice you may need.

A trained dog also removes all waits and delays from the process. The dog is ready to hunt as soon as the season opens, whereas a puppy may be a year or two away from the level of performance you seek (and may never achieve it).

The major drawback to a trained dog is, of course, the price. A started dog will cost from twice to perhaps four times as much as a just-weaned pup of the same breed and breeding. A fully trained dog will cost over five times as much as a puppy, and will vary with the dog's training level and other attributes (class, style, etc.). Important money, especially for the typical American middle class *pater familias or mater familias*.

But a puppy can end up costing even more. If you get a dud, you waste a year or two of your life, as well as the money you have spent buying and maintaining it, and you have nothing to show for your investment. So you get another puppy, and perhaps waste another year or two, plus that much more money. At this point, you have spent what a started dog would have cost you, surrendered two to four years of your life, and still don't have a dog. The time lost will concern you more than the money. Money, after all, is a renewable resource, but time is not.

Here's an even worse scenario: The first puppy flunks the course, but your family won't let you unload it so you add a second pup. Same result. Now you have a houseful of useless birddogs you can't unload, and city ordinances may not allow you to buy another dog. I have known of such situations. If your family will become strongly attached to your dog, you should get a trained dog if you possibly can.

FINDING A TRAINED DOG

Contact breeders and professional trainers of your selected breed. If you don't know any, inquire about them from the various clubs mentioned earlier: field trial, hunting test, and national breed clubs.

Try to locate two or three prospects from which to choose. Request copies of their pedigrees (study Appendix II, "Reading Birddog Pedigrees"), and apply what you learn to the pedigrees you receive. The quality of these pedigrees indicates the value of the animal as breeding stock, which is one pricing consideration.

Assure yourself that any prospect you consider is properly registered with the AKC and/or the FDSB. Which registry you seek depends on the breed you have chosen and the activities you plan to participate in with the dog (see details under "Finding a Litter," below).

Go see each prospect work. Never buy a trained dog without seeing it work—especially not by mail. Even after satisfying yourself that a trained dog works as you want, you should not buy it until you have determined that you have the proper rapport with it. I have known many outstanding dogs that I could not enjoy hunting with, much less living with, because of traits in their personalities. Before buying a dog, spend enough time with it to assure yourself that it represents a marriage made in heaven for you. Ideally, before buying, you should also have a pro (not the one through whom you are buying) evaluate the dog for 30 days (for a fee, of course). During that period, you should visit the pro's place often enough to become well acquainted with the animal.

Before uncapping your pen, find out what follow-up services the seller offers, like help in learning how to handle the dog afield, how to maintain its training, and so on.

PUPPIES ARE FUN

Within the framework of the caveats mentioned above, a lot can be said for buying a puppy. Granted, it's a gamble, no matter how royally bred the youngster may be. But realistically, this is the only affordable option for many. My wife and I raised five children, so I know about skimping. The needs of the family can make money scarce, even if it is replenishable.

Economy is not the only reason for choosing a puppy. Many of us prefer the excitement of bringing a pup along, watching it develop, working through its problems. And if successful, we will feel a greater sense of accomplishment than we would if we had bought trained dogs. Fishermen get the same satisfaction from catching trout on flies they have tied themselves and on rods they have assembled from parts.

Even if you buy a trained dog, you should consider a puppy as your second dog. You already have a dog that can do the job for you, so the pup is not such a risk. If it doesn't work out, you can get another, and another, until you succeed, all without giving up a day's hunting for lack of a dog. From your first dog, you know something about training and handling. You won't make as many mistakes with this puppy as you would have if it were your first.

FINDING A LITTER

If you opt for a puppy, look for a breeder with a reputation for producing the kind of stock you seek. The secretary of the national breed club can help you locate several.

That secretary can also inform you about any hereditary health problems to which your breed is vulnerable—and how to avoid them. Some breeds have serious hip problems. Others suffer from eye problems. Some have a relatively high incidence of bad temperament. You need to know these things.

When you contact breeders, ask for references, especially those whose dogs have matured enough to be trained and hunted. Contact these references. Ask what they like and dislike about their dogs, what health and temperament problems they have encountered, and so on. Ask if they know of others who have bought dogs from the same breeder. You may get some names the breeder would rather you didn't have.

After you select a breeder, request pedigrees of planned litters. Study Appendix II, "Reading Birddog Pedigrees," and apply what you learn to the pedigrees you receive.

Assure yourself that any litter you are considering is registerable with the appropriate registry: the AKC and/or the FDSB, depending on the breed you have chosen and the activities you wish to pursue. If you have chosen the field-bred Pointer, the field-bred English Setter, or the Red Setter, you should insist on FDSB registration. If you have chosen any other breed, you should insist on AKC registration. If you plan to run in American Field–type field trials, you should insist on FDSB registration. But if you want to run in AKC field trials or hunting tests, you should insist on AKC registration. Dual registration is ideal, but not mandatory.

With all that done, choose the litter from which you will select the puppy you hope will grow up to be your personal wonder-dog.

PICKING A PUPPY

You may now start playing with puppies. But how should you go about picking just one?

Before expounding on how to pick the best puppy for you, I suppose I should say a few words about the male/female decision. Frankly, my few words are: Yes, you must get one or the other, but don't fret about it. Get whichever you prefer, and you will be happy with your choice. Get the sex someone else touts, against your instincts, and you will be unhappy with it. Okay, now on to the important stuff.

For many years field trialers have recommended that, after selecting a good litter, you simply reach in and grab a puppy. Wrong, wrong, wrong.

True, field trialers seek competitive dogs, dogs that can win. They can learn to love and live with any animal that fills their trophy cases. True also, no one can tell which pup in a litter will be most apt to become a winner. So maybe the reach-in-and-grab technique works as well as any—*for field trialers.*

But you are trying to select a personal gun dog, not a pot collector. You need to know how to identify the pup that will best suit your individual personality; in short, the pup with which you will have the greatest rapport.

During recent years, several puppy-testing procedures have been developed and publicized. Most of them are for pups in the 7 to 12 week age group, which is when most pups go to new homes. These tests do help identify canine personality traits: dominance/submissiveness, boldness/fearfulness, friendliness/independence, and so forth. That information can help you understand your puppy early on. I recommend that you learn about them and apply such tests to the puppies from which you can choose.

However, the most important selection criterion should be rapport. Play with each puppy in whatever way you wish, test it as you choose, then select the one you just plain like best. Go with your gut instinct here. The puppy you are most strongly attracted to is the best one for you. It may not be right for your hunting buddy, but it is for you. That's the nice thing about a well-bred litter. Every pup is the best one for someone.

Years ago I talked to an elderly Pointer breeder with an outstanding local reputation for breeding wonderful gun dogs. I asked him what his breeding secrets were. He told me that matching each puppy with the right owner was, if anything, more important than the breeding itself.

"I tell the guy to bring his wife out when he picks his puppy," he said. "Then I send the old man down to the kennel to play with the litter while I talk to the wife. I ask her what he's *really* like—and she'll tell me, too, every time. Then, I just match him up with the pup that is most like him."

That's what you're really doing with all these tests and all this playing: trying to identify the pup that resembles you most in personality. That's the best pup for you.

Don't pay for the pup unless you receive the proper registration form (AKC or FDSB). Don't accept *any* excuse for the lack of this form. Wait to buy until the breeder has everything in order to complete the sale. In fact, any difficulties about registration papers at this stage should make you suspicious of the breeder's integrity.

HOUSING YOUR DOG

If you plan to maintain only one dog, you should keep it in the house with you. That way, it will have your company and that of your family. If you put it outside, even in an ideal kennel, it will suffer loneliness. I remember years ago watching helplessly as a delightful Brittany went stir-crazy because it was kenneled alone in a backyard. The owner fed and watered it as he should have and cleaned up after it often enough for good sanitation. But, except during hunting season, he paid no attention to the dog. I talked to the poor animal over the fence frequently, but that wasn't enough. In a couple of years I saw it change from a happy, gladda-see-ya dog to a cold-eyed suspicious slinker.

If you must keep your dog outside, get two dogs. They will keep each other company. Besides, alternating two pointing dogs while hunting gives you fresh dog power all day.

Keep your two dogs in adjacent runs, so they can interact without being able to harm each other if they disagree on some point of canine etiquette. My runs are 21 feet long, 4 feet wide, and 6 feet high. The base is concrete and the fencing is chainlink (including a top). Each run has a doghouse. During the winter, I cover the gates, which are on the north end, with canvas to stop the wind.

My runs are right next to my house and under a large maple tree for shade. I have never understood why so many people put them way out in back. I don't like to wade through snowdrifts in the winter to take care of my dogs. Ditto for heavy summer rains. I can get to my dogs comfortably in any weather. When they bark, I hear them before my neighbors do. I can keep them quieter this way.

TATTOOING FOILS DOGNAPPERS

Research laboratories pay $2 per pound for live animals delivered to their doors, and they don't ask too many questions. After all, this country has always had more strays than we can count.

Not surprisingly, we have full-time dognappers who make very good livings satisfying this demand. The typical professional dognapper picks up strays, of course, but if he can't get enough animals that way, he may steal dogs from backyards, even from locked kennel runs. In this day of two-income families, many neighborhoods are deserted during working hours. If a dognapper finds a dog in a locked kennel run, he risks little by sawing through the lock.

Laboratories will not accept tattooed dogs. A tattooed dog can be traced. Thus, professional dognappers leave them alone. If he gets one accidentally, he turns it loose before arriving at the laboratory—unless the tattoo is on the dog's ear, in which case he might cut off the entire ear!

To foil dognappers, have your dog tattooed on the inside of one upper thigh. Some prefer to tattoo the dog's registration number. Others use their Social Security numbers. Still others make up numbers. To find a tattooist, contact your veterinarian or one of the tattoo registries listed in Appendix III, "Important Contacts."

As an added precaution, you should put a sign on your kennel runs indicating that your dogs are tattooed. That might prevent dognappers from taking your dogs and dumping them miles away.

PART II

TRAINING YOUR BIRDDOG

Overview

Maybe you dream. . . . Here Cecil Gardner's Shorthair delivers the bird beautifully.

At this point, you either have your birddog or you are in the process of acquiring one. Let's say you have just brought him home.

I hope that as you sit there reading, perhaps with your puppy beside you, you dream of the wonderful things the youngster will one day do. Perhaps you see him kiting down a hedgerow, head high, testing the wind. Suddenly he spins and stops in a calendar-art point: tail high, head high, eyes bugged out, one front foot cocked, nostrils flaring, every muscle taut. As you approach him, you say softly, "Good boy. Whoa." You step in front of him, gun ready. Without warning, some 20 to 25 quail detonate almost under your feet and blow out in every direction. BOOM! One quail falls. BOOM! Nothing falls. (Well, I guess you're a realist, even in your dreams.) Your birddog stands staunchly in place, staring intensely where the one bird fell. At your "Fetch!" he races out, snatches up the bird, and tosses it merrily as he returns. He drops it into your hand. You turn the bird slowly, admiring every feather. Then your birddog nudges your leg. You look at him and see his eyes pleading that you stuff that bird into your gamebag and start off after more. So you do. But as you do, you keep repeating to yourself "Wow! What a dog!"

Maybe you dream of struggling through ruffed grouse tangles with your birddog's bell tinkling ahead of you. You bend to avoid this limb, step over this one, squirm under that one, lift another as you duck under it. You stop to wipe the sweat from your forehead and realize the bell has gone silent. He's on point! But where? Let's see, last time you remember hearing him, he was over this way. You struggle in that direction, bending, stooping, ducking cover as you do. Yes, there he is, crouching in a tight point that tells you the bird is very close indeed. Before you reach your dog, the grouse fills the quiet woods with his roaring take-off. Getting barely a glimpse, you toss off a quick snap shot at the bird's sound. You listen for a *kerplop.* Did you hear it, or didn't you? Uncertain, you say "Fetch" tentatively. Your birddog disappears into the underbrush. In less than a minute you hear him struggling back toward you. Bird or no bird? Yeah! All right! He has the grouse in his mouth when he reappears. He drops it in your mitt. "Wow! What a dog!"

Perhaps you dream of cutting your birddog loose in a huge field where pheasants hide (and run). The weeds stand evenly, about thigh-high, everywhere you look. Where will the birds be? Your dog cuts this way and that, using the wind, using his experience, and using his nose. He slows down, points, eases forward, points, moves forward again, and finally locks up tighter than a politician with his own money. You hurry toward your dog. Will the bird hold? You move faster and faster. In fact, you huff and puff a bit. You swing out and around to approach your dog from the front, to help hold the bird. After you take a couple of steps toward your dog, a rooster rockets straight up between you and your dog. All those colors, shining in the sun! You bend over backwards shooting the bird as he levels off at the top of his climb and starts back behind you. Feathers fly everywhere, showering you and your dog, but the bird keeps going. You turn and fire the other barrel. The rooster tips over and heads for the ground. "Fetch!" you scream, trying to give your dog every advantage against what you know will be a strong runner. Fingers crossed, you watch your dog trail the bird zig-zag for 50 or 60 yards. Bingo! Back he comes, with the rooster's iridescent head bobbing from one side of his mouth and his long tail dancing from the other. "Wow! What a dog!"

Such dreams contribute greatly to your training program. Remember them often and they will keep you going when you hit a training snag (as everyone does). When your other responsibilities take you away from training for a while, your dreams will bring you back as soon as possible. Keep dreaming and you'll keep training.

Training is a continuous process, not a series of disconnected steps and phases. Nor is it what mathematicians call linear. You don't always complete all of one phase before starting another. Sometimes you can—and should—work on several phases in a single session. Sometimes you work on multiple phases in parallel for a sustained period of time. Be aware of this, but don't fret about it. Throughout the training chapters I explain when you should be doing what.

I have divided the training program into eight parts and devoted a chapter to each: Puppy Training, Obedience Training, Hunting and Pointing, Force-Breaking—Gently, Staunching on Point, Stopping to Flush, Steadying and Honoring, and Proofing and Maintenance Training. In each chapter, I precede the training coverage with the following background topics: What Is It?, Why Do It?, Prerequisites, Equipment and Facilities, Schedule, and Handling Techniques.

To get the big picture, read the entire training section first, maybe a couple of times. Then you will understand how each chapter fits into the overall plan.

TRAINING BASICS

Developing a birddog involves two complementary processes: encouraging the dog's natural instincts to develop properly, and teaching the dog appropriate responses to a series of commands. Although both are important, you will spend most of your training time on the second process.

It would be wonderful if a person could communicate with his dog as he does with other humans—by words. Then a trainer could simply explain to the dog in words what he wants done, how he wants it done, and why it matters to him. The dog, assuming it retained its great desire to please in spite of its new intelligence, would then do as instructed.

But training doesn't work that way. No, to be successful, you must train your dog through *conditioned responses,* just as Pavlov did. You lead the beast through the proper response to a command and reward him appropriately. You repeat this over and over, in different locations, with different distractions, until he does it always and everywhere through rote repetition. Of course, any time he fails to respond properly, you punish him appropriately (which does *not* mean severely). Thus, he learns that doing things your way brings pleasant results but doing them any other way brings unpleasant results.

The most important reward in your cupboard is praise and appreciation. Your dog wants to please you. When you let him know he has done so, he feels rewarded. Similarly, the most severe punishment you have at your disposal is your displeasure. Use it sparingly.

To train a dog, you must be willing to go through many repetitions (rote drilling, if you will) in many locations. But you can't do too many at any one time, lest you ruin your dog's attitude. You also must be willing to praise your dog lavishly, even if you don't feel like it, when he does things correctly. I have, many times, praised a dog through gritted teeth—when the contrary beast finally got it right after trying everything else he could think of first (getting corrected for each mistake, of course).

One important caveat: All the formal training (rote drilling in the various commands) in the world will not make your dog a *complete* birddog. As mentioned above, you must also help your dog develop his natural hunting instincts. That takes experience with wild birds. So in addition to the "book larnin" you must also give him ample opportunities to study under the tutelage of wild birds. If you can only do that during hunting season, your dog will not progress in bird-sense as rapidly as he will if you can do it year-round. One more thing: When you run him on wild birds, don't hack him around; let him run and hunt and *learn from the birds.*

SCHEDULE

Most beginners worry too much about time. When starting each phase of training, they ask, "How long will this take?" Maybe they unconsciously allow our American workaday time-is-money philosophy to spill over into their recreational lives. Perhaps they suffer too much from the influence of football and basketball, in which the clock is so important.

Bowing (grudgingly, I admit) to this concern for time, I offer an approximation of the probable schedule in each chapter. However, these are just estimates. Don't set your stopwatch by them. Take whatever comfort you can in them, but don't take them *too* seriously. No one will take your dog away from you if you run behind. *And no one will give you a prize if you lap the field.*

You would be happier if you could forget about the clock, even the calendar. Put yourself in a baseball frame of mind. The inning ends when you get the third out. Each training phase ends when your dog can do the work. Not before.

Birddogs are not machines. They are sensitive, often high-strung animals. Although they lack human intelligence—which forces us to train them by conditioning rather than with reason and logic—they share our emotions. They experience fear, they become bewildered, they feel joy, they love, and they hate. They also share many of our physical limitations. They feel invigoration and exhaustion. They suffer headaches and backaches—but they cannot complain verbally. They have good days and bad days. Any training program that ignores these emotional and physical characteristics in order to meet some fanciful schedule will ruin 10 dogs for every one it makes.

Different breeds mature at different rates. Within each breed, some individuals mature more rapidly than others. Rapid maturity is not an unmixed blessing, nor is slow maturity a serious problem. The slower-developing dogs retain their training better, whereas the faster ones need more frequent refreshers throughout their lives.

Some trainers train faster than others. I am one of the slower ones. I value style, slash, and dash so much that I do everything I can to retain it. A person can't put it back after destroying it. Thus, I take more time, deliberately underwork my dogs (to keep them eager), and use as many positive motivators as I can.

So how long will it take you to train your birddog? The only answer I can give comes in two parts, both vague. First, it will take as long as it takes—which depends on both you and your dog. Second, you will never completely finish it, for you will have to do a certain amount of maintenance training all through your dog's active life.

More relevant schedule questions are: *How often should I train?* and *How long should each session be?*

Clearly, the more time you spend training your birddog—without overworking him—the better he will become. However, since you probably work for a living, you cannot spend all your waking hours creating a birddog wonder. Besides, you probably have family and other social obligations that limit your training time even more. So instead of talking about optimal time commitments, let's talk about what you can reasonably do with the time you can devote to training.

Puppy training, obedience, and force-breaking, much of which can be done at home, require frequent short sessions. Two or three brief (10 to 15 minute) periods per day would be ideal. You can get by with one a day. However, don't try to make up the difference by lengthening the sessions. Keep them short.

Field work, at whatever level, takes more time because you must leave home. If you can work in two or three sessions per week (including weekends), you should make excellent progress. Again, don't overwork your dog in any one session. Limit each session to no more than 45 minutes running afield, plus another quarter-hour to half-hour of formal birdwork.

If you work a daytime job, you can only train in the field in the evenings during the months of daylight savings time, April through October. Weekend training gives way to hunting during the fall—as it should. If you live in the northern half of the country, snow and cold limit your training during winter. Thus, you may have to make do with six or seven months of serious training per year. You can get by with that if you train regularly during those months. More would be better, of course, but the realities of life must prevail.

YOUR TRAINING GROUP

If you wish, you can do much of your training alone. However, for certain phases you need an assistant. For example, when your dog is ready to have birds shot over him, you should have someone else do the shooting. That way, you can concentrate on your dog and his manners. Similarly, when you teach your birddog to honor another dog's point, you need a training buddy with his dog.

Besides, most feel that it's more fun to train with a small and *simpatico* group. If you can find one or two other birddog owners who can train with you regularly, your training will be both more effective and more enjoyable. To find folks like that, you should join your local birddog club—the one that sponsors field trials and hunting tests in your area—and get acquainted.

TRAINING GROUNDS

You need as many training areas as you can get. A dog trained in only one pasture will act as if he has never been trained when taken somewhere else.

If you (like me) live in town and don't own extensive training grounds in the country, your biggest ongoing problem will be finding suitable places for training. Here are a few suggestions for managing (note that I didn't say *solving*) this problem.

First, join every hunting dog club in your area that has leased land available to members. Not just the birddog club(s). Most retriever and spaniel clubs will allow you to run your birddog on their grounds as long as you don't interfere with them when they are training their dogs there.

Second, take advantage of every opportunity you get to train on the grounds of shooting preserves in your area. Occasionally, such a preserve will swap training privileges for part-time guide services.

Third, if your area has a hunting club—one of those organizations that leases land for hunting and then sells memberships for reasonable fees—join it, and train on their leased land through the off-season.

Fourth, check with your state's fish and game commission for information on state land open to dog trainers during the off-season.

Finally, drive around the countryside and talk to landowners. Sometimes, if you impress them as a rational human being (not a wild-eyed, city-spawned maniac), they will welcome you on their land. Hey, it's worth a shot.

Wherever you find land for training, treat it and everything on it with respect. Don't do anything dumb! One club in my area lost a marvelous lease through the incredible stupidity of two members. One hot, dry summer, these two nerds took their families out to the lease on the Fourth of July. At dusk, they started shooting fireworks in the pasture. The farmer tossed them out before they started a fire—fortunately—and then terminated the club's lease posthaste. When asked why they did this, one of these two idiots answered, "Hell, we lease the place. We ought to be able to do anything out there we want to!" Dumb, dumb, dumb.

THE PROFESSIONAL TRAINER

Most amateurs fall into one of two schools of thought about pros: the "all" school or the "nothing at all" school. I don't agree with either.

Members of the "all" school feel totally incompetent to train their own dogs. They turn the entire job over to a pro and only see their dogs during hunting season or at field trials. They may fill their trophy cases, but they miss the joy of day-in, day-out associations with their dogs.

Members of the "nothing at all" school feel it would be a disgrace to get help from a pro. When they run into a training problem they can't handle, they either live with it or they start over with a new dog.

As I said, I don't agree with either school. I feel that the pro's greatest usefulness lies somewhere in the middle. You should train your own dog, but when you hit a brick wall, you should seek professional assistance. I have always followed that approach, and I recommend it to you. No one knows everything about birddogs, so it's no disgrace to admit it when you are baffled. In fact, pros go to other pros for help sometimes, just as golf pros do.

YOU *CAN* TRAIN YOUR BIRDDOG

You may have noticed that I have not discussed what it takes to be a dog trainer. I have a couple of reasons for this omission.

First, every time I read such a passage in a book, I suffer a deep feeling of inadequacy. I am intimidated by the list of preternatural personality traits some writers insist a person must have just to train a birddog.

Even now, after having spent many years training many dogs to do many things, I feel that I may not measure up to the author's standards. Clearly, such standards are pure (self-serving) fiction.

Second, I believe any healthy and rational person can train a birddog if he wants to. More specifically, I believe *you* can do it. You need only *know* two things: the techniques in an integrated training program, and your individual dog. I give you the former. Your dog tells you all about himself every moment you spend with him. If you pay attention to him, you cannot miss his messages.

Granted, some people have more talent as dog trainers than others. They have more insight, more creativity, and probably more interest than most. Some ball players play in the major leagues, some at various levels in the minors, and some peak out in slow-pitch softball. But they are all ball players.

If you *want* to train a birddog, you *can* train a birddog. *Vaya con Dios.*

CHAPTER 13

Puppy Training:

Getting the Right Start

Most pups start to point after flushing a few birds, as Doug Meierhoff's Shorthair, Rebel, is doing. However . . .

the trainer can encourage pointing a little, as Doug Meierhoff is doing here, and . . .

it works! Rebel points on his own.

BACKGROUND

What Is It?

During the first several weeks after bringing your puppy home, you can teach him a few useful words, like his call-name (the one you use for him every day, not necessarily his registered name) and two formal commands: *No* and *Hush*. You can introduce him to cover, birds, gunfire, and water. You can awaken his pointing instinct. You can introduce him to play-retrieving with both a dummy and dead birds.

Why Do It?

In this training, you not only build the foundation for all your pup's later work afield, you also build the foundation for your relationship with him. That relationship should be friendly—buddy-buddy, really—but, trust me, one of you will be the boss. If you want the job, apply early, when it's open. That doesn't mean dominating the puppy unmercifully. It doesn't mean being unkind or unfeeling. It just means maintaining control in a friendly but firm way. Adopt the attitude that you are a benevolent monarch. You rule your canine subject, but you assume full responsibility for his physical and mental welfare.

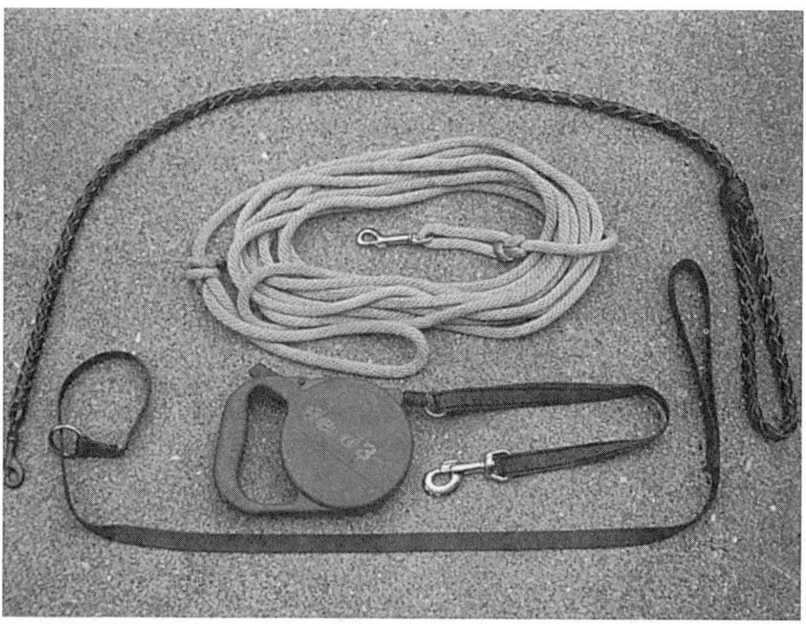

From top: A short lead, a 20-foot checkcord, a Flexi-Lead, and a short slip-collar/lead combination.

Prerequisites

The only prerequisites are a healthy puppy of seven to twelve weeks and a strong desire on your part to learn how to train him.

Equipment and Facilities

You need a collar for your pup. Actually, you need a series of them in graduated sizes to accommodate his growing neck size. Until the pup is fully grown, I prefer the little nylon strap collars with plain buckles. They are cheap and sturdy.

You should have a light puppy lead. This can be a simple nylon affair, maybe five or six feet long. You should have a Flexi-Lead, which releases and rewinds a long lead in a manner similar to that of an automatic fly reel. This will come in handy for taking your puppy for walks, for encouraging a good return in play-retrieving, and as a tangle-free checkcord in the field. Flexi-Leads come in several lengths and strengths. Get one strong enough to handle a mature dog of your breed, and the longest one available. Right now, that is about 26 feet.

You need a puppy-sized retrieving dummy or, better yet, a series of them in graduated sizes. My wife makes mine from pillow ticking and foam rubber chunks. Several mail-order catalogs offer puppy dummies in a variety of sizes and materials.

You need two plastic whistles. Why two? You might blow the side out of one in mid-toot, so you need a readily available backup. Why plastic? In cold weather a metal whistle sticks to your lips and can tear skin off when you remove the whistle from your mouth. Some people, especially those who chew on their whistles afield, cover the mouth end with surgical tubing.

What kind of whistle? Several good ones are on the market today, but the favorites are the Roy Gonia, the Acme Thunderer, and the Fox 40. I favor the Gonia because it is small, easy to hold between the teeth, and has a wonderful range, from a soft *pip-pip-pip* to a blast that reaches out a long, long way.

You need a lanyard on which to carry your whistles. If you carry them in your pocket, you will waste precious seconds fishing one out, and it will sometimes not work because of lint or other materials it has picked up in your pocket. Lanyards come in many styles, from the inexpensive nylon cord models to high-dollar affairs in braided leather, beaded macrame, even braided horsehair.

Eventually, you will feel improperly dressed without your lanyard and whistles dangling from your neck. I've even seen people wearing them at airports. You will acquire quite a collection of them, and you will stash lanyards and whistles here and there for convenience. I have one hanging from the mirror of my truck, one by the back door, and two with my training equipment. Two retired lanyards (with whistles) hang on the wall with other memorabilia from outstanding dogs that live only in my memory.

You need a .22 blank pistol for introducing your pup to gunfire. Some prefer a .22 starter pistol that takes regular .22 blanks, but many trainers use a less expensive pistol that shoots only the quieter "crimp" .22 blanks. Some field trialers use .32 blank starter pistols, which are required in some trials. I use a .32 blank that has been converted to fire shotgun primers. Primers make as much noise as regular .22 blanks, and cost a lot less.

If you decide to play the wing-on-a-string game with your pup (to start sight pointing), you will need a pole some five to ten feet long with a string of equal length attached. You also need a bird wing to attach to the other end of the string.

You need a source for pigeons and quail. Check with the secretary of your local birddog field trial club.

Finally, you need fields (the more the better) with cover and terrain variations, where you can allow your pup to learn all about his place of work. You also need a small stream in which you can introduce him to water.

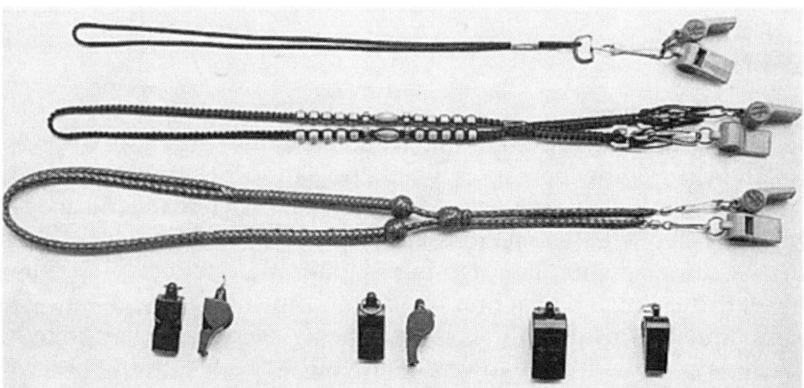

Varieties of lanyards and whistles. From top: a cord lanyard, a macrame lanyard, a braided leather lanyard (all three with Roy Gonia whistles), and a row of other popular whistles (from left): two Fox 40s, two medium Acme Thunderers, one large Acme, and one small Acme.

Schedule

You should start this training almost as soon as you bring the puppy home. If possible, work with him every day.

You should sequence your puppy training steps as follows: Start with familiarization, during which you teach the puppy his name and *No!*, then teach *Hush.* Start his introduction to cover and terrain as soon as he is acquainted with you; introduce him to water (during warm weather only) when he has accepted you as his special human; and do the wing-on-a-string game (if you must) after he has become accustomed to cover and terrain. You can start play-retrieving anytime after he has established his lair and accepted you as his special human, but you might want to wait until after he has shown some indication of pointing instinct (either afield or in the wing-on-a-string game).

Puppy training flows naturally into obedience training (Chapter 14) and hunting and pointing training (Chapter 15). Your puppy may be four months old—or he may be eight months old—before you complete this puppy training and move on. Depends on him. Depends on you.

Handling Techniques

Any handling procedures you need are explained in the appropriate training sections. For the most part, you should just be comfortable, relaxed, and consistent.

TRAINING

Getting Acquainted

First, spend a few days getting acquainted. Everything in your future relationship with the pup depends on rapport. Rapport depends on *mutual understanding and respect.* Each of you must understand and accept the other's role in the relationship.

As long as you allow the pup enough time to sleep—and he will need to do a lot of that at first—you cannot spend too much time getting acquainted. However, if job commitments keep you away from home each day, you will have to wedge in your dog time around your work time. A few minutes each morning and a longer period each evening will do nicely, especially when complemented with generous weekend allotments.

During your time together, you will come to understand your pup and—more importantly—the pup will come to understand you. Dogs read people better, faster, and more thoroughly than people read dogs (which explains in part why people spend so much time working, while dogs mostly eat, sleep, hunt, and procreate). Given ample exposure to you, that pup will do most of the adjusting without you even realizing it.

Introduce him to as many of the situations he will have to cope with throughout his life as possible: how to go up and down stairs; the sound of the doorbell, the TV, the washing machine, the dishwasher, and the trashman; and so on. Take the pup for walks around the neighborhood on his lead or the Flexi-Lead. Let other people make up with him. An occasional trip to a shopping center will do wonders.

The Puppy's Name

The first word you should teach your puppy is his name. Not his long-winded registered name, but a short call-name you will use daily for the rest of his life. I usually make a call-name from part of a dog's registered name. My resident Shorthair is registered as Westwind's Erick Von Greif, so I call him Erick (plus or minus colorful expletives, as the occasion demands). Others choose names that have no relationship to the dog's name. The dog doesn't care, really. It's your choice.

A good call-name should have two characteristics: First, it should be short, no more than two syllables; second, it should not sound like any other word in the dog's working vocabulary, especially the various command words you will teach him: *No, Hush, Kennel, Release, Whoa, Come, Fetch, Give.*

Since you will mostly use your dog's call-name to get his attention, you want a short one. Magnificent Adonis might sound impressive as you carry and pet the little puppy, but over the dog's life, you will find just plain Don more comfortable. With judicious use of your whistle, you shouldn't have to holler at your dog often, but when you must shout—and it may save your dog's life someday—you'll find a short call-name shouts better than a long one. One or two syllables, no more.

Call-names that sound like command words—Moe (*No, Whoa*), for example—will cause your dog to misunderstand you at times, especially at a distance.

Having selected a good call-name, start immediately teaching the youngster to respond to it. If you are a puppy cuddler (as I am), repeat the call-name as you carry the puppy around the house and yard. Over and over and over. Look at it this way: You have to say something while carrying him, so why not say his call-name? That way, he can learn something from your reassuring voice. Use that name when you put his food bowl down, when you let the pup outside or out of his kennel run, when you run away from him in play—in short, every chance you get.

Later you will occasionally use his name when you are displeased. Now, however, use it only under pleasant circumstances. If the pup comes to associate the sound of his name with rewards of various kinds—being held and petted, being fed, being let outside, chasing the boss around the yard, and so on—he will react positively. Conversely, if he comes to associate it with punishment of any kind, he will learn to react negatively to it, perhaps even learn to run away and hide whenever you say his name, or at best ignore you. If you sometimes reward him and sometimes punish him when you call his name, he will become one confused puppy, and it will show.

No!

Initially, the only word the puppy should associate with your displeasure is *No!* A normally inquisitive pup will get into enough mischief to learn quickly that *No!* means trouble—if you use it consistently, without his call name, to correct him.

Back up each *No!* with whatever little force is necessary to gain compliance with your wishes. Puppies of seven weeks to four or five months are easy to handle physically, so you needn't do anything heavy-handed. Simply forcing the pup to do or stop doing something normally suffices. On those occasions that call for stronger measures, you can convince the youngster of the wisdom of humoring you with obedience by giving him a light shaking coupled with words of displeasure. In extreme cases, a swat on the fanny with a rolled-up newspaper will do wonders. However, do not ever strike your dog in the face, especially with your hand. A hand-shy dog can be extremely difficult to train—and he will make you look like a real brute to your friends and hunting buddies when he shies away from your approaching hand, even when you try to pet him.

Hush!

Some puppies are naturally quiet. Others are naturally noisy. Most fall somewhere in the middle. Regardless of which you drew, if you are a city dweller, you must show consideration for your neighbors. That is most easily done by teaching your dog to stop barking on command.

For the command word, I prefer *Hush!* Some use *Stop-That-Noise!*, *Shut It Up!*, or some even more colorful variation. But the simple one-syllable *Hush!* works as well and is easier to articulate when you are sleepy. Whatever word you choose, you must convince your pup that it means "stop barking—*NOW!*"

The problem that prevents most owners from convincing their dogs to stop barking on command is the lapse between the offense and the correction, especially in the middle of the night. By the time the boss dresses and gets outside to correct the dog, the beast has probably stopped on his own. I deal with this by opening the window and saying *Hush!* while he is still barking. Then, I dress and go out. Even if he has quieted down on his own, I grasp and shake his muzzle as I command *Hush!* several times. After a few such incidents, the dog learns that the word *Hush!* means trouble, so he scoots for his doghouse.

That quiets him—admittedly by accident—so I don't go outside to punish him. Eventually he figures out that if he stops barking on the command *Hush!*, nothing bad happens to him, even if he doesn't hide in his doghouse. This takes time and, most of all, consistency.

A stream of water convinces a dog to quiet down better than a shaking, but you can only use water during the warmer months. During the summer, I keep a squirt bottle full of water by the back door. When I go out to correct a dog for barking, I grab that squirt bottle on my way out. Instead of shaking the offender's muzzle as I say *Hush!*, I squirt him in the face with water from a squirt bottle.

One caution: Don't start *Hush!* training too soon after the puppy arrives at your place. Give him time to adjust. Look at it from his perspective: He has been removed from his mother and littermates, perhaps flown several hours on an airplane, picked up by a total stranger, driven to a strange house, played with briefly, and then shoved into an unfamiliar kennel run. No wonder the poor thing howls a bit the first few nights!

Still, you must show your neighbors some consideration. If you take the pup around and introduce him, explaining that he may be a little noisy for a few nights, most people will be understanding. Then, if you get out of bed, go outside, and reassure the pup when he gets too noisy, he won't become totally obnoxious. When he begins to howl, let him out of his kennel run and allow him to follow you around the yard until he is sleepy again. Then, put him back and go to bed. Don't pick him up. Don't pet him. Don't make a fuss over him. Just keep him moving until he is ready to go back to sleep. This rather impersonal approach prevents the pup from feeling that he is training you to come out and console him. After a few nights of this, when he is acclimated to his new environment, you can start *Hush!* training.

Introduction to Cover

Take your pup for romps in all kinds of cover from his earliest days. Let him get familiar with the feel and scent of the conditions under which he will do his life's work. Let him dig for field mice, chase songbirds, catch toads, and, most of all, plow through every type of cover you can find. Let him romp up and down hills, through wooded areas, across ditches, whatever.

If he flushes a bird—or even a rabbit—let him chase it until his heart is content. If it is a bird, you might even praise him as he does, but say nothing if it is a rabbit. The puppy will associate the praise with the bird, not the chasing. It tells him you are pleased when he finds birds.

If he points *anything*—bird, rabbit, mouse, turtle, harmless snake, whatever—praise him softly and let him decide when enough pointing is enough. He will eventually dive in. Fine, as long as he is not pointing something that can hurt him. If he flushes a bird after pointing it, let him chase, praising him as he does. You are letting him develop his hunting instincts now, not training him to be staunch on point (which comes much, much later).

If he points something that can hurt him—a poisonous snake or porcupine, for example—pick him up and carry him away. Leading him away discourages pointing. Later on, you will lead him away when he points undesirable things (like rabbits), specifically to discourage him from pointing them. Right now, you want to encourage any pointing he may do.

Introduction to Gunfire

During these romps afield, your pup will occasionally flush and chase (with or without a point) a songbird or even a gamebird. Great! Wait until he has chased several. Then, when he is some distance from you and highballing after a bird, fire your blank pistol. If he acts startled, ignore him and keep walking. If you console him in any way, you will confirm his suspicion that his fears are well founded. If you ignore him and act as if nothing happened, he will assume you are right and he is wrong. Let him flush and chase several more before shooting again.

Chances are, he will not notice that first shot. If he ignores it, shoot every time he chases a bird.

Introduction to Water

Even if you will never ask your birddog to retrieve waterfowl, you should introduce him to water and let him learn to swim comfortably. You may shoot an upland bird that falls in or across water. If he won't jump in and swim, he won't retrieve it for you.

The ideal place to introduce a pup to water is a lazy, firm-bottomed stream or creek about 20 yards across with shallows on both shores and 5 to 10 yards of hip-deep water in the middle. The stream should be slow-moving, of course, so the pup will not be washed downstream when his feet leave the bottom.

A stream is better than a lake. You should introduce him to water by leading him in. In a lake, you can go only so far. If he refuses to follow you, he wins, for you will have to return to him eventually. In a shallow stream, you can cross and keep going away from him on the far side. He will fear that you are leaving him, so will follow.

Why do you lead him in, rather than, say, tossing a retrieving dummy in for him (assuming he retrieves)? Look at it this way: You wouldn't expect the greatest field hockey player on earth to transfer his skills to ice hockey until he became comfortable on ice skates, would you? Ditto for a dog that retrieves on land, but has never learned to swim.

This introduction should take place in warm weather, of course, and the water should have a comfortable temperature. The only way you can tell what the water is like is to wade in it *without waders.* Slip into some old jeans and tennis shoes, things you don't mind wearing in the water.

Start out walking around the field adjacent to the stream. When both of you are plenty warm, wade into the stream and stand in the shallows. If the water is uncomfortably cool for you, get out and don't let the pup get in. If the water is okay, stay there and encourage him to follow you in. When he does, praise him and walk around in the shallows. Stay where he can walk rather than swim. Continue to praise him as he follows you. You might even sit down in the water and pet him awhile. Before asking him to swim, let him learn that following you walking in water is not very different from following you on land.

When he seems to enjoy walking around belly-deep in shallow water, wade across and encourage him to follow you. If he has shown any reluctance to enter earlier, find a much narrower place for his first crossing, perhaps even one in which he will not have to swim to cross. Eventually, cross in a spot where he must swim a little way to reach you. If he balks, move away from him and encourage him to follow. When he does, praise him lavishly as he splashes his way toward you and really make a fuss over him when he reaches you.

Then walk around in the field near the stream awhile to dry him off. When he seems good and hot again, lead him back across. Go back and forth several times, always praising him while he swims.

Don't worry if he beats the water with his front feet, and above all, don't dream up any clever techniques for curing this problem. He will work through it in time with no help from you. I have heard of inexperienced (and insensitive) trainers tying weights on a pup's front end, wading along pushing down on his head and shoulders, and heaven only knows what else. The only thing such nonsense can do is make the pup hate water. Dumb, dumb, dumb.

Once your pup will follow you readily in this one place, take him across in several different places, even in different streams, if possible. Eventually, you can even have him swim along behind a boat in a lake if you wish. Let him catch up and climb aboard occasionally to motivate the chase.

Remember to repeat this water work now and then throughout the warmer months so your pup doesn't forget what he has learned.

Awakening the Pointing Instinct

If your pup points or even flash-points during his romps in the field, you need not mess with this sight-pointing exercise. In fact, you shouldn't. It's a wake-up call to the pointing instinct at best, not a real training procedure.

However, if your pup chases and chases—and you, being a beginner, are starting to worry about whether he will ever point—to relieve your anxiety you should play the old wing-on-a-string game in the backyard. On a stick or fishing rod some 5 to 10 feet long, tie a string of equal length. Tie a bird wing on the end of the string.

Take your pup out in the backyard and swing the wing around and around in a circle above him. He will chase it, but you should keep it just high enough and just far enough ahead of him to keep him from catching it. When he slows down a bit, drop the wing to the ground. If he points, fine, praise him. If he dives in, snatch it up again so he cannot catch it and swing it around again. Drop it again, and so on. If he points and then dives in (as he probably will), keep him from catching it. If he occasionally catches it, no big problem, really, but try to keep him from it as much as you can.

Now, after you have done this often enough to convince yourself that the little rascal does indeed have some pointing instinct, *hang it up already!* Break the pole if you have to, but stop playing this game. It does nothing to advance your pup's education beyond this point. In fact, it can create problems, for it encourages sight-pointing. Later, in the field, he will creep forward too close to his birds before locking up—because he feels he must see them before pointing.

If you can resist doing this at all, so much the better, but few beginners have that much blind faith in a pup's genes. So try this if you must, but don't continue doing it after you know your pup will indeed point.

Play-Retrieving

Most birddog puppies have natural retrieving instinct, but few beginning trainers understand what that is, let alone how to bring it out.

The so-called retrieving instinct is not, as many think, a tendency to pick up birds and deliver them to the boss. No, no, no, it's something entirely different.

In the wild, a large animal feasts on a kill on site. A small animal, on the other hand, picks up its kill and hustles back to its lair, where it can consume its prize at leisure and without much danger of losing it to a larger animal. Dogs, descending as they do from small animals, retain at least some of that instinct to carry a kill back to the lair.

Trainers turn that instinct into retrieving by becoming a secondary lair for their dogs, using the animal's desire to please the pack leader (trainer) as motivation for the process. *Thus, you cannot bring out your puppy's so-called retrieving instinct until he has established his primary lair and until he has formed a strong attachment to you.*

Every pup establishes a lair, which is that one special place he considers his own, the place to which he retreats to sleep, to meditate on the meaning of life, or just to escape the "slings and arrows of outrageous fortune." For the outside dog, it will be his doghouse. For the inside dog, it will be where he sleeps regularly.

You should not attempt play-retrieving until he feels you are his special human being, his buddy, his boss, the pack leader he must please. Through early familiarization, you become his buddy. Through *No!* and *Hush!* training, you become his boss, his pack leader.

When your pup has shown that he is ready—has a lair and accepts you—familiarize him with a puppy dummy of appropriate size. Hold him by the collar and show him the dummy. This is something new, and many pups are apprehensive at first. Let him smell it and mouth it a little. Control him with his collar and keep the dummy in your hand even as he mouths it. This initial step is one of familiarization. Don't yet try to get him excited about the dummy by teasing him with it. That could frighten him and set training back.

When he has no fear of the dummy—in fact, seems to like it a lot—go near his lair. Release your grip on his collar and tease him with the dummy. Tap it on the ground, wave it around in the air, talk excitedly, and so on. When he is frantic to get the dummy, toss it four or five feet. If all goes well, he will pounce on it, spin around, and head for his lair. Since you are in the way, he must go directly past you. As he does, slip a finger under his collar and gently stop him. *Do not take the dummy.* Just bring the youngster to a stop beside you.

Pet and praise him for several minutes, all the time letting him keep the dummy. If you take it too soon, he will avoid you the next time. In the pup's mind, that dummy is canine property, fairly obtained, and you have no right to it. Respect that feeling. Just praise and pet him and make him glad he chanced by you. After a few moments of this, see whether he is willing to surrender the dummy. If so, take it. If not, continue praising and petting him while he holds his treasure. Eventually, he will let you take it.

Repeat this two or three times, no more. Don't give even the most eager pup more than four retrieves per session.

Okay, that's how it goes if your pup reacts ideally, as most puppies will. However, he may react in any of several less-than-ideal ways. He may not even go after the dummy. He may run to it but not pick it up. He may run to it, lie down and chew on it. He may pick it up and run off.

If he doesn't chase it, or chases it but refuses to pick it up, you may not have done the preliminary work thoroughly enough. He may not yet feel comfortable with this new thing. You may have tossed it before he was adequately excited. Start over and see if the problem goes away. Another possibility: Maybe he is too tired from playing with the kids or the other dogs all day. Confine him for an hour or so before each training session so he will be adequately rested. Or maybe he doesn't feel well. However, if this uninterest persists over several sessions, he may lack retrieving instinct. In that case, you will have to force-break him later on—or settle for a dog that points dead instead of retrieving. If neither option suits you, you should take your pup to a pro for an evaluation. If the pro confirms your suspicions, you should trade this pup in on a new model as soon as you can.

The pup that lies down and starts chewing the dummy will probably grow up to be a tough, independent cuss that will require a heavy hand throughout his training. You should give some thought as to whether you care to deal with such an animal when he is full-grown. If not, get a second opinion from a pro before you swap him off. Solving the immediate problem is rather simple: Go out and take the dummy away from the little outlaw; then put the lead on him and start over. If he does the same thing, haul him unceremoniously back to you, *with or without the dummy.* This type of hooligan is not much given to dropping dummies, or even releasing them without coercion. But if the dummy does fall out of his mouth—and if you ease up on the pressure—he will figure out that he can control you by dropping the dummy. Then, he will drop it as soon as you apply pressure, and mess around picking it up again—over and over and over. Don't let that start. Haul him in, with or without the dummy.

You should also go immediately to the lead with the dog that picks up the dummy and runs off. This dog is aloof and little affected by praise and petting, which makes it difficult to motivate him with anything but force and fear. Frankly, these negative motivators will play a large role in all training for such a dog. If you are too tender hearted to apply copious force, you might consider starting over with a better prospect. If you decide to stick with this one, there is one motivator that will help you through your immediate problem: food. Generally, I don't recommend bribing a dog with treats, but I would make an exception in this case. Use the lead to force him to return to you, and then trade him a piece of dog food for the dummy. This encourages both the return and the release. The anticipation of food may even cause this dog to drop the dummy as he reaches you. Don't worry about it. You will have to force-break him later anyhow and you can deal with that problem then. As he returns more and more voluntarily, cut back on the treats, until you are no longer using them at all—if possible.

If you must go to the lead to get a decent return, stay with it until you have not the slightest doubt about your pup's return. If you remove it too soon, you could teach him to run off when free but to return properly when you use the lead. Definitely not what you are trying to do.

Once you get a decent (off-lead) return immediately in front of the dog's lair, try it a little ways away, but still so you are blocking his path to his lair. Keep your throws short, just four or five feet, and limit the number to no more than four per session. You're working for a reliable return, not distance and endurance records. When your pup returns reliably there, move a little farther away, and so on. When he *always* turns toward you on these short retrieves, rather than toward his primary lair, you have established yourself as his secondary lair for retrieving.

Now you should move some distance from his lair and toss the dummy directly toward it. If you have any doubt about your chances of success in this, start out with the lead attached, so you can force him to come to you rather than scoot into his doghouse with the dummy. If he does this and gets away with it, you almost have to start over. Better safe than sorry.

Next, you can lengthen the throws—gradually. If you have had much trouble getting the initial return, you might want to use the long Flexi-Lead for a few retrieves, just in case. Another precaution is using a long, narrow area in which he cannot help but return to you. I use the 4-foot by 20-foot space between my house and my kennel runs. This helps especially with a dog that returns almost to me but veers off at the last moment—as many do. The narrow passageway prevents the veering. Eventually such a dog will forget about it, especially if I praise him enough before reaching for the dummy.

If a pup veers off after I have moved out of my narrow passageway—as often happens—I run away from him, clapping my hands, talking excitedly to him. The puppy will invariably chase me. When he catches up, I grasp his collar. Then I pet and praise him awhile, but let him hold the dummy as long as he wishes.

That is the big secret with most dogs: Praise and pet them before taking the dummy so they want to return to you more than they want to get away with the dummy.

Teaching Commands by Association

You can simplify your later steadying efforts a little right now by giving your pup a command to retrieve as he chases after the dummy, and a command to return as he does indeed return to you. Although this may sound like a page out of the *Husband's Handbook*—you know, the page that says, "I can make my wife do anything she wants to do"—it is actually training by association. When you command the pup to do what he is already doing, he will associate the command with the action. That will help him understand the command later, when you teach it formally.

For a retrieve command, some use *Fetch!*, others use *Dead!* I prefer—and recommend—the dog's call-name. Why? I want my dog to have a retrieve command different from that used by any handler with whom I am braced. I don't want my dog to break when another handler sends his dog to retrieve. Will using his call-name as a command to retrieve confuse the dog? I've done it with many dogs, and it hasn't confused any of them so far. Like I said, they read us better than we read them.

For a come-in command, I use a whistle signal consisting of two shorts and a long—*Twee-Twee-Tweeeeeet*—trilled, not blasted. Others use a series of short sharp blasts. Choose whatever you like, but be consistent.

CHAPTER 14

Obedience Training:

a.k.a. Yard Breaking

This is how the properly installed chain training collar looks on a dog that heels on the trainer's left. *(Fr. Robert K. Spencer)*

BACKGROUND

What Is It?

The traditionalist birddog trainer, with his background in horse-training (where "breaking" means "training"), calls it "yard-breaking." The newer members among the birddog fraternity call it "obedience." Whichever you prefer, the term means a dog's conditioned responses to a set of commands. The set for birddogs includes *Release, Whoa, Kennel, Come-In,* and *Heel.*

Release tells the dog he is no longer under the constraint of whatever command he last received, that he is free to do as he pleases (within the general limits of good canine citizenship, of course). *Whoa* is birddog-eze for "stop and stand right there." *Kennel* sends the dog into his kennel run, crate, or dog box. *Come-In* tells the dog to proceed directly to the trainer (without passing Go or collecting $200). *Heel* means "walk beside the trainer."

Why Do It?

The most frequent and most serious charge made against birddogs by their owners' hunting buddies is that the dogs ruin hunts by running wild, completely out of control.

I well remember a quail-hunting trip I took with a man with whom I used to work. An out-of-town relative had given this man a two-year-old Pointer shortly before opening day. The relative said the dog was tireless and had an outstanding nose.

We only saw the dog three times all day: When we let him out of the car in the morning; when we returned to the car at dusk; and once about noon when he sailed past us at about 150 yards, blissfully ignoring my buddy's stream of commands—*Come, Whoa, Sit, Down, Heel*—each command followed by appropriate expletives.

The relative had not lied. The dog self-hunted all day and was still quite fresh at dusk. And he had a great nose, for he flushed and chased every covey in the county. Right after we turned him loose in the morning, we saw him flush a big bevy and chase it over the hill—which ended our first sighting of this animal. Although we were in prime Midwestern quail country, we did not see a bird all day. He flushed and chased every last covey.

For inexplicable reasons, my friend (not a dog man) fell in love with this bolting beast! He wouldn't go hunting without him. I didn't hunt with him again that year, of course, but others did, and I heard the reports. One by one, they stopped hunting with him, too.

Shortly before the start of the next quail season, I saw him walking despondently into his office. When I asked him what the problem was, he said someone had poisoned his dog the night before. Heart-broken, he swore off quail hunting because it would remind him of his "wonderful" dog. Of course, he changed his mind a couple of weekends into the season and was completely recovered by closing weekend.

I've always wondered whether one of his hunting buddies poisoned that miserable mutt. I've never asked around. Guess I don't really want to know.

Granted, obedience to a few commands would not have solved all of that dog's problems, especially his bolting. But it would have made it possible to lay hands on the critter and stuff him back in the car before he ruined everything.

If you can control your birddog, your buddies will love to hunt with you, even if your dog makes a few mistakes. If you can't control him, you will end the season singing that old WWII torch song, "I'll Walk Alone."

You instill basic control through obedience training, or yard-breaking. Do it right and the rest of your training—staunching, steadying, retrieving, handling afield—will go well. Slight it and you will never thoroughly train your dog in anything.

Prerequisites

You can—should—start teaching *Release, Whoa, Kennel,* and *Come-In* as soon as your pup knows his name and *No.* For *Heel,* you should wait until the pup is at least five or six months old. This command demands more seriousness and a longer attention span than the typical puppy under that age possesses.

Equipment and Facilities

You need several additional pieces of equipment.

For heeling, you need a chain training collar (sometimes called—erroneously, methinks—a choke collar), and you should learn to put it on your dog correctly. It has been designed to allow you to make little rapid-fire jerk-and-release corrections while heeling. To be effective, these corrections should cause the collar to tighten quickly and release quickly. That way, the dog gets the message at the right time. If you put the collar on backward, it will neither tighten nor release quickly.

To install the collar correctly, mind your P's and Q's. Hold the looped collar in front of you with the ring that attaches to the lead at the lower left. If you slide the other ring up the chain, you form the letter P. Now, reverse the collar so the lead ring hangs at the bottom right. When you slide the other ring up the chain, you form the letter Q. The rule for correct collar installation is this: If you heel the dog on your left, the P configuration is correct; if you heel the dog on your right, the Q configuration is correct.

One word of caution: *Do not allow your dog to wear a chain training collar when you are not with him.* He could catch it on something and hang.

Many birddog trainers use spike collars for much of their yard-breaking. These are leather or webbing slip-collars with a row of metal points lining the inside. Some trainers file the points down and call this a *pinch collar* because it can no longer puncture the dog's hide but can still pinch folds of skin around the animal's neck when tightened up. The principle underlying the use of this collar is that the dog will correct himself. Whenever the dog moves in the wrong direction or at the wrong speed, the collar tightens and the spikes push in on the dog's neck. When the dog returns to the proper place or speed, the collar loosens up.

Frankly, I don't like the spike collar, even with blunted spikes. I've never found it necessary. I am not very big. I am not even, as they say, strong for my size. I am no longer young. Even so, I have trained some pretty big and strong dogs. I have yet to find one that won't respond to the chain training collar, if it is properly installed and used. Perhaps if I were a pro trainer spending most of my waking hours yard-breaking other people's birddogs, I would view the spike collar differently.

You need a basic six-foot lead, in either leather or webbing. For large dogs like Erick, I use a leather lead that is one-half or five-eighths of an inch wide. For smaller dogs, I use one that is only three-eighths of an inch wide.

When you start heeling off-lead, you need a short, light riding crop or a flushing whip with which to remind your birddog where he belongs when he strays.

For teaching *Kennel,* you need a crate or dog box of some sort. Ideally, you should have an outdoor kennel run, too, but that isn't necessary.

Schedule

You cannot do obedience training on a now-and-then schedule. Ideally, you should get in a couple of 10- to 15-minute sessions each day. Many working people cannot manage two sessions a day, so they have to make do with one. That's okay, as long as they do it every day, not just every once in a while.

Train when your dog is fresh, not after field work or a play period. Confine him in a kennel run or crate for about two hours before each session. That way, when you let him out for training, he will be jumping out of his skin to work. Training becomes a reward. He will prance through his drills, especially if you keep the sessions short—and positive.

How long should obedience training take? Well, in one sense, it is never completed. You will give your dog occasional refreshers throughout his active life to keep his responses sharp and immediate. However, the initial training doesn't take a lifetime. An experienced trainer with a smart five-month-old pup could probably complete the course in 10 weeks or less. A green trainer with an average dog might take 20 weeks. Most human/canine teams fall somewhere between those extremes. However, since you do obedience training in parallel with regular field work, it doesn't matter how long it takes. It isn't holding anything up.

One more point on how long it takes: If you start some of this work when your puppy is quite small, as I recommend in some of the training sessions, you will finish much earlier than if you wait until the dog is five months old before starting any training.

Handling Techniques

I cover handling techniques, as necessary, in the training section for each command.

TRAINING

Release—The Obedience Paradox

Dog training is full of seeming contradictions. For example, the very basis of all control is freedom! The dog must understand when he is *not* on command before he can perform reliably when he is on command. Without that understanding, he will take frequent liberties to determine his current status empirically. The dog that knows precisely when he is and when he isn't on command need not experiment.

Thus, you need a specific *release command* with which to free your dog from your commands. For too many years, I have used *Okay,* a singularly poor choice because I use it so often in ordinary conversation. Although I have yet to release a dog by accident, I recommend that you choose something else, something you don't use often, like *Release, Free, School's Out,* or *Happy Time.* Here I will use *Release.*

The release command does more than simply tell your dog he is free of control. *It also allows you to praise and pet your dog without releasing him.* Praise and petting are powerful motivators—for the dog understands that they don't release him.

The dog without a release command will invariably interpret praise and petting as release. Too often one hears such statements as "You can't pet a hunting dog and maintain control." That only means that the speaker doesn't use—or doesn't fully understand the role of—a formal release command.

Since *Release* is so basic to control, it would be nice if you could teach it first. You can't, obviously, for until you teach some other command, you have nothing from which to release him. However, you can do the next best thing: You can teach *Release* second, right after *Whoa.* You can—and should—reinforce it as you teach the other control commands.

Whoa (and Release)

Whoa stands alone as the most important command in a birddog's vocabulary. Throughout your dog's life, you will use *Whoa* more often than all other commands combined. And you will rely more on immediate compliance with *Whoa* than you will on any other command.

You will use *Whoa* whenever you wish to bring your rambunctious birddog under control, whether in the field, in the backyard, or in the house. One birddog owner of my acquaintance had such a habit of raising his hand and saying *Whoa* to control his dog that he unconsciously did it to his wife when he wanted to interrupt her—*but only once.* After she finished explaining the several differences between herself and his Irish Setter, the singular inappropriateness of canine command words between spouses, and the probable consequences of any repetition of that particular matrimonial mortal sin, the poor guy was all but unable to resume using *Whoa* on his birddog.

You will use *Whoa* to staunch your birddog on point. Later, you will use it to steady him to wing and shot. You will also use it to teach him to honor another dog's point. And you will use it as a court of last resort for all occasions afield. If his response to *Come-In* becomes unreliable during the hunting season, you will handle emergencies with *Whoa.*

My Pointer, Jigger, never responded reliably to *Come-In,* at least not from any distance. Oh, his heart was in the right place. He would start toward me promptly. But before he had covered 30 yards, some stray scent—or stray thought—would distract him, and off he would go on a tangent. Sure, if I again tooted the *Come-In* whistle, Jigger would turn toward me again. But I finally gave up trying to bring him in that way. I simply *Whoa*-ed and walked to him, snapped on the lead and heeled him away.

Since *Whoa* is so important, you should really tattoo it into your dog's subconscious. To do that, you should start when he is a small puppy—as soon as he understands his name and *No* (if you proceed slowly enough to accommodate his maturity rate). Continue to work on this command through his entire active life. If you start young enough and persevere long enough, your dog will never suspect he can do anything but stop and stand there when you say *Whoa.*

Pro trainers have developed all sorts of equipment-intensive techniques for teaching *Whoa.* Some involve long tables with cables and pulleys (also used for force-breaking). Others involve checkcords run through rings which are attached to a wall or cemented into the ground. These are all fine if you have room for them in your backyard—and if your spouse doesn't object to such functional sculpture.

However, you don't have to clutter your yard with such unsightly paraphernalia. You can teach *Whoa* as thoroughly with nothing more than a strap collar, lead, and Flexi-Lead.

With your pup on lead, get his attention and command *Whoa.* Since he has no idea what you have in mind, you must position him properly, that is, standing quietly at attention. Lift the lead up tight with one hand while you stroke his belly with the other. If he is particularly

Whoa training. Start near a wall or something that keeps the dog from moving away from you. . . *(Fr. Robert K. Spencer)*

Later, lengthen the distance between you and the dog, but keep him attached to the other end of your Flexi-Lead. *(Fr. Robert K. Spencer)*

When you are sure he will hold, start moving around him, eventually going out of sight. *(Fr. Robert K. Spencer)*

Whoa training should be extended to other practical uses, like before releasing from the house or kennel.However, don't command *Whoa* with the gate or door shut, when you cannot insist on complete obedience. *(Fr. Robert K. Spencer)*

rambunctious, start him near a wall or fence, where he can't move away from you. Hold him in place, repeating "*Whoa*... *Whoa*... *Whoa*." Praise him quietly, too. If he moves in spite of your efforts, say *No*, then gently put him back into the proper position, again command *Whoa*, and continue praising him quietly.

Now say *Release* and ease the pup out of his *Whoa* position. Play with him awhile. Then repeat the sequence again: Command *Whoa*, position him, praise him, command *Release*, ease him out of position again, and play with him. If possible, repeat this about half a dozen times per session. Your puppy will quickly learn what *Whoa* means, what *Release* means, and he will at least suspect that praise doesn't mean freedom.

Whoa him in different places in the yard. Any time he moves, say *No*, reposition him, say *Whoa*, and praise him again.

When he seems to understand the command, *Whoa* him and stand up beside him. If he moves, say *No* and reposition him. Eventually, he will remain in place while you stand up beside him. Next step around in front of him, hold your hand out over him (palm down) and command *Whoa* softly several times. You are now introducing the *Whoa* hand signal.

Always praise and pet him while he is in position. Always free him with *Release*.

Gradually move farther away from him—with him on lead—and move around him until you can walk completely around him at the end of the six-foot lead without him moving. Then use the Flexi-Lead to allow more distance.

When you can walk around the *Whoa*-ed pup at, say, 15 feet without incident, you should start *Whoa*-ing him when he is in motion. Take him for a walk, on lead or on the Flexi-Lead, and when he is close to you, command *Whoa*. He may stop immediately, or he may slow down and stop gradually, or he may ignore you.

If he stops immediately, great! Praise and pet him a little before commanding *Release* and continuing your walk. If he slows down but doesn't stop, use your lead to stop him. Position him where he should have stopped, repeat *Whoa*, and praise him. Don't speak harshly to him, for he was trying to obey. But if he ignores your command, pull him up short, physically place him where he should have stopped, all the time reprimanding him verbally. As soon as he is standing where he belongs, praise and pet him lavishly.

Keep repeating this *Whoa*-in-motion on walks until he stops immediately every time. Then start *Whoa*-ing him from a little farther off (but still on lead). Progress gradually until you can stop him immediately at any distance your Flexi-Lead allows.

The next step, *whoa*-ing him off-lead, is critical. Take him back to where you started this training—in the backyard by the wall or fence. *Whoa* him there, where you can grab him and enforce compliance if he ignores your command—but he probably won't, if you have done all the preliminaries thoroughly enough.

Gradually extend *Whoa*-ing off lead in the backyard until you can stop him immediately anywhere in the backyard at whatever maximum distance your yard allows. Sometimes leave him in place while you walk around in the yard. Sometimes release him from a distance. Sometimes walk to him before releasing him. Use the hand-signal for *Whoa* frequently. Later in the field, it will allow you to hold him in place from a great distance.

I use a couple of little drills for keeping a dog sharp on *Whoa* all through his life. First, each day before I release him from his kennel run for a romp in the yard, I *Whoa* him, open the gate, walk around kicking the ground here and there (as if I were trying to flush a bird), and then release him. I also *Whoa* the dog as I set his food bowl down for him, and make him wait a few seconds before releasing him to eat.

The *Whoa* command is the single most important command in your dog's vocabulary, so train it thoroughly and work on it regularly all through his life. Some trainers also use a single blast on the whistle as a *Whoa* command. The only problem I have with that is that the handler of a bracemate may toot his whistle in a manner that would *Whoa* my dog accidentally. Thus, I prefer to use my voice only for this command.

Kennel (and Release)

Kennel tells your dog to go into his run, crate, or dog box. This command introduces a type of control that makes your birddog easy to live with, easy to hunt with, and easy to travel with.

You can start this training in parallel with *Whoa* training, starting as soon as he knows his name and *No,* as long as you proceed slowly enough to accommodate his maturity rate. Doing it in parallel helps your pup grasp the meaning of *Release.* If you have a kennel run, use it to start this training. If not, use a crate—one with a wire door, so your dog can see you from inside. That is important, as you will see.

Put the strap collar and lead on your pup. Open the gate to your kennel run (or the door to your crate) and command *Kennel.* Again, your pup has no idea what you want, so you should guide him in with the lead. As soon as he is in the run, close the gate. Now stand there and praise him. This reinforces the notion that praise doesn't mean release, for the gate blocks the pup's exit.

After a few moments, open the gate, say *Release,* and encourage him to come out. Play, romp around with him, do anything to make sure he no longer feels restraint.

Repeat the whole process five or six times during each session. Command *Kennel,* pull your pup into the run with the lead, shut the gate, praise awhile; then, command *Release* as you open the gate; play again to make sure he feels completely released. Before long, he will go in on his own when you command *Kennel,* largely because of all the praise he gets there. Once he has shown that he understands *Kennel,* you can apply light punishment for refusals and slow responses. Jerk the lead a little as you put the laggard in. But whenever you have to punish this way, remember to also praise after he is inside. He should come to associate your praise with compliance, even when forced.

After he obeys *Kennel* readily, extend the meaning of *Release.* Until now, the pup has come out when the gate opened, and he probably thinks the gate, rather than *Release,* gives him his freedom. Now you should teach him the error of that thought.

Kennel and praise him normally. Open the gate slightly, but do not say *Release.* He will try to come bouncing out, of course. Shut the gate in his face, commanding *No* rather sharply. Then praise lavishly—this first correction can be a bit of a shock, especially for a sensitive pup. Open the gate again and say *Release.* If he is reluctant to come out, encourage him, even pull lightly on the lead. Then, once he is out, play with him as usual.

Repeat this several times. When you open the gate and the youngster hesitates until you say *Release,* you are making your point. Increase the time you wait before saying *Release.* Naturally, until you are sure of his response, don't open the gate too wide. If he does escape, put him back with the lead on and start over.

The only verbal correction you should give when he tries to escape is a sharp *No.* Don't repeat *Kennel.* You will be a better trainer if you minimize duplicate commands. Above all, don't command *Whoa* when he tries to escape. *Whoa* must mean "freeze in place." When he is inside his kennel, you simply cannot enforce complete immobility. Stick with *No.*

Gradually open the gate wider and wider, and make him remain inside longer and longer before commanding *Release.* Eventually remove the lead, but don't rush this.

Also increase the distance you send your dog when you command *Kennel.* Eventually you will be able to send him into his kennel, off-lead, from anywhere in the yard, and he will stay there until released even with the gate wide open. You should also extend *Kennel* to include dog boxes in vans and pick-ups, stalls in dog trailers, and so forth.

Come-In

From your pup's earliest days with you, you should encourage him to come to you for treats, praise, and petting. Squat down, clap your hands, talk excitedly. When he reaches you, make him glad he came.

Once he understands *Whoa, Kennel,* and *Release,* you can start teaching *Come-In* on a more formal basis—but it still should be fun for him. You will introduce the "must" aspect of the command gradually, after he already has a positive attitude toward coming to you.

Start the *Come-In* by *Whoa*-ing your dog on the Flexi-Lead. *(Fr. Robert K. Spencer)*

Toot the *Come-In* whistle. This picture shows the advantage of the Flexi-Lead over a checkcord for this training. The dog is flying toward the author, but the Flexi-Lead is taking up slack rapidly. *(Fr. Robert K. Spencer)*

Teach him to come on both a verbal command and a whistle signal. Over his life, the whistle will serve you better, because it reaches farther and frightens birds less than the human voice. For a whistle command, I use two shorts and a long, trilled rather than blasted—*Twee-Twee-Tweeeet*. Others use a series of short blasts. Take your choice, but remember to be consistent. For a verbal command, I use *Come*. Others use *Here*, and some even use *Heel*. Again, take your choice and be consistent. Here I will use *Come-In*.

At first, call him to you when he is out running around loose in the yard. Squat down, clap your hands, but instead of talking excitedly, toot the *Come-In* whistle. Better still, wait until he is coming to you because of your clapping before you toot the whistle. That way he will associate the sound with what he is already doing. This is teaching by association, which is the easiest way to introduce a new command, if you can. Alternate the whistle signal and the verbal command.

When he gets to you, of course, make him glad he did. Pet and praise him, even slip him a treat sometimes. Then release him again.

As soon as you can, stop clapping. Just squat down and toot the whistle or give the verbal command. When your pup responds properly, pet and praise him as soon as he reaches you.

Eventually, you can stop squatting down. Just toot the whistle or command *Come-In*. Always pet and praise when he arrives.

When you are certain that he understands this command, introduce it into his regular obedience sessions. Leave him in a *Whoa* stance, walk to the end of the Flexi-Lead, and toot the whistle or give the *Come-In* command. At first he may think you are just tempting him in a new way to break his *Whoa* stance, so you may have to encourage him to come. Fine, do so. Eventually, he will understand that this new command can override even a *Whoa*. However, only call him to you once in every three or four *Whoa*'s, lest he lose some of his respect for that all-important command.

By now, you should start insisting that he *Whoa* when he reaches you rather than just milling around as he has been doing. Call him to you, then *Whoa* him immediately in front of you, then pet and praise him—insisting as you do that he remain standing still. This will aid you later when he retrieves to you. He will stand quietly to deliver, rather than prancing around you just out of reach.

Eventually, you will be able to call him in off-lead from anywhere in the yard. Later you will extend this drill to field conditions, too, but get it tattooed in right there in the backyard first.

One last word on *Come-In:* Do not—ever—call your dog to you and then punish him. If he needs punishment, go to him to administer it. If you call him in and then punish him, what do you think he will do the next time you call him in? Right; he isn't stupid.

Heel

The dog that heels walks beside his handler, typically on the left side. When the handler stops, the dog either stands or sits beside him. This is a convenient skill for any civilized canine, regardless of breed or function.

When stopped, some handlers have their dogs sit beside them, because sitting is a more stable position. Others have their dogs stand (*Whoa*), because they feel that a birddog should never be taught to sit, lest he start sitting on point. I have trained birddogs both ways. I have never had one sit on point after learning to sit at heel. However, I don't teach heeling until the dog has already started pointing properly.

Take your choice. Have your dog sit or stand. Also, take your choice about which side you have him heel on. I use my left side, so all the photos and instructions apply to that method. Those who prefer the right side should have no difficulty figuring out what adjustments they will have to make.

I recommend that you wait until your pup is five or six months old before starting this. If he is unusually soft and sensitive, you should wait until he is seven or eight months old. If you plan to have him sit, wait until he has formed his pointing habits, too.

Your goal is to train your dog so well that he heels reliably off-lead. The slowest possible way to get there—absolutely the slowest—is to try off-lead work frequently before he is ready. Like all control training, heeling is a conditioning process, not a learning experience as we use the term in human education. You condition the dog to perform properly on lead until it becomes second nature.

You condition your dog by rote drill. However, to do this successfully you must adopt the attitude that you are teaching your dog to take full responsibility for knowing where you are and for sticking by your side. That attitude will prevent you from making the most common beginner's mistake, namely, steering a dog with the lead.

If you steer the dog through these heeling drills, he will never be properly conditioned. He will learn to follow the direction of the pressure on his neck. In human terms, you are remaining responsible for his position. If you do not steer him, but correct him appropriately when he strays, he will learn to pay attention to where he should be—in other words, take responsibility for his own position.

The chain training collar is one of the simplest but cleverest pieces of dog-training equipment ever invented. Properly installed (as described above), it tightens up *immediately* when the trainer jerks on the lead and releases *immediately* when the trainer slacks off. Tightened and loosened in a rapid-fire series of sharp jerks, the collar doesn't drag the dog into position. Instead, it induces him to move there voluntarily, and quickly. Since the little jerks cease as soon as he is in place, they encourage him to stay where he belongs. As long as the dog remains in the proper position, the collar is loose, the lead slack.

Please note: A knowledgeable trainer never, never, never chokes the dog with the chain training collar. Instead he uses it to give a series of jerk-and-release, jerk-and-release, jerk-and-release corrections that get the dog's attention without cutting off his wind.

Even so, if the jerk-and-release technique were used alone, this training would be a negative process. The dog would come to heel in a hang-dog manner. A lot of dogs are so trained, I must admit, *and show it!*

You are more fortunate than most, however, for your pup already understands that praise does not mean release. You can praise him when he is doing things correctly without losing control. If you praise when your young charge is heeling correctly (and especially after each correction) he will not only learn more quickly, but he will enjoy heeling—*and show it!*

Now, some good news. Your dog—any dog—can only make six mistakes in heeling: lagging, forging, swinging wide, crowding, jumping up, and lying down. Each calls for a slight variation on the basic jerk-and-release-plus-praise technique:

Lagging: The dog is uncertain. Give fairly gentle tugs and talk encouragingly as you do. When he catches up, praise lavishly. Don't slow down or stop. If you do, you will soon find that he is training you.

Forging: This is a bold, aggressive brute. Let him get ahead of you, then turn and go in the opposite direction. When he hits the end of the lead, administer a series of none-too-gentle jerks. Don't slow down. In fact, you might speed up a bit with this character.

Swinging Wide: This dog is expressing independence. Turn 90 degrees away from him, and when he hits the end of the lead, give a series of jerks. If he is also hard-headed, you might even speed up a bit.

Crowding: This dog is sensitive and feels safer when touching you. Normally, no jerks are necessary. Just bump into the dog frequently. If he is not too soft, give a series of *light* jerks away from you. This dog is trying to do what you want, so praise lavishly whenever he is in place.

Jumping Up: Either this dog doesn't realize that this is training time, not playtime, or he is trying to con you. Either way, give a series of sharp jerks down, say *No! Heel!* and keep on walking. When you praise this dog, do it calmly. Excited praise may incite another demonstration of playfulness.

Lying Down: This can be a real problem. The dog is either frightened or trying a new way of training you. Hard to tell which. If you are sure it is the latter, force the issue. Start walking, command *Heel,* and jerk the dog along. If you are right, he will get up and play by your rules. If not, he will freeze on his belly. Stop then—don't drag him. He is frightened. Find out why and work him through it before continuing.

Okay, so much for collar and lead work. Before you can successfully teach a dog to heel, you must also learn how to walk! Honest. The way you walk can help or confuse him. He will key off your left leg (assuming you heel him on your left side). By moving your left leg consistently, you help him maintain his position. Here are the walking techniques I recommend:

1. When you start heeling from a stopped position, step off with your left foot as you command *Heel.* When you leave your dog in a *Whoa,* step off with your right foot.
2. When you stop while heeling, bring your left leg up to your right as the last step. Also, don't stop abruptly. Slow down gradually.
3. Round your left and right turns. Don't make sharp military turns.
4. When reversing directions, turn away from your dog, not into him.

You now know how to walk and how to correct your dog with the chain training collar. However, you don't do either automatically. You have to think too much about your handling because you haven't formed habits on which to rely. A new trainer and an untrained dog can have unbelievable problems until the trainer has developed some minimal level of competence.

To avoid a poor start in heeling, don't bring your dog into the picture until you are comfortable with your part of the routine. Use a friend, spouse, or child instead. Put the chain training collar on that person's right wrist and heel him until you are comfortable with your job. I have "played dog" for a number of beginners over the years.

With your surrogate canine, practice the basic foot patterns and collar corrections. Have him simulate the six mistakes a dog can make. Make the appropriate correction for each until it becomes instinctive. Practice the little jerk-and-release corrections, and practice the immediate praise, too, no matter how silly you feel about it. However, if any non-doggy person sees this seemingly insane process, you may end your session fleeing from someone with a butterfly net!

When you feel confident in your handling techniques, start heeling your birddog instead of your surrogate. Put the chain training collar and lead on him, bring him up beside you, command *Heel,* and step off walking. He won't have any idea what you expect, but by now he will at least understand that this is a new command he must figure out and help you with. He will gradually learn how to avoid those irritating little jerks on his neck. It is unfortunate that you cannot sit down and explain it to him as you could with a child. Canine nature being what it is, you can only communicate with him through the collar and lead. You can minimize the negative and maximize the positive by praising him at every opportunity. Most important of all: Keep the lead loose whenever he is in place. If you keep it tight, you are steering him, not training him.

It won't take him long to figure out what you want. Then change speeds and directions frequently. Stop frequently and either have him *Whoa* or sit, whichever you prefer. When he is heeling nicely on lead in the backyard, introduce distractions: family members, other dogs (on lead, and not too close), and so on. Finally, take him to a shopping center occasionally—but keep him on lead.

When you feel he will heel off-lead, use your riding crop or flushing whip to tap him when he strays. To use either one of these successfully, pet him with it more often than you tap him with it. That way, he will never come to fear this tool.

Other Commands

Obedience training can include several other commands—*Sit, Down, Stand, Stay*—that are useful for dogs bred for different work (retrievers, spaniels, herding, etc.). Your birddog can learn any of them, but I feel you can better spend your time drilling in the ones he really needs—and working in the field—than teaching him unnecessary obedience commands.

Praise and appreciation facilitate obedience training. *(Fr. Robert K. Spencer)*

CHAPTER

15

Hunting and Pointing:

Awakening a Birddog's Instincts

You must understand the relationship between your dog's range and your transmitter's range. If your dog finds the trap so far out that you can't release the bird, he may injure himself on the trap. He certainly won't learn to point.

If your dog points, great! Approach him from the side. *(Ray Taylor)*

If he creeps forward, launch the bird, and let him chase it. *(Ray Taylor)*

BACKGROUND

What Is It?

In this phase of the training program, you determine whether your maturing pup has a hunting range with which you can live happily ever after. If his range is *a little* uncomfortable one way or the other, you begin tweaking it in or out. If his range is substantially too close or too wide, you have a decision to make.

Here, you also bring out his pointing instinct in the field, primarily by letting him learn the hard way that he cannot catch birds. Finally you begin developing his ground pattern by introducing the basic handling commands you will use all his life to direct him afield.

During this phase, you continue the gun-proofing you started in your puppy training field work. And you introduce him to water retrieving.

Why Do It?

Silly question, really. If you are going to have a working birddog (as opposed to a fireside ornament), you must go through this phase. You must accept or modify his natural range—or swap him off. In poker terms, this is when you must know when to hold 'em and when to fold 'em. Even if you decide to hold 'em, you must decide whether to play 'em pat or draw some cards.

If you are ever to get anything out of him in the field, you must help him learn to find birds with his nose. And you must bring out his pointing instinct—with real birds in the field, not with a wing on a string in the backyard.

If you are ever to control his ground pattern afield, you must teach him some basic handling commands. Now is the time to start. Now is also the time to start him into retrieving from water, if such is your wish. And if you don't continue his gun-proofing, he will lose the little ground he gained in puppy training afield.

Prerequisites

This phase flows naturally and imperceptibly from your puppy work afield. As your youngster matures and becomes comfortable running in the field, especially after he has had a few game contacts (of any kind), he will start showing you his natural range. As you establish control in your obedience training work, primarily through *Whoa, Come-In,* and *Release,* you can start influencing his range in the field, at least a little.

Most pups mature sufficiently for this training at between six months and one year old. Pups that mature rapidly may be ready a bit sooner, and those that mature slowly may not be ready until a bit later, but most can make the transition in the six- to twelve-month timeframe.

Equipment and Facilities

Mostly, you need *birds, birds, birds.* Pros use lots of gamebirds, mostly quail kept in call-back pens scattered about their extensive training grounds. That is the ideal arrangement, and if you have access to such fantasyland luxury, I recommend that you take advantage of it. I won't cover that training process here, for a couple of reasons. First, I've never been spoiled by such "Cadillac" facilities. I have spent my life scrounging for training grounds, usually sharing pasture space with assorted livestock herds that would stomp call-back pens into the ground, even if the landowner would allow me to install them. Second, too many books on the market already describe how to train a birddog under such ideal conditions. Who writes such books? Pros, regular clients of pros, and affluent amateurs who have no idea what life is like out here in the middle-class world.

Don't misunderstand: I envy them their facilities. So should you, but don't despair of training your birddog without them. We middle-class urbanites and suburbanites have developed other options as we struggle along, training on pastureland leased by our clubs, often sharing that limited space not only with other members but with sundry bovines. Not ideal, I admit, but the important thing is that we succeed. Keep that in mind.

Our principal training bird is the common pigeon (a.k.a. commie). The more fortunate among us (myself not included) can keep a few homing pigeons around. Homers save money because they can be used over and over, whereas commies escape after a single use. Having commies fly off may not be expensive for those young enough to trap their own (by climbing and crawling around on top of buildings and in barns), but fly-aways do add up for us creaky old gaffers who buy our pigeons—at $1.50 to $2 per head. Even so, it is much cheaper than buying and maintaining private training grounds with quail and call-back pens.

So you need a source for common pigeons, and a way to keep a few homers if you can. Check around in your club for pigeon suppliers.

Training mostly with pigeons is, let's say, challenging. They do not sit naturally on the ground like gamebirds do. They prefer tree limbs, roofs, and so forth. To keep them on the ground for birddogs, trainers have developed various planting techniques.

The oldest of these is dizzying. Holding the bird by its body, the trainer dizzies it by spinning its head around in a small circle. Then he places it in cover. Ideally, the bird will stay there until the dog approaches, sit there if the dog points, but flush if the dog crowds it—just as a wild gamebird would. But too often, the dizzied pigeon behaves abominably.

Dizzied too little, it flies off before the dog finds it. Dizzied too much, it won't flush at all, so the dog catches it on the ground. Every such incident is a disaster, for it convinces the dog that pointing is unnecessary. *For an older dog, one that is pointing staunchly, dizzied pigeons work fine, but they are too unpredictable for young dogs just learning to point.*

Some trainers have developed ways to shackle a pigeon—for example, with a velcro-held body wrap—so that it cannot fly until unshackled. This, too, works well with a staunched birddog, but has no place in training a youngster.

Dissatisfied with the above techniques, trainers have developed an assortment of mechanical and electronic release traps, which hold an undizzied pigeon in place on the ground until the trainer trips a release mechanism. Some release traps simply open up to let the bird escape at its leisure—which may not be quick enough for a hard-charging pup. Others catapult the birds into the air, forcing them to fly. For obvious reasons, I recommend the latter.

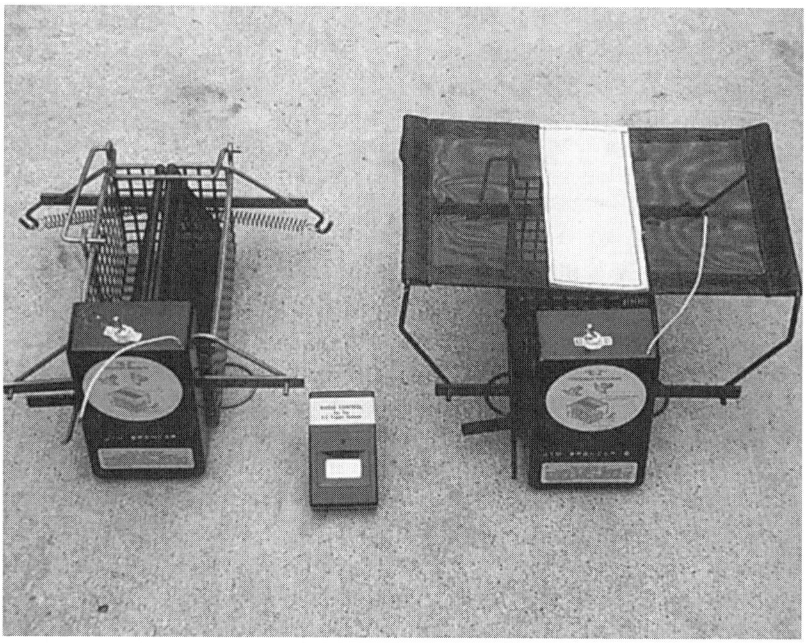

Two E-Z electric remote release traps, one closed, one open, with the remote transmitter between them. This battery-operated trap is economical (for a remote release trap).

Two Tri-Tronics electronic remote release traps, one closed, one open, with the remote transmitter between them. This is a top-of-the-line trap powered by rechargeable NiCad batteries.

Of those that catapult the bird into flight, some are mechanical, some are electronic. To operate the mechanical types, the trainer must either trip a lever with his foot or pull a string. The former is only slightly better than using dizzied or shackled pigeons, for the dog that doesn't point will pounce on the trap before the trainer arrives. The latter—string operated—works adequately for young dogs, since it can be operated at a reasonable distance with a string of appropriate length. Back in the early 1970s, before the electronic models came out, I built a string-operated release trap from scrap metal, screen wire, springs, and an old fly reel (to hold a very long string). It worked quite well, but not as well as the new electronic models. I now keep the old one among the memorabilia in my office.

One company makes an electronic release trap that the trainer operates with a button on the end of a long (50 foot) electric cord. This works better than the string-operated models, but still requires that the trainer be quite close to the trap.

The best—and, unfortunately, most expensive—release traps are the electronic models that the trainer can trigger remotely with a portable hand-held transmitter. With these remote electronic release traps, you can spring the pigeon into the air from a considerable distance.

Several companies manufacture them in a variety of makes and models, at various prices.

I have heard two objections to release traps—both from trainers who have never used them. First, some claim that they hold in bird scent so the dog cannot find the bird. Nonsense! I rub the bird around in the cover before putting it in the trap. But I sometimes forget. I haven't noticed any difference in my dog's performance whether I do this or not. Perhaps I just do it to reassure myself. Second, some claim that the trap, when it throws the bird into the air, might make a noise that would frighten a sensitive young puppy. Again, nonsense! Mine don't make much noise, and I've never seen a pup react in any way. Granted, if I were silly enough to let a pup pounce on the trap before springing it, I might frighten him, or even hurt him, but I don't let the dog get that close before launching the bird.

In short, I believe that the remote electronic release traps are the answer to a middle-class birddog trainer's prayer. In some ways, they work better than quail from call-back pens. You can put the bird exactly where you want it, and it will stay there. When you want it to flush, it will flush. No unwanted wild flushes. No unwanted running. You push the button on the transmitter and the bird is propelled into the air—right now!

Over the years, I have accumulated several such traps of two different makes, one among the least expensive, the other among the most expensive. The cheaper ones operate on lithium batteries (in both trap and transmitter) and work to about 60 yards away, which is normally far enough for the kind of dogs I train. The more expensive ones operate on rechargeable NiCad batteries (in both trap and transmitter) and work to any distance you might want. Frankly, I've never tested them for maximum distance (as I did with my other ones) because my dogs don't run that big.

Electronic release traps are expensive. The cheapest I have found run a bit north of $200. The most expensive run just south of $400. However, if you can possibly afford it, I recommend that you buy a remote electronic release trap—and two or three would be so much better, as I will explain in the training section. If you can't spend that much, settle for those operated by strings, or for the electronic models with the long cords (rather than remote transmitters). Again, two or three would be much better than one. To get more traps on a budget, you might buy one remote electronic model and a couple of string-operated models—or, better yet, train with one or two friends who also have electronic traps, so you can share your combined wealth.

For water retrieving, you need a floating retrieving dummy. I prefer the small white plastic knobbies. They show up well in the water and last forever. Canvas dummies are okay, but don't use them after they start falling apart—I've seen too many dogs develop mouth problems after retrieving old beat-up canvas dummies.

For your gun-proofing work, you need your trusty blank pistol, plus a small-bore shotgun (28 or 20 gauge), and your Big Bertha 12 gauge.

For any kind of field work, you should have a tie-out chain. This consists of a stake you can drive into the ground and a short (6 to 10 feet long) chain with a snap on the end. Attach your dog to the tie-out chain when you are not working him (like when you are helping someone else with his dog). Your dog will be more comfortable than he would be in the dog box.

Schedule

As mentioned above, this training flows naturally from the field work covered in Chapter 13 ("Puppy Training") and from the yard training covered in Chapter 14 ("Obedience Training"). Start your youngster in this work when he is 6 to 12 months old—give or take a month or two depending on his maturity rate—whenever he has shown you that he enjoys running in cover and obeys *Whoa, Come-In,* and *Release.*

Keep him here in this phase until you are satisfied with his range, until he holds point long enough for you to approach him (at least most of the time), and until he understands his basic ground-pattern commands. By then, he should be 9 to 15 months, again give or take a little for his maturity rate.

Handling Techniques

I cover handling techniques, as necessary, in the various training sections.

TRAINING

Range

After your youngster has run in cover enough to be completely comfortable there, and after he understands *Whoa* in the backyard, begin taking a more businesslike approach to your romps afield with him.

From now until he is staunch on point, run him alone. A bracemate will only impede his progress during this critical time. If you were to run him with a more mature dog, your pup might start a bad trailing habit. If you were to run him with another inexperienced youngster, the two might socialize too much or interfere with each other's birdwork. Run him alone, at least for now. Of course you can exercise him with other dogs, but run him alone on birds.

Start each run quite formally. When you get him out of his dog box, snap a lead on him, and heel him to the starting point for your run. When he arrives there, *Whoa* him and make him stand there a few seconds facing the direction in which he is to run. You might even style him up a bit as he stands there—push his tail up, pat his head up, rub his belly to raise his torso up, do all those things trainers do to improve a dog's pointing style. Now unsnap the lead quietly, but keep a finger under his collar—just in case—and make him stand there a second or two longer.

Send him off with a command. I use *Hie-On*. Some use two toots on the whistle. I save that for turning my dogs, but many prefer it for sending a dog out.

After sending him, let him run! Don't hack him around. Don't try to direct him this way or that. Let him run. You want to get a line on his range and natural ground pattern. You can't do that when you are interfering with his thought processes all the time. Let him run.

End each run formally. If possible, run him in a large circle that takes you 20 minutes to half an hour to complete. When you near your starting point again, he should be tired. Fine. Command *Whoa* when you get close to him. If you have trained him properly in the yard, he should obey. If he doesn't, run him down and teach him the error of his ways. If he does obey, praise him, walk to him, snap on the lead, and heel him back to your vehicle.

Don't let him run aimlessly back to your car. He should learn early on to hunt until you stop him, not to seek his dog box on his own. Always stop him while he is still hunting, and heel him back. I made the mistake of letting Erick run back to the truck at first. Results? In his first two hunting tests, as he entered the birdfield, he saw the row of vehicles in the gallery on the hill. Guess what? Yep.

Repeat this businesslike routine every time you take him afield. Start him formally with *Whoa* and *Hie-On*. Follow him quietly. Of course, don't let him get into mischief or danger, but otherwise don't try to steer the boat. End the session formally with *Whoa*. Then heel him back to your vehicle.

Change locations often, so you can observe his range under a variety of cover and terrain conditions. In a relatively short time, he will show you what nature dictates.

If you like his emerging range, wonderful! If he comes reasonably close to what you want, fine; you can adjust him a little in or out as you train him. However, if he runs substantially too wide or too close for your tastes, you should take him to a pro for a second opinion. If the pro agrees with your assessment of the dog's natural range, ask if he can change it to what you want. If he can, consider whether you should put him with the pro for that work, trade him in on a different model, or revise your own preferences in range. Whatever you do, *make a decision.* Don't stumble along indecisively for any great length of time. You only live once, and then only for a short time, and all that.

As I indicated above, if his range comes reasonably close to what you want, you can adjust it a little either way in training without professional help. If he runs a bit too wide, tire him out repeatedly by running him longer. Later, when you start planting birds for him, plant all his birds where he will find them while close to you. Then, if he misses them and runs out too far, stand still, call him back in, and work him to the planted bird(s). He will gradually figure out that birds, for some inexplicable reason, like to be near you.

If he stays in a little too close for your tastes, do just the opposite. Keep him over-eager by running him for shorter periods, and even less frequently. Later, plant his birds a long way from your starting point so he will learn that he must run a long way before finding them. Another trick: Before running him, stake him out near the starting point where he can watch other dogs take off and find birds a long way from the starting point. Leave him there while you go out to plant and shoot birds for the other dogs, all within his sight, but some distance from the starting point. Later, when you bring your dog to the line and *Release* him, he will smoke the cover heading for the distant birdy area.

Pointing

As soon as you decide you can live with your pup's natural range—with or without minor adjustments—you should start bringing out his pointing instinct with planted birds. *You do this by convincing him that he cannot catch birds, no matter how hard he tries.* Once he really believes that, he will start pointing. Some dogs convince more easily than others of course. For this training, homing pigeons will save you money, since you will allow these birds to fly away. Homers will return to your loft, where they will wait for you to use them another day.

If you bought one or more remote electronic release traps that operate at the outer limits of your youngster's range, you can combine work on planted birds with his normal workouts afield. If you bought releasers that do not work at his outer range limit, you must do your bird work separately, keeping him on a checkcord to prevent him from reaching a release trap before you can set it off.

Although you can get by with planting just one bird at a time, you can save a lot of training time if you put out two or three widely separated birds each time. That's why I recommended that you get two or three release traps—or share with a buddy or two.

First, let's assume you have maximum-distance electronic releasers. While you select locations for your launchers and load them with birds, leave your dog in his dog box, where he cannot watch you plant them. *You also don't want him to learn to trail you to the birds,* which can become a real problem. To prevent trailing, drive around to a place near where you want each bird. Get out and plant it, drive to the next location, and so forth. When you have planted all your birds, drive back to the starting point. If that is not possible, walk in a huge circle from your car to where you want the birds. Do not walk near the starting point in this circle, and stay downwind of your dog's probable route.

Always rub the bird around in the cover before you put it into the release trap. As I said, even when I forget to do this, my dogs seem to have no problem finding the bird, but at first you want to give your youngster every advantage—especially plenty of scent.

To help you find it again, flag each bird's location somehow. For example, tie a piece of surveyor's tape on a weed nearby. Dogs are color-blind, so they won't key off the orange tape. However, you can see it at a distance, so you will know when your dog nears the bird. You will also know when he creeps too close—in other words, when you should launch the bird.

Now return to your truck and take your dog to the starting point, which should be downwind from the birds. Release him normally and watch him closely. Let him hunt, but as soon as he shows signs of winding a bird, get ready to launch it.

If he does indeed point, praise him *calmly,* and approach quietly. If he starts to creep forward, great! *That's exactly what you want right now.* Launch the bird and let him chase it. After enough repetitions of this futile chasing, he will figure out that creeping flushes birds. That's precisely what you want him to think, because that's how wild birds behave.

If he doesn't point, or if he merely flash-points and dives in, launch the bird and let him chase it. Enough of these and he will start pointing. That's how a dog learns on wild birds.

Let's assume that you do not have a maximum-distance electronic release trap. To prevent your pup from getting to the trap before you can spring it, you should keep him on a checkcord as you go from one trap to another. When you are close enough to release the trap remotely (that is, when you reach the end of the string or cord, or come within the range of your remote transmitter) release the checkcord and let your dog go in naturally. If he points, praise him as above. If he charges in without pointing, launch the bird and let him chase it out of sight. In other words, as soon as you are in position to release the bird, handle your dog as described in the maximum-distance remote release trap discussion.

Since pigeons normally fly with the wind, each bird will fly away from any other traps you have planted—you are working into the wind, remember? Thus, your pup can chase as far as he can see the bird without the risk of stumbling on your other traps.

When he tires and returns to you, work him to the next trap, and so on. After the last trap, heel him back to the truck and put him up (with a drink of water, for crying out loud!) while you go out and retrieve your traps and markers. Don't leave your marking tapes out there. They could mislead you or another trainer some other day.

If you are training with a group, the trainer who will run next may want to follow along and plant fresh birds in each trap after your pup finishes with it. That saves time between dogs, but it does increase the risk of starting the next dog into a trailing habit. When your dog runs after another dog, if you replant the same trap positions, watch for signs of trailing—nose down, straight-line running—and if your dog does it, change your planting procedure; that is, move the traps after the previous dog finishes.

After chasing enough birds, your youngster will start pointing. How many birds will it take? Beats me. When he starts pointing, he's told you how many. No one else knows what his particular magic number is. When he reaches it and starts pointing regularly, you should start staunching him as described in Chapter 17 ("Staunching on Point").

Ground Pattern

To develop and control your pup's ground pattern, you need to be able to direct him in three ways: You must be able to send him out; you must be able to stop him; and you must be able to turn him left or right at a distance.

You have already started training him to go out on *Hie-On* (or two toots) to start each run. You have already started stopping him afield with *Whoa* at the end of each run. Now, you should start training him to turn on command. You can do this two ways: by association, when he is turning naturally in the field, and by formal training with the checkcord.

During his runs in the field, whenever he finishes one cast and turns naturally to make another, give him your turn command and start walking and waving your arm in the direction he has already chosen. As I said above, I use two toots on my whistle (*pip-pip*). Do this every time he turns naturally, and you will be amazed at how quickly he learns to associate your command with his action.

Then, after each field session, when he is tired, snap on the checkcord—or better yet, the Flexi-Lead—and take him for a short walk. Whenever he reaches the end of the rope, give your turn command or whistle, turn, and force him to go in the opposite direction—*and praise him as he does.* Do this for a few minutes at the end of each session.

For right now, that is all the ground-pattern work you need to accomplish. You will get into more advanced work in later chapters.

Gun-Proofing

During the above work on bringing out your youngster's pointing instinct, you should also continue the gun-proofing you started in your puppy training work. Every time he chases a bird, whether he pointed it or not, let him get some distance away from you, and then shoot. Start

At the end of each session, snap on the Flexi-Lead and teach your dog to turn on either a whistle or verbal command, as Dr. Jeff Herod is doing here with his Shorthair, Kit.

with your .22 blank pistol. If he ignores it—as he should if you have done the preliminaries during puppy training—begin shooting it several times each time he chases.

When he pays no attention to that, move up to the 28 or 20 gauge, but only shoot once per chase at first. When you are comfortable with his reaction to a single shot from your small-bore shotgun, start shooting two or three times (depending on what kind of smokepole you're toting at the time).

When multiple small-bore shotgun blasts don't faze him—guess what?—move up to Big Bertha (your 12 gauge), and start over with a single shot. And so on.

Water Retrieving

If you introduced your birddog to both water and play retrieving in his puppy training, and if you are satisfied with his performance in each, you can now have him make a *few short* water retrieves during the warmer months. Please notice the emphasis on both *few* and *short*. This is introductory work, not a way of demonstrating that your dog can outswim a Chesapeake (which he can't, incidentally, but who cares?).

Use a retrieving dummy for this, of course, either your puppy dummy (if it will float) or a larger plastic or canvas dummy made specifically for water retrieving.

Start out tossing the dummy into shallow water, where your dog won't have to swim to get it. As he gains confidence, lengthen the tosses until he has to swim a few feet until he is swimming 20 to 25 yards comfortably.

After swimming any distance, when he reaches shore again, he will almost certainly stop, drop the dummy, and shake the water out of his coat. The chances are good to excellent that he will *not* pick the dummy back up again. That's why delivery to hand is so difficult in water work.

To avoid this problem for now, you should meet him at the water's edge. When he reaches you, take the dummy before he has a chance to drop it. Later, if you care about good water work, you should force-break him to get reliable delivery to hand, even in water retrieves. For now, just take the dummy before he can drop it. For this, a pond with a sharp dropoff at the shoreline is ideal, for he must swim right to you before landing.

Another nasty habit a sharp drop-off prevents: When they get back to the shallows after a swimming water retrieve, some dogs play with the dummy instead of returning to the trainer. If your dog ever starts this, either move to a pond with a sharp drop-off, or put him on the Flexi-Lead for his water work until the problem is solved.

CHAPTER 16

Force-Breaking—Gently:

Getting a Reliable Retrieve

This German Wirehair, DC/AFC Dunkees Justa Hole n One, CD, MH, retrieves to hand and doesn't harm the bird, as this live quail shows. *(Bernee Brawn)*

BACKGROUND

What Is It?

Birddogs practice two basic forms of retrieving: *natural* and *force-broken.* Natural retrieving is an obvious extension of the play retrieving covered in Chapter 13 ("Puppy Training") into field work. In this chapter, I explain the second option, force-breaking.

Force-breaking is a structured procedure by which you train your dog to pick up, to hold, and to carry a bird on the command *Fetch* and to release it on the command *Give.*

In the slow and gentle six-step process I describe here, you do not introduce force (mild discomfort to induce compliance) until the dog is comfortable with the process and understands what you expect. Step 1 (accept, hold, release) requires no force. Nor does Step 2 (carry). You first use force in Step 3 (reach) and continue using it through Step 4 (pick up). Step 5 (jump) is an optional happy-'em-up process, and Step 6 transfers the skills learned in force-breaking to field work.

Why Do It?

First, you should decide whether you want your birddog to retrieve at all. Some field trialers who compete in nonretrieving trials prefer to omit it, feeling that retrieving may incline their dogs to break to wing and shot in competition.

If you want your dog to retrieve, you should decide as early as possible whether you will rely on natural retrieving or go through the formal force-breaking procedure.

If your dog has little or no natural retrieving instinct, clearly you must force-break him. David Sanborn, a nineteenth-century birddog trainer, developed force-breaking back in the 1880s for just such dogs. It worked for him, and it will work for you. True, it will not make your dog a fetching wonder, but it will induce him to run out and pick up most of your dead birds for you.

If your dog starts out retrieving naturally but loses interest later on, as many birddogs do, you must force-break him. Many birddog trainers speak of force-breaking "for reliability." That means that over the years enough of their natural retrievers have stopped retrieving to convince them to force-break every dog as a precaution.

Even for those blessed with dogs that retrieve naturally for a lifetime, force-breaking offers one advantage: *reliable delivery to hand.* Many natural retrievers drop birds as they approach their owners, *especially when coming out of water.* If you run your dog in trials or tests that require water retrieving and/or delivery to hand, you can save yourself some wasted entry fees by force-breaking.

If your dog shows signs of becoming hardmouthed or sticky, you should force-break him. The *effective* cure for each of these problems is based on force-breaking. What's more, with either problem, the quicker you start the cure, the more reliably it will work. I describe the cures for these retrieving faults at the end of this chapter.

Prerequisites

You should not start force-breaking until your youngster understands (and obeys) the following obedience commands: *Whoa, Heel, Come-In.* You should also wait until you are sure he is a good all-around prospect. Force-breaking requires a lot of work. Why waste it on a dog that won't make the cut?

How old should your dog be before you begin force-breaking? Somewhere between 12 and 24 months, depending on his maturity rate and his progress in the rest of his training.

Equipment and Facilities

For force-breaking, you need a wooden force-breaking buck. I make my own, using one-and-a-quarter inch dowel for the crosspiece and half-inch dowel for the legs. A standard buck is nine inches long with one-inch legs, which is a nice size for most birddogs. I have seen similar bucks offered for sale in dog supply catalogs. If you can't find or make one, you can use an obedience trial dumbbell of appropriate size.

The legs on the buck (or solid ends on the dumbbell) do two things: First, they hold the buck up off the ground for easier picking up in Step 4; second, they prevent him from allowing the buck to accidentally slip out of the side of his mouth as he holds it in Step 1. If he wants to get rid of it, he has to spit it out.

Many trainers, especially pros, have elaborate facilities for force-breaking. The ideal arrangement includes a table at least 12 feet long with a post at each end and a wire strung tightly between the tops of the posts. The trainer puts the dog on the table and attaches the animal to the wire with a short lead. That not only gets the dog up where the trainer doesn't have to stoop and bend as he trains, but it also frees both of the trainer's hands, for the lead attached to the wire limits the dog's mobility.

If you were a pro, force-breaking regularly year-round, year after year, you would certainly benefit from such a facility. Since you are an amateur who would only use it every few years, you might find it an albatross most of the time. You would need both a place to set it up when you use it and a place to store it between uses.

Besides, you don't need a table. I've force-broken more dogs than I care to count, and I've never used one. Granted, I do a lot of stooping and squatting. I have to control my dog's mobility manually. However, these seeming disadvantages help me keep my sessions short—which is critical to success.

Here I will describe how to force-break without a table. If you enjoy the luxury of a special table, you will have no problem making the adjustment.

Schedule

Force-breaking requires at least one short (10-minute) session per day until the job is completed. This is intensive work that you cannot do now and then. How long does it take? An average beginner with an average birddog, training once or twice a day, should finish the job in one to two months. An experienced trainer with an unusually cooperative youngster might finish in three or four weeks. Any trainer with a dog that resists more than average may take longer than two months.

I spent two and a half months force-breaking a crafty Chesapeake. I spent three months convincing a particularly flighty Pointer. But frankly, I don't train by the calendar. I just keep throwing strikes until I get the final out. (Clearly, that Chessy and that Pointer got to me for a few hits and runs. So what? I won both games eventually, even if they weren't no-hitters.)

The key is short, frequent sessions. Seldom should a session last more than 10 minutes, but you can do as many per day as you wish. As I said above, you should do at least one a day, but two is much better, and anything up to four or five well-spaced sessions is better still.

Handling Techniques

Remember two things through this training: *short sessions* and *plenty of praise.*

Back in the mid-1970s, I filmed (on super-8 sound film) the force-breaking of a Golden Retriever named Tina. Each session took one 50-foot roll of film—which runs only three minutes and 20 seconds.

Praise speeds up this training. I have shown that film to many beginning trainers over the years. I have shown it so often that my family has long refused to watch it, claiming that it is devoid of plot, setting, and interesting characters. They especially detest the sound track. In fact, I can clear the house of offspring by simply announcing that I am going to show that film. It works even better than my old Glenn Miller records.

My kids call it the "Good Girl" movie, because I say that so often during the entire 33 minutes of film I saved. My wife tried to count the "Good Girls" once but gave up well past 200.

Yeah, all those "Good Girls" drive my kids out of the house, but let me tell you: Tina never tired of them!

One more thing: Don't become discouraged. At some point with every dog, I have doubted whether I was making any progress. With some dogs that has happened more than once. However, I have found that if I persevere, every dog comes around. You will surely hit such a snag, too, so be forewarned that it's coming, that it's normal, and that you can get past it if you just stick with the program.

In Steps 3 and 4, your dog will go through a necessary period of resentment, which if transferred to field work, would cause him to refuse to retrieve (or blink) his retrieves (assuming you are letting him retrieve naturally in the field). To prevent him making that transfer, take the following precautions:

First, and perhaps most important, use an object in force-breaking that he will not connect with field work—a buck or obedience dumbbell—until he is past his period of resentment. Don't use birds in force-breaking until you have completed all steps with the buck, after which his resentment will disappear.

Second, until you have completed force-breaking, do not use the commands *Fetch* and *Give* in the field.

Third, force-break in the backyard, not in the field. Dogs are very place-conscious.

If you violate any of these simple rules and allow your dog to make the connection between this and retrieving in the field, he will start blinking his retrieves. If that happens, discontinue retrieving in the field until you complete force-breaking, when his resentment will vanish.

TRAINING

Step 1: Accept and Hold the Buck (Pre-Force)

You must maintain physical control over your birddog during force-breaking. As mentioned above, I am assuming you do not have a table to help you with this. Further, I am assuming that your dog does not sit when you stop while heeling. As you can see, I describe the worst case scenario: You do not have a force-breaking table and your dog does not sit at heel.

Put the chain training collar (with the lead attached) on your dog. Heel him to a position next to a wall or fence where he cannot move away from you. Stop there, kneel down beside him, toss the lead over your shoulders, and plant your right foot firmly on the end of it. That gives you complete physical control while freeing both of your hands. This kneeling position will become uncomfortable quickly enough to remind you to keep each session short.

Show the buck to your birddog. Let him smell it, but don't let him mouth it or play with it. It's not a toy, but it's also nothing for him to fear.

Step 1: Accept and hold the buck on the command *Fetch.* *(Fr. Robert K. Spencer)*

The reaction you seek is complete boredom with the buck. As long as he fears it or wants to play with it, you cannot proceed with the training.

Once he shows boredom, open his mouth with your left hand, say *Fetch,* and insert the buck with your right hand. Some use the command *Hold* for this, reserving *Fetch* for reaching and picking up the buck. I have always used *Fetch* throughout this training without a problem.

Keep your right hand under his chin to prevent him from spitting the buck out. Keep it in his mouth for a few seconds, *all the time praising him quietly.* Then say *Give,* remove it, and praise calmly.

Control his various efforts to avoid this training. If he turns away from the buck, bring his muzzle back around with your left hand. If, while holding the buck, he tries to spit it out, as he will (many, many times), prevent it with your right hand. If he tries to run off, control him with the lead.

The rest of Step 1 is simple. Just repeat the *Fetch/Give* process (with praise for both) over and over each session. He will gradually learn to hold the buck voluntarily. When he does, withdraw your right hand from under his chin. Gradually wait longer and longer before saying *Give.*

Whenever he drops the buck, say *No!* and reinsert the buck with a firm *Fetch!* Then, of course, praise him.

When he holds it unassisted for a short time, stand up (but keep your foot on the end of the lead). If he drops it, correct him as above. When he holds it reliably while you stand up, step away from his side (but hold onto the lead). When you can walk to the end of the lead, walk around him.

When he holds the buck through this without correction, introduce distractions. Clap your hands or have a family member come into your training area unexpectedly. These distractions should give you a few opportunities to teach your youngster that he is not allowed to drop the buck until you say *Give*, no matter what.

Step 2: Carry the Buck (Pre-Force)

Next, teach him to carry the buck, first while heeling and then on *Come-In.*

Start out having him hold the buck, as in Step 1. Stand up, command *Heel,* and start walking. He will probably spit it out before taking his first step. Wonderful! That gives you a chance to correct him. If he hangs onto it and heels properly—unlikely but possible—praise him lavishly, but continue walking until he does indeed drop it (which won't take long, believe me). Praise him continuously while he carries it. When he drops it, say *No!,* stop, reinsert the buck with *Fetch!,* and resume heeling.

Your young birddog will gradually realize that he not only *can* simultaneously walk and carry the buck—a great revelation—but that he *must.* Two cautions: First, don't bump the buck out of his mouth while heeling; second, don't be too picky about how well he heels.

When he heels carrying the buck reliably, have him carry it during a *Come-In. Whoa* him, insert the buck (saying *Fetch*), walk to the end of the lead, and call him to you. If he drops it as he approaches, rush at him and correct him as above.

In each session, have him heel with the buck awhile, and call him to you two or three times. Also in each session, continue the Step 1 work—*Fetch . . . Give . . . Fetch . . . Give*—several times. By the time he carries the buck reliably at heel and on *Come-In,* he should also frequently open his own mouth automatically on *Fetch.*

Step 3: Open and Reach (Force)

Through Step 2, you have opened your dog's mouth and inserted the buck. His role on the command *Fetch* has been passive. Granted, conditioning alone has taught him to open his own mouth, but you have not trained him to do that—yet. But when he does start opening his own mouth this way, he is telling you he is ready for Step 3, in which you use force—mild physical discomfort—whenever he fails to open his own mouth on *Fetch.* Over the years, trainers have developed several types of force.

Step 2: Carry the buck, first while heeling . . . *(Fr. Robert K. Spencer)*

The Paw Squeeze: Squeeze the dog's front paw. This will open any canine mouth that hasn't been wired shut. Some trainers rig up cords around the middle toes and simply pull the string instead of squeezing the paw. **Advantages:** The dog has good visibility of the buck. You can easily adjust the pain level. The dog tends naturally to reach down toward the foot that hurts.

Disadvantages: It gives no direct control over the dog's muzzle.

The Lip Pinch: Grasp the dog's muzzle and press his upper lip against his canine teeth hard enough to induce mild pain as you open his mouth.

Advantages: This is a natural extension of the work in the previous steps. You can adjust the pain level to the needs of each dog easily. You maintain complete control of his muzzle.

Disadvantages: Your hand blocks the dog's view of the buck momentarily.

. . . then while doing a *Come-In*. *(Fr. Robert K. Spencer)*

The Ear Pinch: Pinch the little flap on the back of the dog's ear. This will induce enough pain to make the dog open his mouth. Some trainers pinch the ear flap against the ring on the training collar for greater effect.
Advantages: The dog has good visibility of the buck. Little strength is required to induce enough pain to get the attention of the hardest-headed dog on earth.
Disadvantages: It gives poor control over the dog's muzzle. It is difficult to adjust the pain level to each dog's tolerance for, after a few pinches, it hurts a lot no matter how lightly you pinch.

The Choke: Position the chain training collar high on the dog's neck, right behind his ears, and jerk up sharply to open his mouth.
Advantages: The dog has good visibility of the buck.
Disadvantages: It doesn't give good control of the dog's muzzle. It is difficult to adjust the amount of force to each dog's tolerance.

The Electronic Collar: Use mild electrical stimulation to induce the dog to open his mouth.
Advantages: The dog has good visibility of the buck. With the right kind of collar, you can adjust the amount of juice to each dog's tolerance.
Disadvantages: It gives you one more thing to hold with your hands, namely the transmitter. It gives you no direct control over the dog's muzzle. The collar is expensive, and many beginners won't learn how to use it properly.

Erick brings the buck to my hand. *(Fr. Robert K. Spencer)*

Take your pick. David Sanborn, who developed force-breaking, used the paw squeeze. To this day, most birddog trainers use some variation of that technique. Since so many trainers get wildly emotional over their choice of a force method, I won't recommend any. In fact, being nobody's fool, I won't even tell you which one I use! In these instructions, I will simply say "apply force" and leave which type up to you.

Force puts your birddog into his necessary period of resentment. However, with the buildup of Steps 1 and 2, you shouldn't have to apply force often, so it won't last long or become severe.

Kneel beside your dog. Toss the lead over your shoulder, and step on its end. Place the buck immediately in front of his mouth, almost touching it, and say *Fetch*. If he opens voluntarily, insert the buck—*and praise lavishly*. If he doesn't open voluntarily, apply force, insert the buck—*and praise lavishly*. Repeat this over and over through several sessions, until he opens automatically on *Fetch* without force.

Next teach him to reach. Here's a shortcut: Heel him around without the buck. As he moves, put the buck directly in front of his muzzle and say *Fetch*, continuing to move as you do. His forward movement should cause him to reach. Since he is already opening, he will take the buck.

Reach while heeling, moving the buck toward the ground in small increments. *(Fr. Robert K. Spencer)*

Reach while heeling, all the way to the gound. *(Fr. Robert K. Spencer)*

Praise him as soon as he has it, and continue heeling him awhile before taking the buck. Repeat this drill until he is comfortable reaching this way.

With that background in reaching, he should adjust quickly to reaching when he is not moving. Have him stand at heel beside you. With the buck almost touching his muzzle, command *Fetch.* He will probably open but not reach. Fine. Push his head forward with your left hand so his mouth goes around the buck. Praise him. Repeat this until he reaches a little without any help from your left hand.

Once he starts reaching ever so slightly without help, apply force whenever he refuses to reach, even though he may have opened voluntarily. Lengthen the distance he has to reach—*gradually.* Lengthen down, to both sides, even slightly up. Apply force for each refusal. He will soon be reaching almost to the ground.

He may try a new ploy: looking away from the buck before you can say *Fetch.* Don't be fooled, and don't move the buck into his cone of vision. Hold it right where it was, command *Fetch,* and force him to go to the buck if he refuses.

After he learns the joy of avoiding force by acting quickly, he may not wait for you to say *Fetch.* He may reach as soon as he sees the buck. Although that indicates that he is hearing the gospel you are preaching, you shouldn't allow it. Say *No,* and restrain him. He must reach only after hearing *Fetch.*

During this Step 3 work, continue the Step 2 work (carrying) in every session.

When he reaches—reliably—almost to the floor, he is ready for Step 4.

Step 4: Pick Up (Force)

Next, teach your youngster to pick the buck up off the ground. Although this is a natural extension of the reaching in Step 3, many dogs balk here. Until now, you have hand-held the buck every time you have commanded *Fetch.* Now you lay it down first. This subtle difference confuses many dogs.

Misty, a Weimaraner and the first dog I ever force-broke, balked for a month. If I held the buck on the ground, she would pick it up. If I removed my hand, she refused. Since I was inexperienced, I was too soft with her. Today I would save time by applying more force a lot sooner.

To ease your birddog into this, start while heeling. Have him reach for the buck several times while heeling, each time holding it closer and closer to the ground. Finally, "accidentally" drop it. If you are deft enough, he will snatch it up before he realizes what happened. If he does, praise him to the high heavens! If not, force him to pick it up by grasping his muzzle and using it as a scoop. Then praise him.

After he has done this several times, ease him into picking it up while standing still at heel. Have him reach farther and farther out and down until he has to move forward to reach it. Have him return to heel with it after he takes it each time. When he moves comfortably out to take the buck and back to heel, with you still hand-holding it near the ground, place the buck on the ground a couple of feet in front of him. Command *Fetch.* With all the preliminary work you have done, he should comply readily. If he does, praise him lavishly. If not, apply force—and praise him after he succeeds.

Next, place the buck a few feet in front of him, and command *Fetch.* Then place it a few feet to each side, then a few feet behind him. Lengthen the distance in every direction until you have to use your Flexi-Lead to give him enough lead to reach the buck.

When he will go to the end of the Flexi-Lead in any direction, pick up the buck, and return to heel with it, he has completed the basic course with the buck.

Erick picks the buck up from the ground. Looks simple, but it takes a lot of work. *(Fr. Robert K. Spencer)*

Replace the buck with a bird and command *Fetch! (Fr. Robert K. Spencer)*

Step 5: Jump (Post-Force)

Your youngster's period of resentment probably ended late in Step 4, especially if you praised him regularly throughout. If he still resents this work a bit, this (optional) sweetening-up step will bring him out of it.

Start out while heeling. As you move along, hold the buck a few inches above his head and command *Fetch.* He will reach up for it. Great. Praise him excitedly here, for you want to pump him up. Do this several times, higher and higher, until his front feet leave the ground.

Next try it with him standing in front of you. Shorten up the distance he must reach, of course, and increase it gradually. Don't go for any height records here. You want to sweeten him up, not make a high-jumping champion of him. I never hold the buck higher than my shoulder, and I am quite short.

Step 6: Transfer to Birds (Post-Force)

After your birddog has learned to enjoy this *Fetch/Give* routine with the buck, transfer it to retrieving dummies and birds. First in the backyard, then out in the field.

Erick says *Moi?* Why, certainly, boss! *(Fr. Robert K. Spencer)*

One caution: When you move into the field, keep the Flexi-Lead on him until you are sure that he will retrieve instead of taking off to hunt for birds to point. He still has his built-in priorities, and you are messing with them here, so be prepared for some surprises at first.

Hey, you made it! And a couple of times during the process you didn't think you would succeed, right? That's dog training, and you now qualify as a dog trainer. Congratulations!

Hardmouth

To cure hardmouth, repeatedly force the culprit to carry a frozen bird until he begs to be allowed to release it, and then do the same with a normal bird. You can do this in the backyard. Hold a frozen bird immediately in front of young Carcass-Cruncher's mouth and command *Fetch.* He can't hurt it. In fact, if he sinks a tooth in, he will wish he hadn't. Now heel him around until he shows signs of wishing he could spit it out, which may take 30 minutes. Continue another 10 minutes. Fine. Stop, tell him *Give,* and let him rest a few seconds. Then command *Fetch,* stick the frozen bird back in his maw, and heel him around again until he begs for relief.

When you are sure he takes absolutely no joy in the frozen bird, switch to a normal (unfrozen) bird. Make him carry it until he begs for relief—and repeat this process several times. Do this every day for a few days. Then do it again out in the field before you start normal field work. Chances are pretty good he will handle birds you shoot for him very gingerly after this treatment.

That cure will work if anything will. *But you can't use it unless you have first force-broken your dog.* Why? Because you can't force him to carry anything for any longer than he chooses to.

Stickiness

Many people do not realize that stickiness differs totally from hardmouth. It is a separate, unrelated problem. In fact, the sticky dog seldom damages a bird. He just won't release it to the boss. Some deal with it by blowing in the dog's ear or some other stop-gap technique. I prefer to cure it.

To cure stickiness, apply an appropriate level of punishment as you command *Give.* A force-broken dog understands that *Give* is a command, not a request. Thus he will understand why you are punishing him. When young Lock-Jaw delivers to you, grasp (but don't pull on) the bird. Command *Give* and punish him until he not only releases his grip but also backs away from the bird. *Never, never, never pull a bird from a dog's mouth, especially not from a dog that is inclined to be sticky.* Grasp the bird and insist that the dog release and back off, leaving the bird in your unmoved hand.

How should you punish young Lock-Jaw during this procedure? The operative word is *appropriately,* but here it carries a note of decisiveness, even finality. In other words, be more heavy-handed than usual. Some trainers use extra juice from the electronic collar. Others jab the dog's rump with an electric cattle prod. Still others apply a knee *forcefully* to the dog's chest.

Whatever punishment you choose, *your timing is critical.* Command *Give* precisely as you punish. That will insure that young Lock-Jaw understands the connection between the punishment and your command. It will also convince him that getting shed of that bird when you say *Give* is a very good idea indeed.

Here again, the cure just doesn't work if you have not force-broken your dog. The non-force-broken dog doesn't understand that *Give* is a command, not an "if you please."

CHAPTER

17

Staunching on Point:

Minimum Requirement for Birddogs

A staunch birddog holds its point until the handler arrives and flushes the bird. Jigger, a Pointer owned by the author in the early 1970s, points while dragging a checkcord.

BACKGROUND

What Is It?

A *staunch* birddog holds point until the handler arrives to flush the birds. A *steady* birddog continues to hold point after the flush and even after the handler shoots. A steady birddog is, by definition, also staunch. But a staunch dog may not also be steady.

Staunching is a prerequisite for steadying. More than that, however, it is essential for every birddog, whether or not the owner intends to steady the animal. A birddog that is not staunch is simply a flusher from pointing breed stock. It is not a true birddog.

In this chapter, I also describe how you should continue training your birddog to handle afield, that is, to go, to stop, and to turn on command.

Here, too, I explain how to line-steady your birddog for water retrieving for those who intend to use their dogs in this way.

Why Do It?

Until staunch, a birddog is just a flusher with pointing breed ancestry. No hunter can allow such a dog to range beyond gun range. Even the hunter who (for whatever reason) insists that his birddog hunt that close will find a staunch dog a more enjoyable hunting companion. In short, a proper pointing dog should stand his game long enough to allow the boss to flush it, no matter where the boss happens to be when the dog locates the game.

Most experienced birddog owners prefer that their dogs range out to find birds that they (the owners) would not locate, either alone or with a flushing dog (spaniel or retriever). A birddog's functional advantage over a flusher begins just beyond gun range and extends out to whatever maximum distance the hunting conditions and/or the handler's comfort zone allow. To operate out there, the dog must be staunch on point.

While you are staunching your youngster, you should also continue teaching him to handle afield; that is, to go out, to stop, and to turn on command. It will make him a better hunter, and it will give you a greater sense of control when he ranges out to a useful distance.

If you intend to have your dog retrieve from water, you should now begin to line-steady him in that work, per the instructions in this chapter.

Prerequisites

Before you can staunch your birddog, he must be pointing solidly, even if he doesn't always stick around until you get there. He should also obey the basic obedience training commands, especially *Whoa*.

If he retrieves, either naturally or through force-breaking, you will be able to reward his staunch points with a retrieve, at least some of the time. If you plan to force-break him (whether or not he retrieves naturally), you can do this staunching work in parallel with force-breaking.

For the handling work described here, your dog should have a basic background in going out, stopping, and turning on command per the instructions in Chapter 15 ("Hunting and Pointing"). Similarly, if you plan to have him retrieve from water, before you line-steady him according to the instructions in this chapter you should introduce him to water work, per Chapter 15.

Equipment and Facilities

For staunching, you need a small, handheld squirt bottle full of water. You will use this to convince your youngster to let you walk in front of him to flush birds.

For line-steadying in water retrieving you need a belt cord. This is a short (three- to four-foot long) piece of cord similar to that used in old-fashioned Venetian blinds, with a loop on one end and the other end plain.

Schedule

You can start staunching as soon as your dog is pointing solidly, even if he still dives in and flushes the birds. You continue staunching until you have convinced him that flushing birds is your job, not his. How long that will take depends on his temperament, his maturity rate, and the frequency of your sessions afield.

The handling and water retrieving described in this chapter continue what you started in the work covered by Chapter 15 ("Hunting and Pointing"). Both are ongoing processes, with no definable ending.

Handling Techniques

Your most important responsibility in staunching is to keep your youngster's spirits up as you instill this level of control. To keep his spirits up, for crying out loud, *praise him every chance you get!* Under the stress of constraint, your dog may well interpret your silence as displeasure. Don't allow that to happen. Praise him while he stands his game, even as you restrain him with a checkcord or Flexi-Lead. Praise him as you approach him. Praise him as you style him up on point. Praise him especially as you walk in front of him before the flush.

In approaching him while he is on point, swing out and come in from the side where he can see you. Talk soothingly to him—praise him softly—as you approach. When you style him up, kneel down beside him. Then rub his tummy to elevate his body, push his rump forward to intensify his point, stroke the underside of his tail up into a higher position, even rub the hair on his back the wrong way. But as you do, continue praising him. Let him know that when he stands there on point he pleases you immensely. *That brings his basic desire to please you to your assistance in staunching him.*

Look at it this way: Your release trap holds the bird securely; it won't go anywhere until you release it so you can concentrate totally on your dog. If you were using wild birds or released quail from call-back pens, you wouldn't have so much freedom. You would have to worry about accidentally flushing the birds as you messed with your dog. As I see it, you are most fortunate to be unable to afford extensive private training grounds with recall pens and all that. You have to get by with remote release traps, which just happen to give you all the best of it in staunching (and later in steadying). Ain't that a shame! Just do what I do: Try not to grin too widely as you suffer these middle-class limitations.

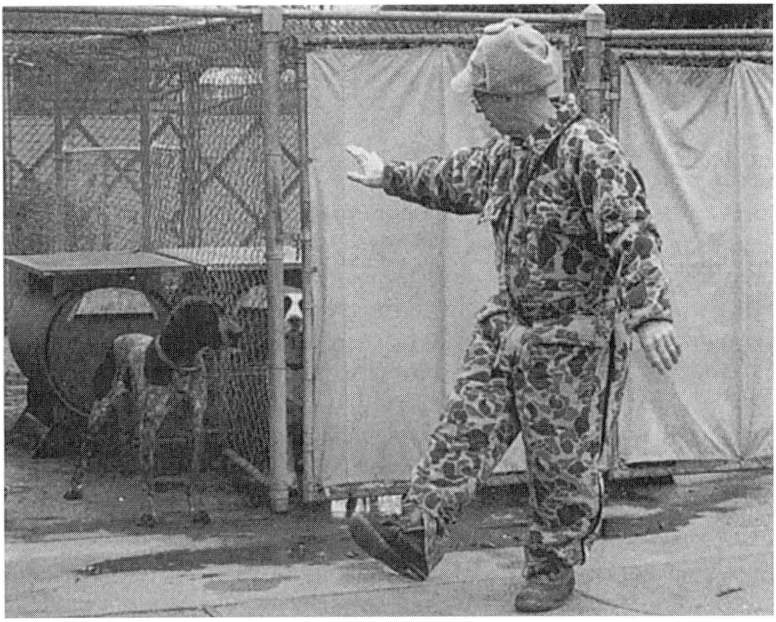

My backyard drill. While keeping the dog *whoa*-ed in his run, I kick around in front of him, just as I will later do in the field when flushing a bird. *(Theresa Spencer)*

TRAINING

Staunching

First, let me describe again a backyard drill that prepares a birddog for staunching. I first covered it in Chapter 14 ("Obedience Training").

My dogs live in kennel runs in my backyard. I let them out morning and evening to run and play in our fenced yard. Before letting a birddog out, I *Whoa* him inside the kennel run. Then I open his gate and walk around in front of him, kicking here and there as I would if I were trying to flush a bird. The dog wants to take off, of course, but can't because of the *Whoa* command. This routine simulates the situation the dog is in when he points and I walk in front of him to flush the bird.

Okay, that said, here are two basic techniques for staunching a birddog. I call one the "Flexi-Lead Technique" and the other the "Checkcord Technique." You should use both before you finish, first the Flexi-Lead Technique, then the Checkcord Technique.

Flexi-Lead technique: When the dog points, swing out wide, keeping the lead tight, and approach from the side. *(Ray Taylor)*

Flexi-Lead Technique: Plant a pigeon in your remote release trap—with your dog out of sight, and without leaving a scent trail to the bird—and then return to get your dog. Snap on the Flexi-Lead (or checkcord) and guide him into a position from which he can scent the bird.

When he points—which he should if he has completed the prerequisites—tighten up on the Flexi-Lead, swing out wide, and approach him from the side. Praise him softly, soothingly, and reassuringly as you do. Keep the Flexi-Lead taut. One of two things will happen: either you will work your way to him and get your hands on him or he will break and rush the bird. Since you are to his side, you can't fully control him with the Flexi-Lead.

If he breaks for the bird, release it, and snub your dog up with the Flexi-Lead as quickly as you can. Do not yell at him! Give him no commands! Just stop him and bring him back to where he was pointing. Now

Whoa him there. Pet and praise him awhile. If he creeps forward, squirt him in the face with water from your squirt bottle. After he has stood there awhile, heel him away, either to the next release trap or back to your vehicle (while you plant another bird).

If he doesn't break but lets you get your hands on him, keep the Flexi-Lead taut with one hand and style him up with the other. Praise him all the while. If he seems willing to stand there, relax the tautness in the Flexi-Lead, and continue petting and praising him. When he breaks—as he will eventually—release the bird, snub him up short, bring him back, *Whoa* him, then pet and praise him again. Use your squirt bottle to discourage creeping. Finally, heel him away.

Some say you should *Whoa* the dog as soon as he goes on point. I prefer to staunch him without *Whoa,* except after replacing him after a chase, as described above—when I intend to enforce it. I introduce *Whoa* more fully later during steadying, when I really mean it. Since so many dogs have been staunched with *Whoa,* it probably doesn't matter much one way or the other, so do whichever makes sense to you.

After he understands the message of the stream of water, use it instead of the Flexi-Lead. Here I approach Erick, pointing without the Flexi-Lead. Notice the squirt bottle protruding from a vest pocket. *(Ray Taylor)*

After a few such enjoyable encounters, your youngster will hold his point longer and longer. When he does, proceed as follows:

After styling him up and praising him, stand up and unsnap the Flexi-Lead from his collar. Now *without a Whoa command* (why give a command you know he will disobey?), step in front of him and ease your way toward the bird. If your dog moves forward even a step, release the bird and let him chase it. Do not yell at him. Just let him go. After chasing the bird out of sight, he will return to you. Good. Stand him where he was pointing, command *Whoa,* and praise him. Walk in front of him again, repeating *Whoa* softly over and over as you do. If he moves, squirt him in the face with a stream of water from your squirt bottle, reposition him with mild displeasure, and start again. When he lets you get all the way to the release trap, kick around in the cover there, just as you have been doing in the backyard in the drill described earlier.

Now give him a pleasant surprise. Pull a dead pigeon from your training vest, toss it in the direction the bird flew, and send him to retrieve it. All this assumes that he retrieves and enjoys it, of course. This is the beginning of a new awareness for him: If he remains in place, he gets a bird in his mouth; if he creeps forward, he only gets to chase a fly-away.

As I walk in front of Erick, I prepare to squirt him if he creeps forward. *(Ray Taylor)*

Once he understands the message you send with your squirt bottle during these rerun situations, you can use it to keep him staunch while you walk past him as he points a bird. But don't rely on it too much. Whenever he seems likely to creep, send the stream of water past his nose from wherever you are at the moment. If he still creeps, let the bird teach him the error of his ways.

When that grand day arrives on which he allows you to walk all the way to the release trap and kick around there, give him a real reward. Release the bird, let him chase it. When he reaches a safe distance, have an assistant shoot the bird for him to retrieve. It will fall like manna from heaven. You should not shoot the bird yourself, for you have your hands full with the dog and the release trap. You shouldn't be carrying a loaded shotgun too.

Repeat this drill every time he points a bird until he is completely staunched. Of course, you may want to switch to the checkcord technique after he is well started. It's easier on you, and gives him more freedom to run.

Checkcord Technique: Plant a bird in your remote release trap, and return to your dog. Snap the checkcord on his collar, take him to the starting point, and release him with your customary formalities. Let him hunt, dragging the checkcord. When he points, hasten to the end of the checkcord, grasp it, and swing out wide so you can approach him from the side.

When you reach him, style him up as described above, with plenty of praise. If he breaks, release the bird and control him with the checkcord. If he lets you walk in front of him, proceed as described above. The only difference here is that you don't have to unsnap the checkcord before letting him chase, because your dog cannot damage it by dragging it as he would if he dragged the Flexi-Lead.

Finishing Touches: Your youngster holds point until you flush the bird in front of him. That makes him a usable birddog, one you can take hunting, one your hunting buddies will rave about, even tell outrageous lies about to their friends and co-workers. Of course, you shouldn't bother them with little details like how easy this training has been. Naw, they probably wouldn't believe you anyhow, so tell them what they want to hear: that you are a birddog training genius of the first order, as is obvious from the performance of your dog.

But back to reality: Notice that you have not been in the least heavy-handed in this training. Your youngster learned to hold point with no punishment from you beyond an occasional stream of water past his nose—okay, now and then you squirted him in the face, just to let him know you could. But you didn't intimidate him. Fact is, the bird did most of the teaching. When your dog did things right, the bird behaved.

When your dog messed up, the bird flew away. Clearly, birds only become reliable assistant trainers when used with remote release traps, but your dog doesn't know that.

You can improve his staunchness in several simple ways: by making him hold point longer while you stand behind him and wait; by approaching him from every imaginable direction—from straight behind him, from quartering this way and that, from the other side of the bird. When he makes a mistake, the bird flies away unharmed. When he does everything right, the bird falls from heaven for him to retrieve. He is acquiring great respect for birds as critics of his performance!

Ground Pattern Work

During the time you spend staunching your young birddog, you should also continue teaching him the three handling commands: to go out farther, to stop, and to turn. For now, just continue the two types of training you have already started: training by association, and formal training with the Flexi-Lead or checkcord.

Whenever you run him in the field, first *Whoa* him, then release him with *Hie-On* (or *pip-pip* on your whistle). Whenever he turns naturally, give him your turn command (verbal or *pip-pip*) and arm signal. At the end of his run, *Whoa* him at a reasonable distance. Either call him in to you or walk to him and snap a lead on him. Then heel him back to your vehicle.

In the next chapter (Chapter 18, "Stopping to Flush"), I explain how to reinforce these handling commands *gently* with the electronic collar. For now, rely on the techniques you have been using all along.

Line-Steadying for Water Retrieving

Your dog has been retrieving from water for some time now and seems to enjoy it. Wonderful, but now you should teach him that he cannot leave to make a retrieve until you command him to do so. This training serves as a good foundation for steadying to wing and shot later on. It also makes your dog something other than a damnable nuisance when you use him as a non-slip retriever, whether for doves or waterfowl.

Attach the loop end of your belt cord to your belt and run the other end under your dog's collar and fold it over on itself. Now grasp the cord so you can control him with one hand. Heel him to the water's edge, command *Whoa,* and hold the belt cord so that he cannot feel any pressure from it. That is very important. Properly used, the belt cord becomes an invisible force to the dog. Until you give the command to retrieve, that invisible force prevents him from moving. But as soon as you send him, the invisible force vanishes. He can leave. Wow! What a magic voice the boss has! Even invisible forces obey him! But the dog won't interpret things that way if he can feel constant pressure on his collar from the belt cord. Keep it slack.

Now, toss the dummy—or better yet, have an assistant toss it so you can concentrate on controlling your dog. When he sees the dummy sail through the air and splash down in the water, he will try to break. Fine! Don't let him. Jerk him back into position, command *Whoa* again with some displeasure in your voice. Make him stand there a couple of seconds before sending him.

That's all there is to it. Oh, sure, it takes many, many repetitions over a period of time and in several places. But the training technique is just that simple.

Don't go for distance records while steadying. You want the dummy floating enticingly close and in plain sight. That makes your dog want to get it. If you give him long retrieves, he may decide "to hell with it!"—and then what will you do? (You'll shorten up and hope he changes his mind, or at least that's what you should do, so why not do that in the first place?)

Of course, don't do water work unless the weather is mild, especially with a young dog. A few dips in icy water may cure him for life.

Here I have the belt cord properly installed on Erick. *(Ray Taylor)*

CHAPTER

18

Stopping to Flush:

Cornerstone of Advanced Bird Handling

Reliable stop-to-flush is more than a nicety of canine etiquette afield, it is the basis for advanced training in steadiness and honoring. Shown here on point is FC/AFC Karrycourts Prairie Fire, owned by Susan Borocy and Jeannie Wagner; honoring, foreground, is DC/AFC Karrycourts Rose O'Cidermill, owned by Jeannie Wagner and George Clark; in back is FC/AFC Karrycourts Toby of Tobie Lee, owned by Terry Harback. *(Jim Basham)*

BACKGROUND

What Is It?

The birddog that stops to flush *whoas* automatically whenever a bird flushes wild. A stop-to-flush differs from a flush and stop about like winning the lottery differs from robbing a bank. A stop-to-flush is a training refinement, not a canine performance fault. The dog was not aware of the bird's presence before the flush and did nothing deliberate to cause the flush. The dog is as surprised as the handler to see the bird in the air. The boss may shoot such a bird without undoing the dog's training.

A flush and stop is a deliberate canine misdeed. The supposedly staunch dog, which should know better, deliberately flushes the bird, then stops in an attempt to induce the handler to shoot it. If the handler does shoot the bird, the dog has won his little con game and will be anxious to play again as soon as possible. After an amazingly few such victories, the dog will no longer be staunch, and may stop pointing altogether.

This chapter also explains how to put the finishing touches on your birddog's ground pattern and water retrieving work.

Why Do It?

The stop-to-flush is more than a hunting nicety. It is the cornerstone for the advanced bird-handling training covered in the next chapter (Chapter 19, "Steadying and Honoring"). Teaching the stop-to-flush first allows you to do 80 percent of your steadying and honoring—including most of the corrections—in nonpointing situations. Thus, you can finish up his steadying and honoring without affecting his style on point.

Putting the finishing touches on your birddog's ground pattern, which is also covered in this chapter, has the rather obvious advantage of making him a more cooperative, more effective hunting companion. Ditto for the finishing touches on water work, for those who intend to use their birddogs to retrieve from water.

Prerequisites

Your dog should be fully staunched on point before you start this training. Although retrieving is not absolutely necessary, it is useful in rewarding the dog for stopping to flush. If you force-break your dogs, it helps to have that completed. If not, you can rely on natural retrieving.

Another prerequisite of sorts is a willingness on your part to discontinue pointing work until you finish this stop-to-flush training. Why? Well, your birddog still chases the birds he points because you haven't yet steadied him. You shouldn't steady him until after he has mastered the stop-to-flush, as explained above. If you allow him to chase when he points but make him stop during this stop-to-flush training, you will confuse the hell out of the poor beast.

For the ground pattern work, your dog should understand these four commands, namely, *Hie-On, Come-In, Whoa,* and *Turn.* For the water work, he should be line-steady.

Equipment and Facilities

I offer you two basic approaches for stop-to-flush training, one with an electronic collar, the other without. If you choose the latter, you need no additional equipment. If you choose the collar approach, you need an electronic collar—but not just any collar, and especially not one of the older models.

Electronic collars today are no longer the crude and undependable instruments of torture they were many years ago. Although some of the old models are still made, today's newer and more advanced collars have features that transform them into gentle, effective training aids. However, even today's advanced electronic collars are no gentler than the person with the transmitter. *Thus, the following types of people should not buy electronic collars:* those with temper problems (if you are in doubt, ask your spouse); those with little patience (again, ask your spouse); those who take canine misbehavior *personally*—as if it were directed at them—and want to retaliate on the dog (ask your training buddies); those who will not take the trouble to learn how to use and how not to use the electronic collar. In other words, anyone who thinks he can simply strap it on the dog's neck and then push the button every time the poor animal displeases him. That isn't training; that's animal abuse.

One more important consideration: Collars are expensive, running from around $200 to over $800. If your budget won't allow both a collar and the remote electronic release traps recommended in Chapter 15, get the traps rather than a collar. The release traps will help you more through the course of your dog's training.

Okay, if after all those warnings you still plan to use an electronic collar, let me give you a little philosophy. You can only do two types of training with an electronic collar: reinforcing and proofing.

Reinforcing: You can reinforce only commands the dog already understands. In this usage, the collar works wonders at a distance, convincing your dog that you have extremely long arms indeed. For reinforcement training, the dog must understand the command, must understand that his disobedience causes the electric stimulation, must understand that he can turn it off by obeying, and must also understand that he can avoid the juice altogether next time by obeying promptly. For reinforcement training, you need not light the dog up like a neon sign. Instead, you need only use sufficient stimulation to get his attention.

Proofing: You can use it to form an unpleasant association in the dog's mind with a certain *object* (snake, skunk, chicken), a certain *action* (chasing deer), or a certain *place* (henhouse). For this usage, you use no command because you want the dog to associate the discomfort with the thing you want him to avoid, not with you. You may use more stimulation here to make the lesson stick quickly.

Above all, you do not use the collar in *teaching* any command. *It is not a teaching tool.* It is a reinforcing and proofing tool, nothing else.

What kind of collar should you buy? I have had personal experience only with various Tri-Tronics models. However, I'm sure other makers produce effective and reliable collars, too. Let me talk in terms of features rather than makes and models.

You should insist that your collar have variable intensity control so you can adjust the level of stimulation to the sensitivity of your dog, specifically, *to the lowest level he notices.* Various collars have four to fifteen levels controlled by collar plugs and/or transmitter buttons. You should get a collar with at least four levels, and if you can afford a collar with more, get one. Avoid any collar with only one level, regardless of its other features.

You should also insist on a collar with an automatic turn-off, after, say, 10 seconds. Anything you can't get through to your dog in 10 seconds will also elude him in 30 seconds. Such a dog needs more training, not more reinforcement.

Electronic collars come with two types of power sources: rechargeable NiCad batteries, and replaceable alkaline or lithium batteries. I prefer NiCad, but either will do the job.

Some collars have features I don't like, like an automatic warning buzzer and a praise sound. The automatic warning buzzer (which sounds before each stimulation) not only complicates a trainer's timing but also makes it extremely difficult to assess each dog's sensitivity to electricity because most dogs react to the sound whether they feel the electricity or not. I have found teaching the dog to understand the intent of the praise sound too difficult to mess with. I prefer to praise vocally—and often. However, some trainers like these features.

So much for the collar. For putting the finishing touches on your birddog's waterfowl retrieving, you need about a dozen duck decoys.

Schedule

In theory at least, you can begin stop-to-flush training any time after you finish staunching your dog on point. However, if he is unusually soft, you should wait until he is mature enough to cope with the mild pressure required here. Such a dog should be allowed, even encouraged, to chase long enough to become as birdy as possible before advancing into this training.

If you have an unusually tough dog, you should begin stop-to-flush work immediately after staunching.

You can do the advanced ground-pattern work and water-retrieving work covered in this chapter as you teach him to stop to flush.

Handling Techniques

I cover any specific handling techniques in the appropriate training sections.

TRAINING

Introducing the Electronic Collar

If you have opted *not* to use the collar, skip this. If you have decided to buy a collar, you should introduce your birddog to it very carefully, according to the instructions given by the manufacturer. The Tri-Tronics booklet, titled "Three-Action Introduction," offers a sound method that should work with any good collar. My own method is only a slight modification of that one.

Introducing a dog to the collar properly requires three things: First, you must prevent him from becoming collar-wise; second, you must determine the appropriate level of stimulation for your particular dog; and third, you must teach him how to respond to stimulation.

Preventing Collar-Wiseness: A collar-wise dog obeys properly only when wearing the collar. When it is removed, he disobeys. This is much easier to prevent than to cure. First, accustom him to wearing a reasonable facsimile of the collar (a dummy collar) until he no longer notices the added weight—24 hours a day for a couple of weeks—*before using the real collar.* Second, after you begin using the real collar, put it on him for every training session, whether or not you intend to use it. You can put aside the dummy collar when you start using the real collar. However, you should always train with the real collar on him.

Determining the Appropriate Stimulation Level: The appropriate level of stimulation, which varies from dog to dog, is the lowest level to which the animal reacts noticeably but not excessively. It is far below the level that shocks him into vocalizing or reacting vigorously. The appropriate level irritates the dog just enough to make him prefer to turn it off through obedience, but not enough to intimidate or panic him. To determine the appropriate level for your dog (after he has worn the dummy collar for a couple of weeks), put the real collar on him and experiment with the different levels of stimulation, *starting with the lowest.* If he ignores the lowest level, try the next lowest, and so on. When he reacts ever so slightly—by cocking his head, looking around quickly, or some such movement—he has told you which intensity is correct for him.

Teaching the Meaning of Stimulation: To teach him how to respond to stimulation with each collar command, first teach the command thoroughly without the collar. Then, with him on lead, strap on the collar and reinforce the command with stimulation as follows:

Start stimulation an instant *before* you give the command, and stop it as soon as he complies. For example, start stimulation just before you say *Whoa,* and end stimulation as soon as he stops. *Then praise him.* If you started stimulation after the command, you might zap him as he begins to obey, which would confuse him. Continue this sequence—start stimulation, command, end stimulation—until his more rapid obedience shows you he understands that he can turn off the stimulation by complying with your command.

Once he understands how to turn off stimulation by obedience to the command, change your timing. Give the command first, and only zap him if he is slow in responding. That will teach him how to avoid stimulation completely—by obeying quickly.

You should introduce your dog to the collar with each command in the backyard before using it with any of them in the field. Why? Well, if you only introduce the collar with one command (say, *Whoa*), your dog may think that he should always perform that one action (stopping) when stimulated. Later on, when you try to teach him to *Come-In* with the collar, he may become confused and *Whoa* instead. If you introduce all these commands with the collar initially, he will learn that obeying, regardless of command, turns off the stimulation. He won't think only one action works.

I recommend that you introduce the collar with the following commands initially: *Come-In, Whoa, Kennel, Turn.* Really tattoo each of them with the collar in the backyard before using any of them in the field.

Stop-to-Flush

If your birddog retrieves, either naturally or through force-breaking, he will learn stop-to-flush more easily and quickly. However, if you are one of the few who prefer dogs that don't retrieve, you can still teach the stop-to-flush. Simply skip over the next section, which explains how to extend retrieving into an elementary stop-to-flush.

Pre-Training for Dogs that Retrieve: If you have line-steadied your dog for water retrieving, as described in Chapter 17, he is ready to move into this rudimentary work immediately. If you have not line-steadied him, do so now—although you need not involve water if you prefer not to. Simply follow the directions in Chapter 17 for line-steadying with the belt cord, but keep the retrieves on land, preferably with little or no cover, until he is completely line-steadied.

After line-steadying, go to a place with little or no cover, snap your Flexi-Lead or checkcord on your dog's collar, grab a retrieving dummy, and start walking around. Now *Whoa* him somewhere, anywhere. Stand directly in front of him, facing him. Get his attention, and hold your hand up in the *Whoa* position.

Now toss the dummy high over your head and directly behind you. If he breaks, stop him *before he gets to the dummy.* Block him with your body—that's why you threw it directly behind you. Use the Flexi-Lead to stop him, then haul him back to where he belongs, uttering a few unpleasantries as you do. Walk out and pick up the dummy.

Whoa him again. Face him again. Toss the dummy behind you again. Do this right there where you started until he stops breaking. Even after he has learned to remain steady, only let him retrieve about every other time. Walk back and pick up the dummy every other time. That convinces him that he won't always retrieve—a holy thought you should encourage, if you want to keep him steady.

When he handles this consistently well, start tossing the dummy off to the side instead of behind you. Then start tossing it straight over his head. All through this work, never let him get to the dummy when he breaks, and only let him retrieve half the time when he remains steady.

When he will stand there no matter where you throw the dummy, try it while he is moving. Let him run on the Flexi-Lead. When he comes toward you (so he can see what you are doing), toss the dummy behind you, straight away from him. As he starts toward it, command *Whoa!* and enforce compliance. Never let him get to the dummy if he breaks, and let him retrieve about half the time when he doesn't. Next, make the toss off to the side while he is moving. When he can handle that, toss it right over his head (while he is moving), holler *Whoa!*, and control him as necessary with the Flexi-Lead.

After he understands the drill on the Flexi-Lead, go through it with the dog running free, as Paul Beauchamp is doing here with Betsy. First he tosses a dummy away from her . . .

. . . then eventually tosses a dead pigeon right over her head.

In a short time he will obey your *Whoa* command with the dummy in the air well enough for you to remove the Flexi-Lead. Go through the entire exercise again with him running free.

Next, repeat it with a dead bird—with the same sequence (behind you, off to the side, over his head). Finally, repeat part of it with a live, clip-wing pigeon that can flutter but not fly. However, don't toss the clip-wing over his head, lest the bird come down on top of him—which you don't need, believe me.

After these drills, your dog should at least suspect that the sight of a bird in the air means he should put the brakes on. He may even stop before you *Whoa* him some of the time. Great! Not necessary yet, but wonderful if he does it.

Stop-to-Flush Without Electronic Collar: If you went through the above preliminary training, your job will be much simpler. But even if you didn't, all is not lost. You can start right here.

As mentioned in the prerequisites, you should discontinue pointing work until you have completed this stop-to-flush training. Your dog still chases flushed birds after pointing them, and that will make this training very confusing to him.

Take your dog to a place with light to moderate cover. Slip two or three strong flying pigeons—homers would be better if you have them—in your vest, snap the Flexi-Lead or checkcord on his collar, and start walking. When he is looking your way, release a pigeon to fly off. As soon as he moves toward it, command *Whoa!* If he ignores you, snub him up with the Flexi-Lead, and haul him back to where he should have stopped. *Whoa* him again. Release another pigeon. This time he may well remain in place. If not, repeat the correction. Then, release another pigeon.

Do this every training session until he stops when you command *Whoa,* even with a flying bird tempting him to break and chase. When he stops at the sight of the bird in the air, before you can say *Whoa,* try him off the Flexi-Lead—but have him drag a checkcord, just in case. Then, if he weakens, run him down and bring him back.

When he stops reliably while dragging a checkcord, and if he retrieves, have an assistant shoot the birds (not homers here, of course) and let him retrieve about half of them, just as above.

Next, plant a bird in your remote release trap, just as you have done while staunching him. However, put the Flexi-Lead or checkcord on him and bring him near the trap from the upwind side, *so he cannot scent the bird.* When he is looking in the direction of the trap, release the bird and command *Whoa!* He should stop, but if he doesn't, control him with the Flexi-Lead.

Repeat this drill until he stops automatically when the bird goes up, without a *Whoa* command. When he will do that, try him without the Flexi-Lead, but dragging a checkcord. Do not proceed until he stops automatically (without *Whoa*) and reliably (every time) for several sessions, preferably in several locations.

When he has proven himself adequately, introduce a little fun—retrieving—into the game, if your dog retrieves. Switch from homers to commies, have an assistant shoot the birds, and let your dog retrieve about half of them.

Stop-to-Flush With Electronic Collar: You shouldn't use the electronic collar for any training in the field until you have introduced it (per the instructions above) for the following commands: *Come-In, Whoa, Kennel,* and *Turn.* If in addition to that you have also completed the above pre-training for dogs that retrieve, you will find the rest of this stop-to-flush training almost trivial. If yours is a non-retrieving birddog, you will have to work a little harder, a little longer.

As mentioned in the prerequisites, you should discontinue pointing work during this stop-to-flush training. Chasing pointed birds when they flush—which you shouldn't stop yet—will confuse him in this training.

Stick a few pigeons (homers, if possible) in your vest, strap the collar on your dog, and turn him loose. When he is running toward you, and fairly close, turn a pigeon loose to fly away. If your dog stops automatically (from the pre-training), great! If he chases the bird, command *Whoa,* and use the collar to insist on obedience. Praise him, walk over to him, and cast him off in a new direction. If he swerves and starts to chase the bird (a delayed chase), command him to turn, and reinforce the command with the collar.

Continue this until he stops automatically, without a *Whoa* command, when you release a bird to fly away. Many dogs will start slowing down when they see the boss reaching in his pocket for a bird. That's a sure sign the dog is getting the picture.

Next, plant a pigeon (a homer, if possible) in your remote release trap. Work your dog around to it so he will approach it from the upwind side—*where he cannot scent the bird.* If necessary, lead him to it on the Flexi-Lead or checkcord. When he is reasonably close to the trap, release the bird. By now he should stop automatically. If he doesn't, command *Whoa* and, if necessary, reinforce it with the collar. And so on, *until he stops automatically whenever a bird pops up.* Don't proceed until he stops without a *Whoa* command *reliably*—which means every time, folks.

When he does stop both automatically and reliably, give him a little fun. Switch from homers to commies and have your assistant shoot the birds. Let him retrieve about half of them.

Advanced Ground Pattern Work

If you have opted for the electronic collar, and if you have introduced your handling commands with it, you can now use your collar to reinforce those commands in the field. Introduce the collar to reinforce the

When he is reliable in the preliminary work, plant a pigeon in your release trap and bring your dog to it with the wind, as Dr. Jeff Herod has done here with Ben. (Notice bend in cover, indicating wind direction.) When you release the bird, your dog should stop like this.

Hie-On command, just as you introduced it to reinforce *Whoa, Come-In, Kennel,* and *Turn.* That done, when he potters around, tell him to *Hie-On,* and if he ignores the command, zap him. When you want to turn him, give your *Turn* command or whistle. If he ignores it, zap him. And so on. In general, you should correct him with a series of short zaps rather than one long one.

Do not hack (over-handle) your birddog, lest you destroy his initiative. You won't shoot many birds over a mechanical mutt that is so absorbed in obeying commands that he doesn't hunt for birds. Don't command *Hie-On* unless he is really pottering around. Don't turn him when he is making a purposeful cast. Don't call him in except at the end of a run afield, before you heel him back to your vehicle. Don't *Whoa* him unless you have a good reason. In short, let him concentrate on hunting and finding birds. Don't distract him with unnecessary commands.

You will get one sure-fire handling opportunity after each stop-to-flush, at least at first. When you cast him off after a stop-to-flush, he will chase the fly-away instead of going where you send him. That is a delayed chase, which is not much of an improvement over a regular chase, really. Use your collar to insist that he do things your way.

If you have decided not to buy a collar, you should continue the same handling approaches you have been using—training by association and specific training on the Flexi-Lead after each training session. In addition, handle your dog in the field as necessary. If he ignores you, run him down and convince him you are serious. You will get your share of exercise until you convince him not to attempt the delayed chase. You, too, should avoid over-handling, lest you destroy your dog's initiative. However, when you have to run the dog down to correct him, you are not so apt to give him needless commands.

Advanced Water Retrieving

If you plan to use your birddog for nonslip retrieving in waterfowling, you should introduce him to decoys before his first season. He should ignore decoys. If he doesn't, he might spend precious time messing with your blocks while a lively cripple makes good its escape.

Introduce decoys in the backyard. Spread out a dozen or so blocks, and heel your birddog around through them—*on lead with the chain training collar*—correcting him every time he so much as sniffs one. Say *No! Heel!* and jerk the lead appropriately every time he even glances at a decoy. Heel him around among them this way for several sessions, until he understands that decoys are beneath the dignity of a waterfowling dog.

Next, *Whoa* him near the spread and toss a retrieving dummy off to one side, where he can retrieve it without going near the blocks. If you have any doubt about him, use your Flexi-Lead at first. If he veers toward the decoys, going or coming, correct him appropriately and control him with the Flexi-Lead. When he makes this retrieve without incident, toss the dummy straight over and beyond the decoys, so that he must go through them both ways. When he retrieves that one satisfactorily, toss the dummy right into the middle of the blocks.

Okay, when he demonstrates proper decoy etiquette on land, move to shallow water, where you can reach him if he errs. Toss the dummy first off to the side, then beyond the blocks, then into the middle of them.

Then repeat the drill in swimming water. Put your blocks out with short anchor cords, lest your dog tangle in them as he swims past. That is a hazard he really doesn't need right now.

CHAPTER 19

Steadying and Honoring:

The Finishing Touches

After doing a stop-to-flush with the wind, the dog should hold steady to point when the bird goes up, as Dr. Jeff Herod's Ben is doing here.

BACKGROUND

What Is It?

This chapter covers the finishing touches in bird handling, namely steadying to wing and shot and honoring (or backing). Although treated separately throughout the chapter, the two are closely related, as you will see.

Steadying: The *steady* birddog, often called "steady to wing and shot," not only holds point until his handler flushes the bird(s), but also remains in place through all the ensuing excitement, namely, the flush, the shot(s), and the fall(s). He remains in place until either sent to retrieve or sent on to hunt again. What's more, the steady dog does not perpetrate a delayed chase. When sent on to continue hunting, he does not take off after the birds that flushed. Instead, he hunts in the direction indicated by his handler.

Honoring: A birddog *honors* (or *backs*) the point of another dog by stopping and assuming a pointing pose when he sees the other dog on point. The honoring dog does not move forward to pick up the scent of the birds himself—that is a fault called "stealing a point"—but stops wherever he happens to be when he first sees the other dog on point.

The honoring dog remains in place until sent on to hunt again. He does not break at the flush or when the pointing dog is sent to retrieve.

Why Do It?

Steadying: Many experienced birddog owners say that steadying to wing and shot is unnecessary, which is true; that, in fact, most birddogs hunt a lifetime without being steadied, which is also true. They also claim that an unsteady dog retrieves more reliably because he gets to the downed bird more quickly—a claim that is open to debate.

However, anyone who has ever owned or even shot over a steady birddog will tell you it is very handy, even if it's not an absolute necessity. How so? In the words of Elizabeth Barrett Browning, "Let me count the ways."

First, the steady dog offers a safety advantage afield. When you flush birds in front of him, he won't—in his mad rush to chase them—take your legs out from under you as you mount your gun. Granted, an unsteady dog doesn't do that often because the hunter is seldom directly in its path, and even when he is, the dog often darts around him. However, it can happen, it does happen, and when it does, it causes gun accidents.

Second, the steady dog doesn't flush birds out of gun range while chasing fly-aways. This is a common problem with unsteady dogs. Every hen pheasant, every missed shot initiates a long chase. A dog chasing full-tilt through the cover is not hunting, so may well charge through other birds, thereby flushing them out of range. What's worse, he will probably then chase those birds in a new direction, perhaps flushing even more birds, and so on.

Third, the steady dog doesn't keep you from shooting at low-flying birds. Quail especially tend to skim the top of the cover. A chasing dog may be too close to such a bird to allow you to shoot safely. Some hunters don't hold their fire due to imperfect vision, excessive excitement, or poor judgment, so veterinarians around the country treat canine birdshot wounds every fall. Many of these dogs do not survive, and some of those that do never regain their full capabilities.

Fourth, contrary to the claims of many, the steady dog marks falls better than the chasing dog. Absolutely! Standing still, he can see where the bird comes down much better than he could if he were bouncing up and down while chasing. Granted, the chasing dog gets to the easy retrieves—the ones that any dog will get anyhow—more quickly, but he frequently mismarks the difficult falls. The steady dog drops many more of those birds into his boss's outstretched mitt than does the freewheeling chaser.

Want more reasons to steady your birddog? Okay, here are three more quickies: The steady dog is easier to handle afield, the steady dog is easier to cure of chasing deer and livestock, and the steady dog retains his staunchness on point more reliably.

Had enough yet? Well, just in case you haven't, here's another: Steadiness is required in the higher levels of most dog games—field trials, hunting tests, and so forth. If you plan to do anything with your dog during the eight or nine months when you can't hunt, you must steady the beast.

Oh, yeah, I almost forgot to mention that *steadying* is so easy that anyone who enjoys messing with birddogs will enjoy doing it. Although it takes a lot of repetitions of a few drills, it is conceptually no more difficult than, say, teaching a dog to heel.

Honoring: When two or more dogs hunt together, they can untrain each other quickly unless each dog will honor the points of the other dog(s). The non-honoring dog steals points, frequently crowding and flushing birds in the process. It doesn't take much of that to induce the pointing dog to crowd and flush his own birds before his bracemate beats him to it. Before long, they are just wide-running flushing dogs out of pointing breed stock.

Of course, if you never hunt your dog with another dog, you needn't teach him to honor—unless you want to participate in off-season dog games (which you should).

Prerequisites

Steadying: Before you can steady your birddog to wing and shot, he must be staunch on point, and he must stop to flush reliably.

Honoring: Before you can teach your birddog to honor, he must be staunch on point and must stop to flush *reliably.* Although not absolutely necessary, you should consider delaying this training until you complete steadying your dog to wing and shot.

This is an electronic silhouette in the up position, with an open release trap and the transmitter that operates both.

Equipment and Facilities

For steadying, you need no additional equipment. However, for honoring, you should have at least one silhouette of a birddog on point. You will use this in combination with your remote release trap to induce your dog to honor as an extension of his stop-to-flush training.

Some dog supply catalogs offer these silhouettes for sale. A couple of companies make electronically operated silhouettes that lie flat on the ground (out of sight) but can be popped up with a remote transmitter. These are ideal, but they are also expensive. If you can afford one, buy it. If not, either buy a plain stake-into-the-ground model or cut one out of a piece of plywood with your trusty jigsaw. Rig it up so you can stick it into the ground easily. Then paint it to represent whatever breed you prefer.

For the final stages of steadying, you also need another steady dog. This is one of those training areas in which a small group is almost essential.

Schedule

You can start steadying any time after your dog is staunch and reliable at stopping to flush. You can start teaching him to honor as soon as he is steady to wing and shot.

How long does it take? In one sense, it takes the rest of your birddog's life, for you will have to give him touch-up training occasionally throughout his active life. However, it shouldn't take too long to do the initial training. I can't give you a precise schedule, for that depends on your dog's temperament, your temperament, the frequency of your sessions, and so on.

Handling Techniques

I cover handling techniques as necessary in each training section below.

TRAINING

If you have done a thorough job of teaching your birddog to stop to flush, steadying him and teaching him to honor are almost trivial. You simply extend his stop-to-flush training to a couple of new situations: when you flush a bird he is pointing, and when another dog points a bird in his view.

Even so, this training does take time. As usual, you train your dog by rote drill, repeated frequently over a period of time in a variety of places.

However, remember that the entire process is conceptually much simpler than, say, dressing yourself in the morning. So hang in there and you will have a beautifully mannered birddog, one your buddies will rave about.

Steadying to Wing and Shot

Because of your stop-to-flush training, your birddog now understands that he should stop in his tracks every time he sees a wild-flushing bird go up in front of him. However, you discontinued pointing work while you taught him this.

Now, in steadying him, you simply teach him that he must also remain in place when a bird goes up in front of him—after he has pointed it. Before you discontinued pointing work while you taught the stop-to-flush, you allowed him to chase pointed birds when you flushed them. Naturally, he still thinks that is okay, so you must convince him otherwise—which you can now do without undue pressure.

Just as I offered separate sets of instructions for those with and without electronic collars in Chapter 18 ("Stopping to Flush"), so I will offer separate instructions here for steadying to wing and shot. The two are identical, except for how you correct your dog when he breaks. Follow whichever applies to your situation, although you should read both.

Without the Electronic Collar: You should make the transfer from stopping to flush to steadiness as obvious *to the dog* as possible. You can do that more easily with your remote release trap and pigeons on your club's lease than you could with 10,000 acres of prime bird cover at saturation level with wild gamebirds.

Plant a bird (preferably a homer) in your remote release trap. Snap the Flexi-Lead or checkcord onto your birddog's collar, and lead him to the bird from the upwind side, where he cannot scent the bird. Do a normal stop-to-flush. Fine; now put him up while you plant another bird in the trap—*without moving the trap*. Now use the Flexi-Lead to bring him to the trap from the downwind side, where he can scent the bird. After he points, style him up, praise him and so forth, as you usually do.

Holding the Flexi-Lead or checkcord firmly, walk in front of your dog. Tell him to *Whoa*, but do it softly. Kick around quite a bit—put on a theatrical performance—as if you were trying to flush a tight-sitting bird. This should tense your dog up to make him at least think about breaking when the bird goes up. Now, release the bird with your remote control. If he remains in place, great! Praise him lavishly.

However, he may break. Fine, let him break! But, when he almost hits the end of the Flexi-Lead, command *Whoa!*, and brace yourself. When he hits the end of his rope, he will flip over and go splat. Say nothing, but haul him back and *Whoa* him where he should have remained. Style him up and *praise him*—that's right, praise him—for a few moments. Now heel him back to your vehicle and put him up while you plant another bird in the trap—again *without moving the trap*.

Repeat the entire procedure, stop-to-flush and all, right there until he remains in place as the *pointed* bird flies away. With all the preparation he has had, and with the sudden stop after his initial break, he should figure out what you want very quickly. He will also make the connection between his stop-to-flush training and what you are doing with him now.

In your next session, repeat the entire lesson, but with the release trap in a different location, even in a different field. Keep working this way until your dog remains reliably in place through the flush anywhere. Then you can dispense with the stop-to-flush warm-up.

The rest should be obvious. Switch from homers to commies. Have your assistant shoot the birds, but keep your dog on the Flexi-Lead. If he remains steady, let him retrieve about half of them. If he breaks, use the Flexi-Lead to keep him from getting to the shot bird.

Don't remove the Flexi-Lead for several sessions after he has convinced you that he no longer needs it, and go back to it immediately any time he breaks.

With an Electronic Collar: Plant a bird (preferably a homer) in your remote release trap. Bring your dog near it on the upwind side where he cannot scent the bird. Release him and do a normal stop-to-flush drill. Now put him up again while you plant another bird in the trap, *without moving the trap*. Bring your dog near it on the downwind side, where he can scent the bird after running a little distance. Release him to find and point the bird. Style him up and praise him. Walk in front of him, telling him softly to *Whoa*. Kick around theatrically, pretending to flush the bird. Then release it. If he remains in place, great! Praise him.

If he breaks, do nothing until he has run a short distance. You do not want to zap him too close to where the bird was, at least at first. When he has gone a few yards past the trap, give him a series of momentary stimulations until he slows down and stops—or starts back to you. Take him back to where he should have remained, *Whoa* him there, and *praise him.* After a few moments, put him up while you plant another bird in the trap. Repeat the entire lesson, stop-to-flush and all, but start zapping him a bit sooner this time if he breaks. After a few such lessons, he will begin to see the light.

The rest is obvious. Repeat this lesson in each session, changing locations often. When he remains steady reliably, eliminate the preliminary stop-to-flush, switch from homers to commies, have your assistant shoot the birds, and let your dog retrieve about half of them.

The finished product. Jim Adams's Shorthair, AFC Megan V, MH, stands like a rock as a quail buzzes away and Jim prepares to shoot. This level of performance takes work, but most who have achieved it say it's worth all the effort.

Honoring

Many birddogs have a natural inclination to honor. Others don't. Either way, if you plan to run your dog with another dog, either in hunting or in off-season dog games, you should *train* your dog to honor or back another dog's point—on sight, without a *Whoa* command.

You can do this easily by transferring your dog's stop-to-flush training into honoring. However, you should wait until you have also steadied him, so he will remain in place through the flush and retrieve by the other dog. To help him do this, you should give him a quiet *Whoa* before the flush.

In the initial work described below, you teach your dog to honor your silhouette of a dog on point. In the finishing touches described thereafter, you introduce other (real) dogs to the program.

Initial Work (With or Without an Electronic Collar): The only difference in this work for those with and those without electronic collars lies in how they correct the dog for making mistakes—which should be few here for dogs that are steady to wing and shot.

If you have an electronically operated silhouette, set it up (lying flat) anywhere in your training area. If you have a stake-out silhouette, set it up in a location in which your dog will not see it until he gets quite close to it. In either case, plant a bird (preferably a homer) in your remote release trap immediately in front of your silhouette.

Now snap your Flexi-Lead or checkcord on your dog and lead him around to where you set up your silhouette—from the upwind direction, where he cannot scent the bird. If you have an electronic silhouette, pop it up and almost immediately release the bird. If you have a stake-out silhouette, release the bird almost as soon as your dog sees the silhouette. Either way, insist that he stop to flush (which he should do without help by now, for crying out loud).

If you have two or three silhouettes and release traps, you can set them all up and lead your dog from one to the other, giving him an honoring lesson at each. If you have only one set-up, you will have to put him up while you move your silhouette and release trap and reload the release trap.

After a few lessons, your dog should stop as soon as he sees the silhouette—because he expects the flush. When he stops this way, *praise him to high heaven,* for that is what you are trying to teach him. However, don't release the bird immediately when he stops automatically. Wait him out. He will eventually creep forward. Great! Release the bird. He will stop, thinking he somehow caused the flush. After enough lessons like this, he will come to believe that if he moves forward after seeing the silhouette, he will cause the bird to flush.

Gradually increase the distance between your dog and the silhouette, so that he honors from farther and farther away.

Finishing Touches: Your birddog honors the silhouette on sight at any reasonable distance. Now you should bring other dogs into your program so your dog will learn to honor them on sight and so learn to remain in place through the shot(s) and retrieve(s).

Do not ask your dog to honor the points of an unsteady dog, lest the other dog teach your dog (by example) to start breaking again. For this work, you need a fully steadied dog, preferably one with at least some experience in running braces. If you can't find one any other way, contact a pro and pay to train with him.

Start out simply. Get the other dog on point, then lead your dog to a position in which he can see the dog on point but cannot scent the bird. He should stop automatically. If he doesn't, stop him with the lead. *Don't proceed until he stops automatically and reliably.*

Next, with him honoring (on lead), say *Whoa* softly. Then have the other handler walk in and flush the bird. Have an assistant shoot it. Keep your dog in place—with the lead if necessary. The other handler should send his dog to retrieve, and you should insist that your dog remain in place. Praise him for doing so, even if you have had to help him remember with the lead.

After that, you should let your dog point and retrieve a bird of his own. In fact, you can rotate dogs between pointing and honoring for the entire session.

The rest should be obvious. Continue working with other dogs in various locations. Discontinue using the lead when your dog convinces you he no longer needs it.

When your dog is steady and honors, you have joined an elite group of trainers. You have a fully-broke birddog, one you can hunt anywhere and take pride in, one that will be the talk of the town in your circle of hunting buddies. Congratulations!

A point honored by two dogs. Paul Beauchamp's Betsy points as his Heidi and Dr. Jeff Herod's Ben back. Again, work like this is worth all the time and effort the trainers expended.

CHAPTER 20

Proofing and Maintenance Training:

No-No's and Reminders

Maintenance training will keep your birddog sharp on point, as Frank Lallas's English Setter, Beeky, shows here. *(Frank Lallas)*

BACKGROUND

What Is It?

Proofing: The outdoor world has many *no-no's* for birddogs: *no-no* critters, like snakes, chickens, and livestock; *no-no* activities, like chasing rabbits and deer; and *no-no* places, like highways and henhouses.

When a trainer "'splains a no-no so's the dog can understand it," he is said to be *proofing* the beast. Proper proofing must be convincing, so it is not necessarily gentle, although it need not be brutal. Most owners would rather put their dogs through a few traumatic training sessions than go through the only other options, like watching their dogs die from the bite of a poisonous snake or the weight of an 18-wheeler.

Maintenance: Just as a golfer's game falls apart if he doesn't practice often, so a birddog's training deteriorates if he doesn't get frequent refreshers. Maintenance training is to dogs what practice is to golfers.

Why Do It?

Proofing: Although you don't have to proof your dog against every inappropriate animal, activity, and place, you should teach him to avoid those he will most likely encounter afield. If you live where poisonous snakes are unheard of, you shouldn't waste training time snake-proofing your birddog. But if you live where they are a real risk, you would be foolish not to. Ditto for all the other no-no's.

Maintenance: By now, you have invested a lot of time, and a bunch of money, in developing a birddog that anyone would be proud to own. If you don't continue working with him regularly, he will gradually backslide into his former state, namely that of an untrained mutt. In fact, a dog that has first been instructed in the ways of canine virtue and then allowed to resume his evil ways is usually more of a liability than is his untaught counterpart. After getting away with disobedience awhile, he will be more difficult to retrain than he was to train in the first place. And he will be less reliable thereafter, too, for the thought that he might get away with disobedience will always lurk in his mind.

Another reason for doing regular maintenance training is that it's fun for both of you. Your dog loves to work, especially now that he knows what you want all the time. You enjoy training him, too, or you wouldn't have persevered this far.

Prerequisites

Proofing: To proof your dog against most hazards, you should use the electronic collar. That means you should first introduce your dog to the collar according to the instructions in Chapter 18.

Maintenance: The only prerequisite for maintenance is a fully trained dog, which you should have by now.

Equipment and Facilities

For proofing, you need an electronic collar, either your own or someone else's. You need no new equipment or facilities for maintenance training.

Schedule

Proofing: You should proof your birddog against the hazards you expect him to encounter afield before his first hunting season as an adult dog. You may or may not need to do a refresher before each succeeding hunting season.

Maintenance: You ease into maintenance training almost without noticing it as your dog completes his formal training. You should continue maintenance training throughout his active life.

Handling Techniques

No special handling techniques are necessary for either proofing or maintenance training.

TRAINING

Proofing

First, you should decide which hazards to proof your dog against. Then prioritize them and start proofing with the most serious.

Snakes: To snake-proof your dog from poisonous snakes, you must use a defanged poisonous snake. A nonpoisonous snake doesn't give off the same scent, so it just won't work. Thus, I recommend that you do *not* attempt this proofing yourself. Instead, take your dog to a pro who specializes in this type of proofing.

Many pros snake-proof dogs for a nominal-to-reasonable fee. They have the facilities (a defanged snake and an electronic collar) and the expertise to do the job quickly and correctly.

Some pros put on snake-proofing seminars. Dog owners bring their dogs and snake-proof them under the direction of the pro.

Even after completing the program, your dog will not be completely safe from poisonous snakes. All a pro can do is teach him not to mess with snakes. Your dog may still be bitten by a snake he does not smell as he runs in the field—like one he approaches from the upwind side, one he races past while making a cast to an objective, or one he stumbles onto while making a retrieve. In other words, you still must exercise some judgment in where you run your dog. Even so, if you hunt in country where poisonous snakes are a problem, you should have your dog snake-proofed, perhaps every year or so.

Farm Animals: Follow the same procedure for any and all farm animals you want to proof your dog against—cattle, horses, chickens, sheep, whatever—but take one animal at a time.

For this, you want to use more juice than you do for reinforcement training. Put a higher-numbered-intensity plug into your collar (or make whatever adjustment it requires to increase the level of stimulation). Start out with just one level higher and increase it as required.

Put your dog on the Flexi-Lead and approach the farm animal you wish to proof him against. When he moves toward it, say *No!* firmly, give him continuous stimulation, pull him back away from the animal, and then discontinue stimulation. Repeat this, without the *No!*, until your dog moves toward you as soon as you approach the animal.

Wait a week and repeat the lesson. Keep this up until you are confident he will leave the animal alone.

Chasing Deer or Rabbits: Here, too, you should use more juice than you have for reinforcement training. Start with one level more of intensity and increase it only if your dog doesn't respond properly.

Take your dog into an area in which he will encounter the deer or rabbit. Turn him loose—assuming you can do so safely, that is, without risk of injury to the dog from automobile traffic, etc.—and follow along behind him. When he kicks up a deer or rabbit and starts chasing, give him a series of stimulations, each two or three seconds long, until he stops and returns to you. Repeat this until he looks at the deer or rabbit and seems to say "To hell with that beast! I know when I'm well off."

You should use the collar during your dog's first hunting season, just to make sure your lesson has really taken effect. Thereafter, use the collar during at least the first few days of each season, just to be sure.

Places: If you want to proof your birddog against certain places—highways, henhouses, etc.—use the electronic collar with more juice than you have used for reinforcement training. Start off with one higher level of stimulation and go higher only if necessary.

Put the dog on the Flexi-Lead and lead him toward the hazard. As soon as he gets too close, zap him with a series of two- or three-second stimulations and turn him back with the Flexi-Lead. When he turns, stop stimulation. Repeat as necessary until he loses all interest in the place you want him to avoid.

If you are proofing against highways, you should also consider avoiding the occasion of sin yourself by not hunting or training in close proximity to such dangerous areas. However, if you have a big-running dog, he might still find a highway when you least expect it—and when you cannot see him. So a little highway-proofing may save his life someday.

Maintenance Training

As I said above, you slip into maintenance training almost without realizing it. You simply continue your regular training sessions year-round after your dog has completed his basic education.

Since he handles birds properly, you need not use your release traps all the time. Just dizzy your training birds and toss them into the cover. Of course, if your dog shows any sign of forgetting his manners, you should revert to the release traps and stay with them long after he seems cured.

In this book, I have explained how you should teach your birddog all the manners he needs to be an effective hunter. *He still has a lot to learn about wild birds: where they are most apt to be, how they react to his approach, how close is too close, and so on.* You can help him understand his adversary better by hunting him frequently during the season. Even during the off-season, you can help him by running him often where he will encounter wild birds (except during the spring nesting season, of course).

One special maintenance training problem you will face: Your dog will get sloppy during hunting season, and you will not notice his laxity immediately in your excitement over the birds. When he commits a fault serious enough for you to notice—a flush and stop, a break and chase, stealing a point from a bracemate—you have an important decision to make: Should you stop hunting and correct him, or should you ignore it and straighten him out again after the season ends?

If you correct the problem immediately, you can do it more quickly and completely. But it will cut into your hunting season, which is already too short for most of us, right? If you wait until after the season, your dog will get worse and worse during the rest of the season, and will be much more difficult to retrain later—and the retraining will not be as permanent as would immediate retraining be. Tough decision, and one we all face frequently. Your decision will depend on how much time you get to hunt each year, how important impeccable canine manners are to your enjoyment of a birddog, how serious the problem happens to be, how responsive your dog is to training, and on and on.

I won't make a recommendation. In my own case, I usually opt to stop hunting while I work out the problem. But then, I have shot a lot of birds over the years. I know they will be there when I start hunting again. Also, I know how much more quickly and effectively I can put the fix on my dog if I do it right away. You may have a different perspective, a different value system, a different hunting background, and so on. So make up your own mind—but do that fully understanding the trade-offs.

Maintenance training will keep your birddog sharp in retrieving, as Walter Furesz's German Wirehair, Ch. Marta Von Pines, shows here. *(Walter Furesz)*

PART III

ENJOYING YOUR BIRDDOG

We train birddogs, not just for the enjoyment (which is considerable), but mostly so we can shoot over them—as Glen Hershberger is about to do with his English Setter, Champ. Because seasons are so short, we also participate in off-season games, like field trials and hunting tests.

Training a birddog is fun in and of itself. You get out in the country. You watch your dog and the dogs of your training buddies progress from session to session. You shoot birds for your buddies' dogs. And you stand around and talk before and after each session.

However, you didn't undertake birddog training for its own enjoyment. No, that's a fringe benefit. You probably started training because you wanted to develop a good hunting dog for your tastes and conditions. At least, that's how most of us got started.

In this section, Chapter 21 ("Hunting") gives you several suggestions about how to hunt more successfully with your birddog: when to take your youngster hunting the first time; how to handle him during his first season, and thereafter; ways to transport him and keep him safe from theft; things you should take along for his care; and so on.

The trouble is, hunting seasons don't last long—just three, maybe four months from early fall through winter. That leaves eight or nine months with not much for your birddog to do. Not surprisingly, you are not the first to encounter this problem. Also not surprisingly, those who have been here ahead of you have developed several solutions for you: field trials, hunting tests, and working certificate tests. I call them "dog games," not derisively, but just to keep their significance in perspective.

Chapter 22 ("Field Trials") describes our oldest birddog dog games, competitive field trials, which we Americans have been holding since 1874. Most field trials in this country are conducted under the umbrella of the Field Dog Stud Book (FDSB). FDSB is associated with the American Field Publishing Company, which publishes the excellent weekly birddog field trial tabloid, *The American Field*. Field trial clubs around the country conduct over 900 FDSB pointing-breed trials every year. The second most popular format is that of the American Kennel Club (AKC), of which we have over 400 pointing-breed trials a year.

Chapter 23 ("Hunting Tests") explains the relatively new noncompetitive AKC dog games that have become extremely popular in their short history (started in 1986). Being noncompetitive, they are less demanding than field trials in terms of the time and money commitments required to participate. Also, being new, they have not yet developed stabilizing traditions, as have the older dog games. The rules have already undergone one major rewrite. Judging is not as consistent from test to test as one would like, but it is improving and will one day become as standardized as that of field trials. Those involved in the hunting test movement are making history, which can't be done without bouncing over a few bumps.

Chapter 24 ("Working Certificate Tests") explains the older noncompetitive testing programs of several pointing-breed national breed clubs. Taken together, these make up a fascinating study in the thinking of grass-roots birddoggers. Each national breed club has developed its program independently, and they differ in format, in content, in levels of difficulty, in every way a collection of related dog games can differ. Look on these tests as the experimental theatre of birddog dog games. They show what the major breed fanciers think pointing-breed dog games should contain. Some of these innovative features will eventually find their way into field trials and hunting tests.

You can't be around birddog owners long without hearing negative comments about dog games. The major complaint is that they are too artificial. They "jest ain't 'nuf like huntin' fer me." In some ways, this is true—unavoidably true. Games require rules to maintain fairness. Rules introduce procedural artificialities: judges, marshals, galleries, horses, bird planters, official gunners, fixed courses, sometimes a set "birdfield," and on and on. Then, too, most dog games use planted birds, which carry human scent and are often placed in unnatural locations. Finding suitable grounds is often impossible, so many trials are run in places most hunters would bypass. Then, too, most dog games are held during the off-seasons, when cover and scenting conditions are unlike those of the fall hunting season. So no one can argue with the person who says they are artificial.

However, dog games do offer birddog owners *something* to do during the eight or nine months every year when they cannot hunt. The question then becomes not: Is this game like hunting?; but Is this game better than nothing? Can a person entertain himself and improve his dog by participating? Any reasonable person would answer, "Yes, he can. Indeed he can."

In the musical *South Pacific,* some women-starved sailors sing a delightful song called "There Is Nothing Like a Dame." In that song, one line goes like this:

> *"It's a waste of time to worry over things that they have not.*
> *Be thankful for the things they've got!"*

Why not view dog games that way? Even if they are artificial, they are lots better than nothing during the off-season. They keep the dogs trained and in shape. They motivate, educate, and entertain the owners. I've never seen a dog that was harmed as a hunter by participation in dog games, but I've seen many dogs atrophy between hunting seasons for lack of work.

Further, I've never heard anyone who has been successful in a dog game complain about its artificiality. No, it's the loser or, more often, the guy afraid to enter his dog. Either way, you can bet the complainer's dog couldn't find a pound of hamburger in the middle of the kitchen floor. That should tell you what such complaints are really all about.

Make up your own mind. Don't stay away from dog games because of what you hear from nonparticipants. Read this section with an open mind. Then, attend some dog games, watch what happens, ask questions, and think what each dog game can and cannot do for a hunting dog. Then make up your own mind.

CHAPTER

21

Hunting:

The Main Event

Pro Clarke Campbell of Maynard, Iowa, and his German Wirehair, Bud, after a successful day's pheasant hunting. *(Glenda Campbell)*

YOUR DOG'S FRESHMAN SEASON

You don't have to—in fact, you shouldn't—wait until your birddog is fully trained before hunting him. No, within reason, the sooner the better. If you have him under good basic control (with at least the *Whoa* and *Come-In* commands) and if he points staunchly (well, sorta), and if he loves the sound of gunfire, hey, take him along. If he retrieves, or even points dead, so much the better. Such a dog can help you a lot, even if he's just a pup. You will help him a lot, too, by taking him hunting as early as possible. His nose will tell him stories beyond your understanding about the ways of wild birds. And he will remember those stories far better than he will remember any training you give him. After all, he was bred to find birds.

On the other hand, if you don't follow a few precautions, you may spoil him for life during his first few trips afield. He is young and impressionable—susceptible to whatever impressions, good or bad, you give him of hunting. You will help him form good impressions if you look on these first-season trips more as training sessions than as actual hunting trips. Consider any birds you bag as bonuses.

If you can hunt him alone, do so. I mean just you and your dog, with no other hunters and no other dogs. That will allow you to concentrate on your training responsibilities. What's more, it will take the peer pressure off you. Especially if this is your first dog, you have probably told your hunting buddies how great young Blink-N-Bolt has been doing in training. We all do this. I have done it long after I should have known better—and every time the dog I bragged about has embarrassed me. Somehow every dog knows when and how to humble a boastful owner.

Hunting alone will also prevent your hunting buddy from undoing your training by shooting bumped or wild-flushing birds, by shooting too often too close to your dog, by interfering when your pup retrieves your buddy's bird to you. Not every hunter understands that a dog takes every bird to the boss, regardless of who shot it.

I took advantage of that once years ago when I took a friend hunting with Misty, my Weimaraner. On the way out of town, I explained how Misty worked, what to do, what not to do. Then, I added this: "You know, sometimes you and I will shoot at the same bird and not know which one of us actually hit it. Don't worry about that today. Misty always knows, and she will retrieve each bird to the person who shot it. She's really an amazing dog that way."

My friend knew little about dogs, so he believed me. Of course, Misty brought every bird to me. My aviary body count was progressing nicely until Misty brought me a bird I had not shot at. Then, my friend about shot me! Not really, but he was skeptical of anything I told him about Misty's talents thereafter.

Hunting your birddog alone the first season also prevents problems other dogs can cause. A young dog can form a nasty trailing habit, that is, following the other dog instead of hunting on his own. Unless both dogs honor reliably, your dog could start stealing points and enjoying the one-upmanship of it. Similarly, if both dogs are unsteady and disagree on which should retrieve shot birds, your youngster could develop a hardmouth problem—or an inclination to fight. Better to hunt him alone during his first season.

If you have a 20 or 28 gauge shotgun, use it instead of your Big Bertha 12 gauge. And shoot only once at each bird. If you miss, forget that bird. Better to let a few fly away than to create a gun-shyness problem. Even if you have gun-proofed him in training, you could undo your work by shooting too big a gun or by shooting too often during his first hunting season.

If you shoot only the birds your pup handles properly, he will learn (and remember) what you expect of him much more easily. If you shoot at every bird that flies—wild flushes, birds your pup bumps (deliberately or accidentally)—he will develop a very casual attitude toward pointing staunchly. If he flash-points and flushes a bird, hold your fire. If you shoot it for him, he will repeat the same procedure on the next bird. Eventually, he will do this on birds that are too far away for you to shoot at. Better by far to pass up shooting at any bird he mishandles. Console yourself with the thought that you don't need the meat to feed your family, that hunting is just recreation, and helping your dog learn now will contribute to your long-term enjoyment.

If you must shoot at every bird that flies—and some people just must—you will have to keep your dog within shotgun range all the time. Better yet, you should think about switching to a flushing dog—a spaniel or retriever designed to quarter within gun range and put birds in the air immediately. Such dogs are much easier to control this way than are pointing dogs.

Don't try to steer the boat too much. In training, you have known where the birds were planted, and sometimes you have had to handle your dog into the proper area. That's fine in training, but don't let it become a habit that carries over to hunting. Let your birddog take you hunting, not the other way around. Relax and follow along where he leads you—as long as he isn't getting into trouble. He can't learn to hunt if you hack him all the time. If he doesn't learn to get out and hunt, you will never get much out of him.

Don't run your youngster too long without stopping to rest. If you have two dogs, rotate them about every hour. That way, you always have a fresh dog ahead of you, and you won't sour your pup by overworking him.

YOUR DOG'S POST-FRESHMAN SEASONS

After a good freshman year, young Blink-N-Bolt should be a pretty salty hunting dog. You can dispense with many of the precautions you practiced initially. You can take other hunters along. You can shoot Big Bertha—and more than once if you need to. You can run him with a bracemate.

If you wish to hunt with other people, as most of us do, don't go with too many at a time. Two or three hunters and one or two dogs make a nice party. More of either hunters or dogs gets pretty unwieldy. Dogs forget their manners, and so do hunters sometimes.

On the way out of town, review with your hunting buddies what you would like to have them do and not do when hunting with your dog. For example, I prefer that no one shoot at a bird the dog flushes (even accidentally—who can tell every time?) rather than points. Stops to wild flushes? No problem for hunters who can recognize the difference between these and bumped birds, but few who don't own dogs can tell.

If you switch to the 12 gauge, check your dog's reaction to your first shot before you start filling the sky with birdshot. He should show no reaction at all, especially if you have shot it over him during preseason training. But check it anyhow.

If you run him with other dogs, limit it to one other dog at a time. If your dog is staunch and steady, don't brace him with one that isn't—unless you enjoy redoing major areas of your training program every year. If your dog retrieves, don't brace him with unsteady dogs, lest they get into a serious debate over fetching rights.

More often than not, you will have better hunting if you rotate dogs rather than brace them. You will have a fresh dog all day, and you will avoid a lot of unexpected mishaps.

CONDITIONING

Before every hunting season, you should condition your birddog. If you train regularly year-round, he will be in top shape during hunting season (and so will you). But if you take the summer off for other pursuits, like fishing, your birddog will be flabby by early fall. You can bring him back into condition by training regularly then and especially by swimming him every day or so. You can swim him by tossing retrieving dummies in a pond for him, or by having him swim along behind a boat while you row. Rowing is also good exercise for you. Stop now and then and help him aboard by getting his front feet up and then bracing the back of his head with your hand. That will give him the leverage he needs to scramble into the boat. Let him ride awhile. That will motivate him next time you swim him behind the boat.

This is the dog box in the bed of my pickup. It is steel, lined with wood interior, has controllable ventilation, and can be padlocked to the truck. The stall doors can also be padlocked.

TRANSPORTATION

You need a suitable means for transporting your birddog when you go hunting. Some people let their dogs ride in the car with them. Some use crates inside station wagons or vans. Some use dog boxes in the beds of pickups. Some pull dog trailers. Any of these is fine as long as the dog has adequate ventilation (especially in warm weather) and adequate protection from wind, moisture, and cold in colder weather.

Every year I see dogs running loose in open pickup beds. Veterinarians tell me they patch up a lot of dogs (the luckier ones) that have jumped out at inopportune times. More recently, I have seen dogs hooked up to cables in pickup beds. This arrangement prevents untimely exits, but it leaves the animal vulnerable to weather and flying debris. I see no excuse for carrying dogs loose in open pickup beds, whether tethered or not. Anyone who can afford a dog, a shotgun, and a pickup can afford a suitable dog box or trailer.

In selecting your method of transportation, you should consider the matter of crime prevention. Every year I hear stories about dogs that have been stolen from unattended vehicles during hunting trips. I use a wood-lined, steel dog box in the bed of my pickup. It has two dog stalls, each of which can be locked with a padlock. In addition, I chain and padlock the dog box to the pickup. When I take more than two dogs, I pull a glass-fiber two-dog trailer. It can be padlocked to the pickup and each dog stall door can be padlocked. Anytime I leave dogs in my vehicle unattended (like when I'm hunting with another dog or eating lunch in a restaurant), I padlock every dog in its stall. I also padlock the dog box and trailer to the truck. Granted, simple padlocks wouldn't stop a determined thief (what would?) but they do protect my dogs from casual thefts, which account for most hunting dog losses afield.

IMPEDIMENTA

You will need several items of equipment for your dog when you take him hunting. Naturally, you should carry a slip-lead in your pocket and a couple of whistles on a lanyard around your neck. I keep extras of such things in my truck all the time, just in case I leave my favorite ones at home.

Carry plenty of water for him, and don't forget a water bowl, too. Dogs do better on water from home than they do drinking the water found in the areas in which they hunt. Depending on how many dogs I take, I carry one or more plastic 2.5-gallon containers of water. In the field, I carry a plastic bottle full of water so I can give my dog a drink when we are far from the car. I use old dish detergent bottles, which I have rinsed out again and again until I can drink from them without noticing a soapy taste. Some people prefer old plastic syrup bottles.

Since your dog is working pretty hard, you should take a little food along, too. Feed him—not too much—when you stop for lunch. *But never feed your dog chocolate.* Such a treat may give you a quick charge of energy, but it can kill your dog. Chocolate is toxic for canines, and it doesn't take much to be fatal.

If your dog has long hair, you need some way to remove burrs. I carry a spray can of PAM cooking oil and a dog grooming tool called a *mat rake.* A mat rake has long, curved teeth that are sharp on the inner edge to cut hair around mats and burrs. I squirt a little PAM on each burr, then insert the mat rake under it and lift it out. It slides right out. Other people rub human hair oil on their dog's coat before going hunting. That also facilitates burr removal, but it leaves the dog pretty greasy.

Some carry a canine first aid kit. I don't. Nor do I carry a human first aid kit. I figure that, in any emergency, the patient (human or canine) will be better cared for if I rush him to the nearest source of professional health care. Fortunately, in this country, we are never far from such services. On the other hand, in 40-some years of hunting, I've never had to handle a medical problem.

If you decide to carry a first aid kit, talk to your veterinarian about what it should contain. That will vary depending on where you live. But just accumulating all the proper equipment is not enough. You must learn when and how to use each item. And you must stay abreast of changes in recommended equipment and procedures. If you want to be an amateur veterinarian, you should be an informed one.

SPECIAL PRECAUTIONS

If you take your birddog dove hunting early in the year, hunt only near a pond or stream, where he can stay wet and cool. Never, never, never walk doves up far from water during warm weather. Dogs overheat more quickly than do humans. I almost lost a Golden Retriever walking up doves one September. One minute he was hunting fine, but the next he was wobbling and staggering uncontrollably. Fortunately, we were near a river. I carried him to it and laid him in the shallow water, where he remained for 30 minutes before trying to get up again.

If you hunt ducks with your birddog, even in mild weather, give him plenty of opportunity to run around and dry off between retrieves. If he sits beside the blind soaked, he may chill. If you hunt ducks in really cold weather, leave your birddog home and take a retriever. Granted, the wirehaired birddogs can handle severe ducking weather and water better than the rest, but if this kind of hunting is your bag, you really should consider adding a retriever to your canine collection.

ONE MORE ADMONITION

Have fun, my friend, have fun. All these precautions may seem overpowering as you sit there reading them. But I only intend them to remove potential problems from your path as you set out to hunt with your birddog.

You bought him and you have trained him so you could have fun hunting with him. Now's the time to do it. Enjoy!

CHAPTER

22

Field Trials:

Our Traditional Birddog Pastime

A brace about to start at an AKC field trial. Judges Bob Erbe (left-most horseman) and Greg Lamar (right-most horseman) watch as scouts Fran Krommenhoek (on foot at left) and Lenn Forbush (on foot at right) prepare to cast the dogs off. Handlers pro Terry Krommenhoek (second horseman from left) and pro David King (second horseman from right) get ready to ride.

Birddog field trials in this country date back to 1874. Today American pointing-dog fanciers conduct about 1,400 trials (over 400 AKC and over 900 FDSB) per year nationwide. No matter where you live in America, you can find birddog field trials nearby. To facilitate more widespread participation, most trials are scheduled on weekends and are conducted by clubs organized for that specific purpose. Depending on its affiliation, each club conducts its trials under either AKC or FDSB rules.

Field trials are competitive. Most are divided into two or more separate competitions, called *stakes.* In each stake, the entered dogs compete only against each other. Each stake has entry restrictions, which are indicated (to the initiated) by the stake name. These restrictions, intended to provide fairer competition among participants, may apply to the handler and/or the dog.

Restrictions on the handler address either the person's status as a professional or amateur or his mode of transportation. Stakes with names that include the word *amateur* are for amateur handlers only (although the dogs may be professionally trained). Stakes with names that include the word *open* are for all handlers, amateur or professional. In stakes with names that include the word *walking,* handlers may not ride horses (although the judges do, and sometimes the gallery also does).

Restrictions on the dog address either the animal's age or its past accomplishments. Stakes with names that include the words *puppy* or *derby* have an upper age limit for the dogs (although AKC and FDSB limits differ). Stakes with names that include the words *gun dog, shooting dog,* or *all age* have no upper age restriction (although all stakes in AKC trials have a lower limit of six months). AKC trials with names that include the word *limited* (in conjunction with *gun dog* or *all age*) are restricted to dogs that have previously won or placed in a corresponding stake (or won a corresponding derby stake). Trial-giving AKC clubs use limited stakes to control the number of dogs entered in a gun dog or all age stake when past experience indicates that an unlimited stake might become too large to run in the allotted time.

With all this said, here are some illustrative examples of stake names and their implied restrictions: an AKC amateur walking derby stake is for amateur handlers on foot with dogs that fall within the AKC derby age limits; an FDSB amateur shooting dog stake is for amateur handlers with no restrictions on the dog; an AKC open limited all age stake is for amateur and professional handlers with dogs that have previously placed in an AKC open all age stake or won an AKC open derby stake.

At any given trial (AKC or FDSB), each dog/handler team may enter any or all stakes for which they meet the restrictions. One handler may enter several dogs in any stake. One dog may run in two or more stakes with different handlers—such as in the open all age with the pro trainer and in the amateur all age with the amateur owner.

The courses over which the competing dogs run may be set up in several ways: single course with birdfield; single course without birdfield; multiple courses with birdfields; multiple courses without birdfields; continuous course.

A single course with birdfield consists of a back course and a birdfield. The birdfield, where birds are planted for each brace of dogs, must be at least five acres, and should be about ten acres. The birdfield is located at the end of the back course. The back course must be long enough to allow the dogs to run the required time in their heats. Ideally, the back course should go around in a large circle, so that the birdfield is near the starting point of the back course. That minimizes the time the judges must spend between braces getting from the birdfield to the starting point.

A single course without birdfield is like the above course except that it has no birdfield. Birds are planted throughout the back course for each brace. Ideally, this course should be circular, for that minimizes the time the judges must spend between braces getting from the end to the start of the course.

Multiple course layouts (with or without birdfields) are just like the corresponding single courses. Clubs with ample grounds and large entries resort to multiple courses to allow more time for each stake.

A continuous course layout consists of three or more single courses without birdfields laid out end to end, preferably in a huge circle so the last one ends near the start of the first one. Birds are planted throughout the courses. When the first brace finishes their heat on the first course, the second brace is put on the ground to run their heat on the second course, and so on. This arrangement minimizes the time spent between braces.

Some trials are run on native birds, but most on planted birds. Although any gamebird may be used, quail are most popular, followed by chukkar and pheasants.

In all stakes, the dogs run in braces, that is, two at a time. If a stake has an odd number of dogs entered, the judges select a nonentered dog to run as the bracemate of the bye (extra) dog.

Depending on the stake, the handlers may ride horses or walk. The judges (usually two, but three in major trials) follow on horses. The judges are accompanied and assisted by the marshal, who also rides. Behind the judges and the marshal, the gallery of spectators follows along, usually on horses (for better visibility of the running dogs). If the handlers ride horses, they dismount and handle on foot when they reach the birdfield (if one is used).

The stakes are scheduled on the course(s) one after another, per the schedule given in the premium list. Once a stake starts, all entered dogs run before another stake starts on the same course.

AKC FIELD TRIALS

Stakes

AKC calls their bread-and-butter trials *member trials* and *licensed trials.* The two differ only in the relationship between the AKC and the trial-giving club. Only clubs that are members of AKC (which is a "club of clubs") can conduct member trials. AKC authorizes (licenses) nonmember clubs to conduct licensed trials. Most trials are open to all AKC-recognized pointing breeds, although a few are limited to a single breed.

Some trials are retrieving trials and others are not. In a retrieving trial, the dogs in the all age and gun dog stakes must retrieve the birds shot over their points. Handlers do not shoot the birds. The sponsoring club designates "official guns" to do all the shooting of live ammunition.

AKC trials may include any of the following stakes: open puppy, open derby, open gun dog, open all age, open limited all age, amateur puppy, amateur derby, amateur gun dog, amateur all age, amateur limited all age. Sometimes the puppy, derby, and gun dog stakes are restricted to walking handlers.

AKC puppy stakes are for dogs between six and 15 months old. AKC derby stakes are for dogs between six and 24 months. All other stakes—the various gun dog and all age stakes—are for all dogs over six months, with no maximum age limit. The difference between a gun dog and an all age stake lies in the expected range of the dogs. All age stake dogs run much wider than do gun dog stake dogs.

Pro Mike McGinnis's setup at an AKC field trial. His dogs are staked out comfortably. His horses are saddled and secured to the side of his trailer.

Requirements for Each Stake

The minimum requirements vary from stake to stake. To win or place, a dog usually must perform significantly above the minimum requirements. Here are both the minimum requirements and what the judges look for in each stake.

Puppy: Each brace runs a 15- to 30-minute heat (with eight minutes in the birdfield, if one is used). A puppy should hunt enthusiastically. On encountering birds, it should at least flash-point, but need not be staunch. When the bird flushes, the handler must fire a blank pistol to demonstrate that the puppy is not gunshy. However, birds are not shot and puppies are not expected to retrieve. Most puppies that place do point staunchly, although they may chase with reckless abandon at the flush. Judges look for potential more than for performance. The bold puppy that runs a class race and points with breathtaking style, even though it sins significantly in manners and bird handling, makes a better impression on the judges than does a better trained ho-hummer of a dog.

Derby: Each brace runs a 20- to 30-minute heat (with 10 minutes in the birdfield, if one is used). A derby dog should hunt enthusiastically and cover the ground reasonably well. It should point, but need not be completely staunch. When the bird flushes, the handler must fire a blank pistol. However, birds are not shot and derbies are not expected to retrieve. Most derbies that place point staunchly, and many are steady (even though that is not supposed to influence the judges). As in the puppy stake, the judges look mostly for potential, but here they seek more control, more training, more bird sense. Even so, class and style mean a lot.

Gun Dog: Each brace runs a 30-minute heat (with 10 minutes in the birdfield, if one is used). A gun dog should hunt intelligently within reasonable foot-handling range. It must point, be staunch, and steady to wing and shot. It must honor its bracemate's points. In retrieving trials, it must retrieve. The judges look for the completely finished birddog of moderate range here. Class and style still carry a lot of weight, but the dog must hunt biddably within the normal range of a walking hunter (even though the handlers may be on horses).

All Age: Each brace runs a heat of 30 minutes to an hour (with 10 minutes in the birdfield, if one is used). An all age dog should perform as a class birddog with substantial range. It must point, be staunch, and be steady to wing and shot. It must honor its bracemates' points. In retrieving trials, it must retrieve. Here, too, the judges look for the completely finished birddog, but in this stake it should move out to greater distances than in the gun dog stake. In general, AKC all age stake dogs range about as far as FDSB shooting dog stake dogs, but not as far as FDSB all age stake dogs.

After all the dogs in a given stake have run, the judges may place the dogs or, if they need another look at some of them, they may call back those dogs for a second series. In the gun dog and all age stakes, they may also call back any dog that didn't have an opportunity to honor or retrieve (in a retrieving trial). In such a situation, since both honoring and retrieving are required for placements, the judges call back such dogs and set up honoring and/or retrieving situations in which to evaluate them. Judges will not call back a dog that has not found and pointed a bird in the first series, or a dog that has failed in any other way that makes it ineligible for a placement.

The second series is for dogs in contention for placements. A dog that failed to find a bird in the first series has eliminated itself and cannot be given a second chance. But a dog that has pointed a bird and otherwise performed creditably may have had no opportunity to honor or retrieve through no fault of its own. Perhaps the guns missed the bird it pointed, so it had no opportunity to retrieve. Perhaps its bracemate went birdless, so it had no opportunity to honor. In such cases, the judges call the dog back for a chance to prove itself.

Placements and Titles

The judges award four places in each stake. They may withhold places if they feel no dogs merited them. They may also award a Judge's Award of Merit (JAM) to any unplaced dog they feel did outstanding work.

AKC awards points toward the Field Champion title to the winner of each open stake. The number of points given (which ranges from one to five) depends on the number of dogs competing. Currently, it takes four to seven dogs for one point, eight to 12 dogs for two points, 13 to 17 dogs for three points, 18 to 24 dogs for four points, and 25 or more dogs for five points. To become a Field Champion (FC), a dog must earn 10 points in at least three open stakes, with at least one three-point win, and with no more than two coming from open puppy and two from open derby stakes. In addition to those requirements, four breeds (German Shorthair, German Wirehair, Vizsla, and Weimaraner) must earn at least four points in retrieving stakes, and two breeds (German Wirehair and Weimaraner) must pass a water retrieving test.

AKC awards points toward the Amateur Field Champion (AFC) title to the winner of each amateur stake, and (if the entry is large enough) to the second and third placers also. Currently, the points for first place are the same as in the open stakes (above). The points for second place are: one point with 13 to 17 dogs competing; two points with 18 to 24 dogs competing; and three points with 25 or more dogs competing. Fourth place gets one point if 25 or more dogs compete. To become an Amateur Field Champion (AFC), a dog must earn 10 points in at least three amateur stakes, with at least two first places, one of which must be a three-pointer in an all age or gun dog stake. In addition to those requirements, four breeds (German Shorthair, German Wirehair, Vizsla, and Weimaraner) must earn four points in retrieving stakes, and two breeds (German Wirehair and Weimaraner) must pass a water retrieving test.

National Championship Field Trials

The AKC allows the national breed club sponsoring each breed to conduct an annual national championship trial and an annual national amateur championship trial. Entries are restricted by the national breed clubs to dogs that have earned a certain number of points during the year in AKC member and licensed trials. The winner of a national championship trial becomes a Field Champion and also earns the title National Field Champion (NFC), preceded by the year in which the title was won. The winner of a national amateur championship trial becomes an Amateur Field Champion and also earns the title National Amateur Field Champion (NAFC), preceded by the year in which the title was won.

These trials are the annual big deals of each breed that holds them. Dogs that have long since earned both FC and AFC titles in regular trials continue to compete year after year just to qualify again and again for the nationals. This keeps the level of competition in regular trials quite high.

My First AKC Field Trial

Back in 1960 I entered my German Shorthair, Cy, in the puppy stake of the Sunflower German Shorthaired Pointer Club's spring trial. Cy was some kind of animal. He ran big for a Shorthair in those days. His break-away was spectacular. He was bird crazy. That's about all a dog needed then to do well in a puppy stake.

Well, turns out there was one other thing he needed, namely a proper introduction to horses. Although this was a walking trial, the judges rode. The first time Cy ever saw a horse was at the start of his heat in that trial. Some dogs ignore horses naturally. Cy wasn't one of those. Some spook at their first sight of such huge animals. Cy didn't fall in that category either.

Cy had a simplistic attitude toward unknown objects, regardless of size. Each such object had to fall into one of three basic categories: objects of affection, objects for pointing or food. Now, clearly, these horses didn't fit in either of the first two, so they had to be something to eat.

Cy's break-away was memorable that day. When I turned him loose, he attacked the larger of the two horses. I suppose he felt his bracemate could handle the smaller one, at least until he (Cy) polished off the big one.

The horse took umbrage to Cy's attentions. It bucked and kicked. It spun this way and that, bucking and kicking in every direction. The judge was, as cowboys say, "pullin' leather" and screaming at me to "Get that _______ dog under control!" Cy was circling the spinning horse, lunging at him whenever he saw an opening. Cy was also verbally abusing his opponent in a voice any Coonhound would envy. I was circling, too, trying to grab Cy's collar, but I was always a step behind.

This riot went on for several minutes before I managed to grab Cy's collar. Amazingly, neither the horse nor Cy were injured in any way. The judge and I were shaken, but otherwise undamaged.

Oh, yes—I know you are wondering—Cy didn't place in that particular trial. Some judges just have no sense of humor.

FDSB FIELD TRIALS

Stakes

Most FDSB field trials are non-title competitions, often called *feeder trials* because the placers may qualify for bigger trials at which championship titles are awarded. All FDSB trials are conducted under the rules of the American Field Publishing Company, which maintains all records of these trials and publishes them in its weekly tabloid, *The American Field.*

FDSB trials may include any of the following stakes: open puppy, open derby, open shooting dog, open all age, amateur puppy, amateur derby, amateur shooting dog, amateur all age. Retrieving is not required in FDSB trials, but the handler must shoot a blank pistol at the flush after each point.

The age limits for FDSB puppy and derby stakes follow equestrian traditions. Puppy stakes run between January 1 and June 30 are for dogs whelped on or after January 1 of the preceding year. Puppy stakes run between July 1 and December 31 are for dogs whelped on or after June 1 of the preceding year. Thus, FDSB puppy stakes allow dogs up to 18 months old. Derby stakes run between July 1 and December 31 of each year are for dogs whelped on or after January 1 of the preceding year. Derby stakes run between January 1 and June 30 of each year are for dogs whelped on or after January 1 of the second preceding year. Thus, FDSB derby stakes allow dogs up to 30 months old. The other stakes—open shooting dog, open all age, amateur shooting dog, amateur all age—have no restrictions on the dog.

Requirements for Each Stake

The minimum requirements vary from stake to stake. To win or place, a dog usually must perform significantly above the minimum requirements. Here are both the minimum requirements and what the judges look for in each stake.

Puppy: Each brace runs at least a 15-minute heat (with eight minutes in the birdfield, if one is used). The puppy should hunt enthusiastically, establish a solid point, and remain staunch, but need not be steady. The judges look mostly for potential, especially in bird-hunting instincts, class, and style.

Derby: Each brace runs at least a 30-minute heat (with eight minutes in the birdfield, if one is used). The derby should hunt enthusiastically and demonstrate some knowledge of where to find birds. It should establish a solid point and remain steady, but need not be steady. It should honor its bracemate's points. Here, too, the judges look mostly for potential, especially in bird-finding instincts, class, and style.

Shooting Dog: Each brace runs at least a 30-minute heat (with eight minutes in the birdfield, if one is used). The shooting dog should be a finished birddog with a range suitable for a walking hunter (even though the handlers may ride in this stake). It should hunt the course intelligently, handle biddably, point staunchly, remain steady to wing and shot, and honor its bracemate's points. Class and style are essential.

All Age: Each brace runs at least a 30-minute heat (with eight minutes in the birdfield, if one is used). The all age dog should be a finished birddog that runs wider than the shooting dog, but without going out of control. It should hunt the course intelligently, handle kindly, point staunchly, remain steady to wing and shot, and honor its bracemate's points. Class and style are essential.

Most FDSB feeder trials are single-heat affairs with no callbacks. Of course, judges may call back dogs they need to see again if they wish. Usually, however, they make their placements at the completion of the first series.

Placements and Titles

In FDSB feeder trials, the judges place three dogs. However, these placements do not lead directly to any titles. FDSB titles can only be earned in trials designated as championship trials. To enter a championship trial, a dog must have won or placed in some number of other trials. The exact requirements vary from championship to championship. In many cases, wins and/or placements in feeder trials do qualify a dog to run in a championship trial.

Some field trial clubs award points toward club trophies—Puppy of the Year, Shooting Dog of the Year, Amateur Handler of the Year, and so on—to dogs and handlers that win or place in feeder trials. In many clubs these awards are highly prized by members.

Championship Trials

The major annual FDSB trials are championship affairs, each with its own entry prerequisites, running format, and title.

The oldest and most prestigious is the annual National Championship Trial held at the Hobart Ames Plantation near Grand Junction, Tennessee. Dating back to 1896, this is the premier FDSB championship trial, the one every trial enthusiast dreams of winning. Entry requirements are complex, but generally involve annually winning (not just placing in) one or two trials which have been designated as National Championship Qualifying Stakes. The heats in the National Championship are three hours long, so only two braces run each day. With more than 50 entries, it takes a number of days to complete this trial. The winner receives many impressive trophies and a large (several thousand dollars) cash purse.

Another prestigious championship trial is the National Free-For-All Championship, which dates back to 1916. The dogs must first run a one-hour qualifying heat and then, if called back, run a three-hour championship heat. A real test of endurance.

Many, many other championship trials are conducted each year around the country. Some involve a specific species of bird, such as the National Open Pheasant Championship, the U.S. Open Chicken Championship, the National Grouse Championship, and so on. Some are for young dogs, such as the National Derby Championship and the Continental Open Derby Championship. Some are regional trials, such as the Georgia Open Quail Championship, the Southern Championship, and the Oklahoma Open Championship. Each championship has its own entry requirements, its own length of heats, its own specific performance standards, and its own purse for the winners. In most cases, both a champion and a runner-up champion are named. Also, in most cases, the judges may withhold the title(s) if they feel no dogs deserved them.

The winners of these events earn the title Champion, modified by the specific trial in which the title was earned, like 1993 National Champion, or 1993 Georgia Open Quail Champion.

Futurities

This is another trial format that is quite popular. Here's how a futurity works. Before a litter is born, the breeder nominates it for the futurity to be held during the litter's derby year. To nominate a litter, the breeder must pay a forfeit of so much money. Then he or the people to whom he sells the pups must make additional forfeits to keep each puppy eligible. When the dogs are between derby age (six and 24 months), those eligible may run in the futurity trial for which they were nominated. The purse, which includes a percentage of all the forfeits and of the entry fees, is split between the breeders and owners of the placing dogs.

The most prestigious futurity is the American Field Futurity, which has been running annually since 1903. In it, four dogs are placed and a large purse is split between the owners and breeders of those dogs.

We also have futurities for specific birds, such as the Pheasant Dog Futurity, and futurities for specific breeds, such as the Brittany Futurity and the German Shorthair Futurity. We have a futurity for shooting stake dogs, the Shooting Dog Futurity. And on and on.

Other FDSB-Affiliated Trials

Several other organizations conduct trials that, although somewhat different from the mainstream FDSB formats, are recognized and approved by FDSB. Each of these organizations has a slightly different view of what constitutes the ideal birddog—mostly in the areas of retrieving, steadiness to wing and shot, range, and foot handling. They have different trial procedures and different judging criteria, but they fall within the acceptable range of FDSB. Most of these organizations conduct various qualifying and championship trials.

Among these organizations are the National Shoot To Retrieve Association (NSTRA), the National Bird Hunters Association (NBHA), the American Bird Hunters Association (ABHA), and the United States Complete Shooting Dog Association (USCSDA). Those interested in more information about their trials should contact the secretary of each organization. They are listed in Appendix III, "Important Contacts."

My First FDSB Field Trial

I first handled a dog in an FDSB trial back in the early 1970s. I had trained Jigger, a classy Pointer of shooting-dog range, rather well. He understood *Heel, Whoa, Fetch,* and a special command—*Git!*—that I used to send him out farther ahead of me. I taught him this command with a slingshot and a pocketful of marbles. Whenever he cut back toward me, I shot a marble at him. As it hit or whistled past him, I hollered "*Git!*" Jigger was nobody's dummy, so, after a few hits and near misses, when I said *Git!*, he *Got!*

I entered him in the puppy stake at a trial conducted by the Wichita Birddog Association in February near Beaumont, Kansas. Most Kansas Februaries are better suited for indoor activities, but that year the weatherman outdid himself. It was freezing. "Oh, well," I thought as I arrived at the trial grounds, "I'll only be out on the course for half an hour. No big deal." As it turned out, I'm no prophet.

I had previously handled birddogs only in AKC walking stake trials, so I was quite surprised to see that this was a horseback trial—one in which everyone rode. *Surprised* may not be quite the right word. *Stunned* comes a little closer, and I can think of several that come closer still, but precision may not be everything here.

You see, I have a genetic problem when it comes to horses. I'm missing a horse gene. I'm definitely a carrier, but not an exemplar of that particular gene. My mother, who grew up on a ranch, could—and probably still can, even now at almost 90—ride any horse she can get on top of. My kids, all of whom grew up in the city, share that talent. They just jump on and take off. Amazing.

But not me. I peaked out as a rider galloping a broomstick around the neighborhood playing cowboys as a kid. Sure, I've been on enough horses as an adult—fishing in the mountains, and so forth—but it never works out as well for me as it does for most folks. The horse senses who's boss—and it isn't me—and so does whatever it pleases.

When my brace was called at that February FDSB trial, I handed Jigger over to a friend while I climbed aboard the horse they had for me. Being a short-legged little rascal, I couldn't reach either stirrup. When the wrangler asked me if I wanted him to shorten them, I foolishly said "No, I'll just be up here for 20 minutes or so and we'll be walking along. Besides, you'd just have to lengthen them again for the next handler. No, don't bother." He looked at me quizzically.

The judges told us to turn them loose, so we did. One of the judges was Bruce Alden, with whom I had been acquainted since the early 1950s, when we both had Weimaraners.

Jigger took off like a shot, and started making nice casts left and right. I shifted this way and that with every step the horse took, but we were hardly moving, so it wasn't too uncomfortable. Besides, he had been around the course several times, so he needed no guidance from me. "Hey," I thought, "these horseback trials aren't so bad after all."

Then, Jigger inexplicably cut back toward me. Big no-no in field trials. But I was ready for him. Leaning forward, I hollered *"Git! Git! Git!,"* just like in training.

And he *got,* too. Trouble was, so did the horse! That was the first time in my life a horse ever did what I said—and I wasn't even talking to it! But it *got* and then some. Since my feet were free of the stirrups, my only fixed connection to the galloping steed was through the saddle horn. But that was enough, you see, for in just a few bounds, the horse and I were in perfect synch. When his back went down, my fanny went up, and when his back came up, my fanny went down. Splat! Bam! Smash! Ouch! The extreme cold made each contact especially painful, and I had lots of contacts in no time.

I hollered the only word I knew in horse-talk: *"Whoa!"* The horse slowed down and stopped. But so did Jigger! So I hollered *"Git!"* at Jigger, and he *got,* but so did the horse. I hollered *"Whoa!"* at the horse, and it stopped, but so did Jigger. And so it went for 20 minutes on the back course. I alternated hollering *"Git!"* and *"Whoa!,"* and both animals obeyed every command. My fanny was numb, and my entire spinal column ached.

Once I glanced around and saw Bruce Alden. He is one of the nicest, most tactful people I have ever known. Watching the circus I was staging right in front of him was almost more than he could handle. He didn't want to laugh and embarrass me, so he must have been holding his breath. All I know is he was hunched over a bit and turning blue when I looked around. But I was too busy *Git*-ing and *Whoa*-ing two animals to offer him any comfort or advice.

On reaching the birdfield in this trial, the handlers dismount and work their dogs on foot for the remaining eight minutes. For me, reaching the birdfield seemed like one of the major milestones of my life. I slid my aching, numb anatomy down from the saddle—gratefully—but things didn't get any better. You see, my legs were rubber, so I couldn't stand up. I sat there in cover almost as high as my head while Jigger and his bracemate raced this way and that, occasionally almost crashing into me.

Fortunately, Jigger found no birds. If he had, he would have been on his own, for I couldn't move. Eventually, someone called time. I tried again to get up, this time successfully. I *whoa*-ed Jigger, walked over to him, snapped a lead on him, and walked back to the car. As we approached the collection of gaping mouths in the gallery, I pulled my hat down over my eyes, fixed my gaze on the ground, scurried to my car, loaded up and got out of there. I figured I had to give Bruce Alden an opportunity to laugh before he exploded.

Oh, yeah—I almost forgot—Jigger didn't place in that trial either. I guess the judges were too busy watching me to see him. However, he was obeying every *Git!* and *Whoa!* command perfectly.

SPECTATING AT YOUR FIRST TRIAL

Many beginners are intimidated by the mystery, the pageantry, the traditions, of field trials. Many participants are, well, as transfixed as they might be going through a major religious experience. Everyone is so busy. And the typical beginner gets the impression that he is the only person present who doesn't understand what is happening and why. I have recounted my first attempts to handle dogs in field trials to help you see things a bit differently. I hope after reading what a fool I have made of myself running dogs, you will at least take a chance and spectate at a trial in your area. I think you'll enjoy it.

To locate a nearby field trial, ask birddog owners in your area. Failing that, check with your veterinarian, who probably can at least direct you to someone who competes in trials. If not, contact the AKC and the FDSB for the name and address of the secretary of the affiliated club nearest your home.

Once you have located a trial, by all means attend it. Wear clothing appropriate for the season, preferably including something bright orange for visibility. In warmer weather use insect repellent. Get there early, ask what spectators should and shouldn't do, where on the trial grounds you should and should not go. If it is a horseback trial, and if you want to see better, rent a horse (if you dare). Afoot or on horseback, follow along behind the marshal, always staying with the rest of the gallery. Once you start following a brace, continue following until they complete the course. If you leave early and try to take a shortcut back to your car, you may interfere with a dog or create a safety hazard for the official guns.

As a general rule, don't ask the handlers questions immediately before or after their dogs run. This is a competition, after all, and they are absorbed in their dogs' performances. Don't ask the judges questions, at least until after they have completed their judging assignments by awarding the placements. Even then, preface your questions with an explanation that you are new to the game and are seeking information, not expressing disagreement with their decisions.

Above all, attend with an open mind. Ask questions, and don't argue with the answers even if you disagree. Think of yourself as a guest, not a commentator. If your idea of an ideal birddog differs substantially from that of the people you talk with, keep it to yourself. You are there to learn. If you keep your mind open, you may learn more than you anticipated. You may even refine your thinking on birddogs a little—or a lot.

CHAPTER

23

Hunting Tests:

Our Fastest Growing Game

A point and a back in the master level at an AKC hunting test. Dr. Jeff Herod's Shorthair, Ben, points as Ray Taylor's Arky backs. The judges (on horseback) are Kent Douglas (left) and Doug Meierhoff (right). Only the judges and marshals may ride. The handlers and gallery must walk.

AKC HUNTING TESTS

The AKC initiated its noncompetitive hunting test program for pointing breeds in 1986. Many birddog owners, unaware of this program's place in the overall scheme of things, have misunderstood it. Many field trialers view the very concept of hunting tests as an attempt to establish a set of easy titles to rival in stature the challenging field trial titles. Not so, but such is the perception of some field trialers.

To understand the birddog hunting test program, you should look at it as one front in a broad movement toward noncompetitive testing. This movement started with retriever tests during the early 1980s. The AKC, yielding to enormous pressure from retriever owners, plus competition from the United Kennel Club (UKC) and the North American Hunting Retriever Association (NAHRA), initiated a retriever hunting test program in 1985. It became immediately, and remains today, the fastest-growing program in AKC history. Impressed by its success in retrievers, the AKC initiated a similar program for pointing breeds in 1986. Another exploding success. They started a spaniel program in 1988. Another winner.

The concept of noncompetitive testing programs is still gathering momentum. The AKC has implemented similar programs for Beagles, sight hounds, and herding dogs. They have even started a basic pet testing program called Canine Good Citizenship tests.

All of these programs have the same essential elements: noncompetitive testing, graduated testing levels, and after-the-name titles. Each has been more successful than anyone would have predicted.

Eventually, the AKC (or some agency) will initiate similar programs for working breeds and terriers. Search and Rescue dog testing is another possibility, with real humanitarian implications. Clearly, the noncompetitive testing concept has found a receptive audience in modern American society.

Why? Look at American society. Since the end of World War II, America has developed a massive middle class with sufficient leisure time and disposable income for hobbies. Before WWII the middle class (if you can call it that) had neither. The post-WWII American middle class has expanded recreational pursuits in this country to a level unknown in any society in the history of the world. Purebred dog ownership is just one example.

Birddog field trials, started in 1874, were never designed for this middle class, which didn't exist back then. Being purely competitive, field trials demand a significant commitment of both time and money. Even for those able and willing to commit the necessary resources, field trials can be frustrating. Each trial is an all-or-nothing gamble. In every stake at every trial most competitors "fail," and many of them suffer what poker players call "that good second-best hand syndrome." Their dogs do well, sometimes exceptionally well, but another dog does better and picks up all the marbles. Everyone else goes away empty.

A noncompetitive testing program is not all-or-nothing. It offers many possible goals, several levels of achievement, and allows every participant to succeed simultaneously. Each handler/dog team tries to measure up to a written standard, not to outdo the other participants. With no pressure to win, people pull for each other—from the heart. That makes the atmosphere at a test relaxed and friendly, which most modern American middle classers need desperately in their recreational pursuits. The workaday world is sufficiently competitive for most of us, thank you.

Why is participation growing so rapidly? Well, the market for these tests, namely the post-WWII middle class, had been searching for such a recreational outlet for about 40 years before the hunting test programs started. Now that it is here, people are jumping in *en masse,* playing catch-up, so to speak.

AKC has promoted its hunting tests as programs designed for hunters. True enough, but they appeal to a much broader range of dog owners: borderline field trialers, obedience trialers looking for a new challenge, show-dog breeders wanting to test their stock in the field. All this additional participation is good news for the pointing breeds and their fanciers. The new titles help everyone evaluate breeding stock.

The program is too new to be totally stabilized, of course, but it is becoming more so as the years go by. We are still building hunting test traditions, which can be a painful process. The rules, even the performance standards, are not applied consistently from test to test, judge to judge. Field trials went through the same growing pains many decades ago, only over a longer period of time and with fewer people involved. The instant popularity of hunting tests adds to the confusion.

But things are improving. In 1989 the AKC initiated formal judges' clinics and has conducted them around the country ever since. In 1991, the rules for pointing breed hunting tests were revised, clarified, and improved.

Although field trials will always remain popular, especially among highly competitive people, hunting tests will become the more popular activity before the turn of the century. Hunting tests have something positive to offer every birddog owner. Hunting test titles will become major factors in breeding programs.

Testing Levels

Hunting tests offer three graduated testing levels, called *junior, senior,* and *master.* In each level, a dog can earn an after-the-name title indicating its level of accomplishment. Although graduated in difficulty, these levels and titles are not progressive, in that a dog doesn't have to start at the bottom and work up. A dog can run in the senior or master without first earning the lower level title(s).

In all levels, dogs are run in braces on single courses, with or without birdfields (minimum of five acres, if used). At least two birds per brace must be planted. Any game bird may be used. In all levels, only the two judges and the marshal can ride horses. The handlers and the gallery must walk.

In the junior level, each brace runs for 15 to 30 minutes, including birdfield time (if a birdfield is used). A junior dog should hunt enthusiastically within a comfortable range, find a bird, and establish a point. It need not be staunch or steady. The handler must fire a blank pistol when a pointed bird flushes, but birds are not shot for junior dogs, nor are they expected to retrieve.

In the senior level, each brace runs for 30 to 45 minutes. A senior dog should hunt enthusiastically within a comfortable range. It must find and point a bird. It must be staunch to flush, but may break at the shot. Official guns, not handlers, do all shooting. The dog must retrieve, but not necessarily to hand. It must honor, but may be held in place during the flush and its bracemate's retrieve. If a dog qualifies otherwise but has no opportunity to retrieve and/or honor, the judges call it back and set up the appropriate situations for testing these abilities.

In the master level, the braces run for 30 to 45 minutes. A master dog must give a finished performance in every way. It must hunt enthusiastically and intelligently within a comfortable range. It must find and point a bird, be staunch, be steady to wing and shot, retrieve only on command, and deliver to hand. Official guns, not handlers, do all shooting. The dog must also honor its bracemate's point(s) and remain steady through its bracemate's retrieve(s). If a master dog otherwise qualifies but has no opportunity to retrieve and/or honor, the judges call it back and set up appropriate situations for testing these abilities.

The AKC hunting tests for pointing breeds do not include a retrieving test in water.

Titles

Per AKC custom, hunting test titles, being noncompetitive, are placed after the dog's name (in pedigrees, advertisements, etc.). The titles are:

Junior Hunter, abbreviated as JH: To earn this lowest level title, a dog must qualify in four licensed junior level tests.

Senior Hunter, abbreviated as SH: To earn this middle level title, a dog must qualify in five licensed senior level tests. However, if the dog has previously earned the JH title, it need qualify only four times for its SH.

Master Hunter, abbreviated as MH: To earn this highest level title, a dog must qualify in six licensed master level tests. However, if the dog has previously earned the SH title, it need qualify only five times for its MH.

These titles make reading pedigrees much more enlightening than it was when the only field titles were NFC, NAFC, FC, and AFC. Since they are noncompetitive, with specific requirements for completion, every good dog can succeed, given a reasonable number of chances. Furthermore, each dog can succeed at the level the owner finds comfortable. For example, those who do not want to steady their dogs to wing and shot can participate at the junior and senior levels—and earn appropriate titles.

However, hunting tests do not allow dogs without ability to earn titles, as some field trialers seem to fear. The dog must do the work, even if it doesn't have to do it better than all the other dogs entered. That eliminates the frustrations associated with the field trialer's "good second-best hand syndrome."

While no analogy is perfect, it is reasonable to say that a birddog with a JH title is the ordinary hunter's dog, the dog that doesn't get much training between seasons but does get a lot of exposure while hunting. This dog is self-taught, but may well have a lot of natural talent. The SH birddog is the ordinary hunter's "brag dog." This animal has good manners on birds, retrieves, and honors. The MH birddog is the ordinary hunter's dream dog, the one he would like to own if it didn't take so much off-season work to train such an animal and keep it trained. This dog does it all in the uplands, and does it with kindliness and manners.

The Mechanics of a Hunting Test

AKC field trial clubs conduct most hunting tests. National breed clubs also conduct them, especially at their annual national specialties. Some local breed clubs whose primary interest is conformation showing also conduct hunting tests. And a few all-breed hunting dog clubs include hunting tests for pointing breeds in their diversified programs.

A typical birddog hunting test, with all three testing levels, can be completed in one day. Consequently, many clubs hold "back-to-backs," that is, two separate tests on successive days, usually Saturday and Sunday. A back-to-back draws a larger entry, because people will travel farther to run when they can earn two qualifying scores.

Different clubs run the three testing levels in different sequences. Some clubs run them in different sequences on each day of a back-to-back. However, all clubs complete one level before starting the next, unless they have two courses available, in which case they can run one level on each course simultaneously.

Since only the two judges and the marshal may ride horses, those in the gallery walking along behind may not be able to see as well as they would like. That's why many clubs position the birdfield near a hill from which spectators can see quite well.

In a single course with birdfield, which is the most common arrangement, the bird planters and official guns stay near the birdfield throughout the test. As soon as each brace starts its heat, the bird planters walk through the birdfield planting birds randomly. Then they return to their position out of but near the birdfield. When each brace of senior and master dogs enters the birdfield, the official guns move out into the birdfield, and one follows each handler.

If a senior or master dog qualifies in all other respects but did not have an opportunity to honor and/or retrieve, the judges call that dog back to give it a chance to demonstrate its ability in that (those) area(s). Some judges call the dog back immediately after its brace finishes. Others wait and do all callbacks after the last brace of that testing level. Either way, they set up a situation to allow the dog the opportunities it didn't get. For example, if the dog didn't get to honor (usually because its bracemate failed to find a bird), the judges will have a bird planted and another dog led up to within pointing distance. After that dog is on point, the callback dog is released to hunt near the pointing dog. If on first seeing the pointing dog the callback dog honors as it should, it passes that requirement. Similarly, if a dog did not have an opportunity to retrieve (because the official guns missed the bird(s) it pointed during its brace), the judges have a bird planted, then have the call-back dog released near it. After the dog establishes a point, the handler flushes and the guns shoot, successfully this time everyone hopes. If they miss again—very unlikely—the entire callback procedure must be repeated. No dog may receive a qualifying score unless it has satisfactorily completed all the requirements.

In some clubs, the hunting test secretary posts the judges' scores for each dog where everyone can see them after each brace. This is easy to do because the judges must use a standardized score sheet that contains the five categories in which the dog must be judged: hunting, bird-finding ability, pointing, trainability, and retrieving. The standard for each category varies with the testing level (and retrieving is not scored in junior, of course). But the scoring system is standardized. Each judge must give the dog a numerical score (between 0 and 10) in each category. The scores given by each judge in each category are averaged. Those averaged scores determine whether each dog qualifies. To qualify, a dog must have an overall average score of at least seven, with no category being scored lower than five.

The hunting test secretary gives orange qualifying-score rosettes to the dogs that earn them. Customs vary from club to club as to when the rosettes are passed out. Some do it immediately after each brace. Others do it at the end of each testing level. Still others do it at the end of the day.

Spectating at an AKC Hunting Test

The gallery cannot ride, so unless the test grounds offers a vantage point from which the gallery can see the dog work, visibility may be a problem, especially if the cover is high. Thus, birddog hunting tests are pretty iffy as spectator sports.

Most clubs do everything they can to make watching possible and enjoyable. If they can, they arrange the entire course around the base of a high hill, from which the gallery can see everything. If that is impossible, they situate the birdfield at the base of a hill, from which the gallery can see at least the work in the birdfield. However, I have been at tests where the birdfield cover was so high that the gallery could not see anything except the judges, the marshal, and their horses' heads. This can be frustrating, but each club does the best it can in its selection of test grounds.

Sometimes the gallery can see quite a bit while walking behind the judges through the back course and from the edge of the birdfield. The gallery, of course, cannot enter the birdfield. If the land is flat and the cover not too high, a person can see a lot of dog work just tagging along behind.

Whatever you do as a spectator, follow the rules of common sense and common courtesy. If you follow a brace of dogs, stay with them until they are finished. Don't wander around on the course, and don't take any shortcuts back to your car. Ask questions, but do so quietly, lest you interfere with the proceedings. Don't ask questions of a handler immediately before or after he runs his dog. If you see some dogs staked out somewhere, don't pet them or otherwise mess with them without permission. If you want to ask a question of one of the judges, wait until he is finished with his judging assignment—which will only be after he is off his horse. And preface your question with assurances that you are not challenging or arguing, but just inquiring.

NAVHDA TESTS

The North American Versatile Hunting Dog Association (NAVHDA) also sponsors noncompetitive tests for pointing breeds. They have patterned their tests after those offered in European countries, especially Germany. Thus, they test not only a birddog's upland hunting abilities (hunting, pointing, honoring, and retrieving), but also its water retrieving talents and its tracking and trailing abilities. They use fur as well as feathers, too, so some of this work is pretty hound-y.

They call their dogs *versatile hunting dogs* rather than birddogs because of the greater range of their abilities. Although these dogs may do more things satisfactorily than will our straight birddogs, they will not typically do the standard birddog work with the same class and style we look for in a pointing breed. Have you ever heard of a one-man band having a number on the charts?

I consider the versatiles a separate classification within the sporting group, just like spaniels and retrievers. That is why I have not included the training for their tests in this book. That is why I am not giving any details about these tests.

However, many of the breeds eligible to run in NAVHDA tests are AKC-recognized pointing breeds, so I am mentioning that these tests exist. In Appendix III, "Important Contacts," I have listed a NAVHDA contact for those interested in getting more information about the organization and its tests.

CHAPTER 24

Working Certificate Tests:

Our National Breed Clubs' Contribution

Working Certificate Tests were designed to prove the working ability of show-bred dogs of certain breeds. *(M.A. Samuelson)*

The AKC wasn't first to recognize the need for some form of noncompetitive field-testing program for sporting breeds. No, the AKC was a Johnny-come-lately. The various national breed clubs began recognizing—and addressing—this need shortly after World War II. Pointing breed clubs, retriever clubs, and spaniel clubs initiated their own noncompetitive programs, with varying names and formats. I lump them all together as *working certificate tests,* because the sponsoring national breed club issues certificates to the owners of dogs that successfully participate in these tests.

The impetus for these programs came from the dog-show world. Breeders whose primary interest was conformation sought a way to demonstrate and document the basic field ability of their stock without making the commitment of time and money required to compete in field trials.

Working certificate tests have caught on both within and beyond the sporting breed world. Herding breeds have had them for many years. So have sight hound breeds. The Newfoundland Club of America conducts a most interesting program. It has two types of tests, water-dog and draft-dog. In the water-dog tests, Newfies retrieve items from the bottom of a lake and perform a variety of water-rescue feats: take a lifesaver to a "drowning" stranger; carry a line to a boat and pull the boat ashore; and swim ashore with a limp stranger hanging on. In the draft-dog test, they pull and maneuver carts through a curved obstacle course, pull carts loaded with freight, and so on. Fascinating tests.

Within the sporting group, most national breed clubs have had working certificate tests for many years, but none are so diverse and innovative as those found among the clubs sponsoring pointing breeds. Retriever club tests follow a predictable pattern of nonslip land and water retrieving tests, varying only in the degree of difficulty—from the basic test of the Labrador Retriever Club to the extremely challenging three-level program of the American Chesapeake Club. All spaniel tests, except for that of the American Water Spaniel Club (AWSC), are identical flush-and-retrieve tests of the most basic kind. The AWSC program is a four-leveled stemwinder that includes everything in the AKC spaniel hunting test program and a whole lot more.

However, the tests conducted by the various pointing breed clubs vary widely from breed to breed. They differ from one another as much as retriever tests differ from spaniel tests. Why? Well, American retrieverites agree in general on what their dogs, regardless of breed, should do afield. Ditto for spanielites. But no such agreement exists among pointing breed aficionados. That is (partially at least) why we have so many more pointing breeds than retrievers and spaniels combined in this country.

Pointing breed fanciers find it easier to express their differing performance preferences in the requirements for working certificate tests than in FDSB or AKC field trials or AKC hunting tests. The FDSB and the AKC must move slowly in implementing changes because their changes affect so many people, so many organizations. Just the logistics of communicating with all affected parties takes enormous time, and getting any kind of consensus may take years. However, a national breed club is small and cohesive. Its members can be as creative as they choose, and change things as rapidly as they choose, in their working certificate test programs.

Consequently, a person can get a better picture of Americans' varying tastes in pointing breed performance by studying the sundry working certificate test programs than by studying the field trials and hunting test programs of our major registries. That's one reason I am presenting several of them in some detail.

I have another reason: Working certificate programs are the proving grounds for ideas that may or may not find their way into our major registries' programs. For example, the AKC's hugely successful hunting test program—for pointing dogs, retrievers, or spaniels—contains little that wasn't first implemented into working certificate programs by national breed clubs. For example, the feature that has contributed most to the success of the hunting test program—*noncompetitive testing*—has been part of every working certificate program I have ever observed or studied.

Let's look at several of the more interesting working certificate programs.

GORDON SETTER CLUB OF AMERICA (GSCA)

The GSCA offers a basic birddog program in which a dog may earn two titles: WD (Working Dog) and WDR (Working Dog, qualified in retrieving stakes). To earn either title, a dog must qualify in three different tests under three different pairs of judges. After a dog earns a title, the owner may place the letters after the dog's name in pedigrees, advertising, etc.

The GSCA requires a novice or green-broke stake at each of their field trials, and they encourage trial-holding clubs to use that stake for qualifying dogs for their working certificate titles. The stake is run under derby rules. Dogs need not place to qualify, but they must satisfy the test requirements. Judging is done on a point system, as follows:

WD Test: Point (30 points); Responsiveness (30 points); Run (20 points); Range (20 points). Total points: 100.

WDR Test: Same as WD, except with the addition of 20 points for retrieving, for a total of 120 points.

In both tests, the dogs are not required to honor, but may earn up to 20 bonus points if they have the opportunity and do honor. To qualify, a dog must earn at least half the points offered in each category. The GSCA has a comprehensive set of written guidelines to assist judges to evaluate performance and score the dogs properly.

Qualifying scores earned in both types of tests apply to the WD title, but only retrieving tests apply to the WDR. So a dog with two qualifying scores in retrieving tests and one in a nonretrieving test would earn the WD, but not the WDR. To earn its WDR, it would have to qualify a third time in a retrieving test.

ENGLISH SETTER ASSOCIATION OF AMERICA (ESAA)

The ESAA offers a basic two-level program in which dogs can earn HD (Hunting Dog) and HDX (Hunting Dog Excellent) titles. The HD title is the lower level, with less challenging requirements. The ESAA conducts special tests in which dogs may earn legs (qualifying scores) toward these titles. To earn either title, a dog must qualify three times under four judges (who are approved to judge AKC field trials). Also, each placement in an AKC licensed derby stake counts as a leg toward the HD, and each placement in an AKC broke dog (gun dog or all age) stake counts as a leg toward the HDX. Dogs that earn FC or AFC titles in AKC field trials automatically qualify for the HDX title. After a dog earns a title, the owner may place the appropriate letters (HD, HDX) after the dog's name in pedigrees, advertising, etc.

These tests are run on a single course with a birdfield. Each brace of dogs runs a 20-minute heat with no more than eight minutes in the birdfield. Horseback handling is not allowed. In an HD test, the dog must hunt enthusiastically at a reasonable foot-handling range, must handle kindly, must point, and must be shot over, but need not remain steady to wing and shot or honor. A retrieve is desirable but not mandatory. In the HDX test, the dog must show all the traits expected in the HD, plus steadiness to wing and shot. It must also honor if the occasion arises, and a retrieve is desirable but not necessary.

WEIMARANER CLUB OF AMERICA (WCA)

The WCA conducts a comprehensive rating test program that has two divisions: shooting dog and retrieving dog. Each division has three graduated testing levels, each with its own title. Shooting dog division titles are: NSD (Novice Shooting Dog), SD (Shooting Dog), and SDX (Shooting Dog Excellent). Retrieving dog division titles are: NRD (Novice Retrieving Dog), RD (Retrieving Dog), and RDX (Retrieving Dog Excellent). To earn any of these titles, a dog must qualify once in the appropriate test at a WCA-sponsored rating test. After a dog earns a title, the owner may place the appropriate letters after the dog's name in pedigrees, advertising, etc.

The general requirements for the shooting dog division are as follows: Judging is on a pass/fail basis; dogs run in braces; a birdfield is optional; horseback handling is optional, at the discretion of the host club; and any recognized gamebirds or pigeons may be used. The specific requirements for each shooting dog level are as follows:

NSD: Each brace runs a 15-minute heat including no more than five minutes in the birdfield (if one is used). To qualify, a dog must demonstrate a desire to hunt, boldness, initiative and search, and reasonable obedience; it must also indicate the presence of game, but need not point.

SD: Each brace runs a 20-minute heat including no more than five minutes in the birdfield (if one is used). To qualify, a dog must demonstrate all the abilities in the NSD, plus it must find a bird and establish a point, and it must be shot over with a .22 blank pistol. But it need not be steady to wing and shot, or retrieve, or honor.

SDX: Each brace runs a 30-minute heat including no more than eight minutes in the birdfield (if one is used). To qualify, a dog must be a finished, fully broken birddog. It must hunt at a reasonable range, point staunchly, be shot over with a shotgun of 20 gauge or larger, remain steady to wing and shot, retrieve on command, and honor.

The general requirements for the retrieving dog division are: Judging is on a pass/fail basis; recognized gamebirds, ducks, or pigeons may be used; a freshly killed bird shall be used for each NRD entrant in the land series; dead or shackled birds may be used for RD and RDX tests, but at least one live bird will be shot for each dog in the land series; each live-bird thrower shall be backed by two gunners; guns shall be 20 gauge or larger shotguns or .22 blanks; in land tests, the cover should be sufficient to hide the bird but not so high and/or dense as to block the judge's view of the dog; handlers may not throw objects to encourage the dogs to enter the water, etc.; all shots will be fired after the throws; in water tests, bank-running shall not be penalized if it is considered "intelligent use of land," but shall be penalized if it is simply "avoiding the water"; in all water tests, the handler shall remain within a 12-foot circle that is three feet from the shoreline. The specific requirements for each level are:

NRD: On land, the dog must complete (within five minutes) one single marked retrieve that falls between 20 and 40 yards from the "line" (starting point for dog). In water, the dog must complete (within five minutes) one single marked retrieve that falls between 20 and 40 yards from the line. The dog need not be steady, but must be restrained until the bird lands. The dog must bring the bird back within the handler's circle, but need not deliver to hand.

RD: On land, the dog must complete (within 10 minutes) a wide-spread (60-degree) double marked retrieve, with the first fall approximately 50 yards and the second fall approximately 20 yards from the line. In water, the dog must complete (within 10 minutes) a wide-spread (60-degree) double marked retrieve through eight decoys, with the first fall approximately 50 yards and the second fall approximately 20 yards from the line. In both series, the dog must be steady (but a controlled break is permissible) and deliver to hand.

RDX: On land, the dog must complete (within 10 minutes) a wide-spread (60-degree) double marked retrieve, with the first fall approximately 60 yards and the second fall approximately 30 yards from the line. In water the dog must do two separate tests: a triple marked retrieve (within 15 minutes), and then a single blind retrieve (within 10 minutes). In the triple marked retrieve, the first fall shall be approximately 40 yards, the second fall approximately 60 yards, and the third fall approximately 20 yards from the line, and eight decoys shall be spread 30 to 60 yards from the line. The blind retrieve shall be approximately 50 yards and through eight decoys. In all tests, the dog must be steady (controlled breaks are not allowed) and deliver to hand.

Clearly, the WCA has an ambitious program, especially in the retrieving dog division. And they have been using it at least since the early 1950s (when I first learned about it). Speaking as a person with considerable retriever training experience, I must say that the RDX water tests are extremely challenging. Among the retriever national breed clubs, only the American Chesapeake Club working certificate program has a more demanding set of water tests.

THE VIZSLA CLUB OF AMERICA (VCA)

Several national breed clubs offer versatility titles to dogs that have significant accomplishments in conformation, obedience, and field work. This is totally different from the versatile hunting dog programs offered by NAVHDA and by the Wirehaired Pointing Griffon Club of America (WPGCA). The word *versatile* as used by NAVHDA and WPGCA means "all around hunting dog, one that hunts birds in the uplands, retrieves (and trails) ducks in water, and tracks and trails fur."

The word *versatility* as used by these national breed clubs means a combination of bench, obedience, and field accomplishments. The Weimaraner Club of America has such a program. So do the Irish Setter Club of America and the Vizsla Club of America. Each program is impressive. Each is unique in its details, but they all share a common goal of identifying those dogs that represent the best in their respective breeds—the dogs with good conformation, good field ability, and good obedience responses.

I have selected the VCA's format here for three reasons: I have covered the WCA rating test program; I have covered two setter club working certificate programs; and, in my opinion, the VCA program is the best versatility program of the bunch (although they are all good). Okay, here's how it operates.

The VCA versatility program has separate requirements, certificates, and titles for conformation, obedience, and field. As a dog satisfies each set of requirements, it receives the appropriate certificate and title. The three titles are: CC (Conformation Certificate), OC (Obedience Certificate), and FDC (Field Dog Certificate). If a dog earns all three, the VCA awards it a Versatility Certificate and the VC title. When a dog earns any of these titles, the owner may place the appropriate letters after the dog's name in pedigrees, advertising, etc. Here are the requirements in each category:

Conformation: An AKC show championship title satisfies this requirement. Other Vizslas (18 months of age or older) may satisfy it by passing the VCA Conformation Test three times under three different judges. In each test the dog is evaluated on the following categories (each worth 20 points): height, temperament, general appearance, head and neck, and running gear. To pass, a dog must receive at least 80 percent of these points, and at least 50 percent of the points in each category. Although this test is not intended to identify potential show champions, it does identify good specimens of the breed.

Obedience: An AKC obedience trial title (CD, CDX, UD, OTCH) satisfies this requirement. Other Vizslas may satisfy it by passing the VCA Obedience Test three times under three different judges. The exercises (which are similar to those in obedience trials) are heel on lead (20 points); heel free (20 points); stand for examination (30 points); recall (30 points); and stay (30 points). To pass, a dog must receive at least 50 percent of the points in each exercise.

VCA has added clever innovations to accommodate field trainers. During the heeling exercises, the dog may either sit or stand when the handler stops (unlike AKC obedience trials, in which sitting is mandatory). Many birddog trainers prefer that their dogs not sit, lest they sit on point. Similarly, in the recall (come-in command), the dog may stand or sit in front of the handler when he arrives. In the stay exercise, each dog may stand, sit, or lie down, at the handler's option.

Field: The AKC field titles (FC, AFC, MH, or SH) satisfy this requirement. Other Vizslas may satisfy it by passing the VCA Field Dog

Test three times under three different judges. In that test, the dogs run a 10- to 15-minute back course followed by five to eight minutes in the birdfield. A dog must show desire to hunt and reasonable responses to its handler. It must find and point a bird and retrieve it (at least three-quarters of the way to the handler). It need not be steady to wing and shot. The judges score the dog on the following categories: application and desire (30 points); pointing (30 points); retrieving (30 points); and responsiveness (30 points). To pass, a dog must receive at least 80 percent of the available points and at least 50 percent of the points in each category.

This program has several nice features. First, regular AKC titles satisfy the various requirements but are not the only way to satisfy them. A dog can earn a VC with three AKC titles, or with none. Second, the obedience test allows field trainers to qualify their dogs without teaching them to sit while heeling or when coming on command. Third, this program introduces noncompetitive conformation evaluations. All other versatility programs insist that the conformation requirement be satisfied in AKC dog show competition—with at least class wins. The VCA program alone allows a person to have his dog's conformation evaluated without competing against other dogs, without the preparation associated with the show ring, and without any knowledge of show-ring handling techniques.

THE FUTURE OF WORKING CERTIFICATE TESTS

Some express concern that the success of the noncompetitive AKC hunting test program will damage or even destroy the noncompetitive national breed club working certificate programs. Without question, AKC titles mean more than breed club titles. Also, AKC hunting tests are more readily available throughout the country.

However, let's hope working certificate tests thrive and grow alongside hunting tests. They fill a need in the dog world because they are more specialized (by breed), more flexible, easier to modify, and more experimental.

The VCA versatility program illustrates one particularly attractive experimental direction working certificate tests are taking now. For the first time in this country, a dog can earn noncompetitive titles in conformation, obedience, and field. If extended to more breeds, this concept could reverse, or at least minimize, the show/field split that plagues so many sporting breeds today. A breed splits for a variety of reasons, but mostly because of the extremely high level of competition in both dog shows and field trials. Just winning consistently in one or the other is all the challenge many can handle. Breeders despair of winning consistently in both dog shows and field trials, so they throw up their hands and specialize in one area or the other. Specialization leads inevitably to a breed split as surely as form follows function. However, if noncompetitive conformation titles were widely available—as are noncompetitive field titles (in the hunting test program) and noncompetitive obedience titles (a dog can earn the CD, CDX, and UD titles without placing)—many breeders would be encouraged to strive for dual- and triple-purpose stock.

But how will noncompetitive conformation titles become widely available if national breed clubs don't take the lead? The AKC seldom initiates a program until some other organization has proven it to be a winner. Thus, these working certificate programs continue to serve a useful purpose in the world of dogs. Long may they live and prosper!

CHAPTER 25

Keeping Everything in Perspective:

Enjoy, Enjoy, Enjoy

Enjoy! Enjoy! Enjoy—as the author does with Erick. *(Ray Taylor)*

PAX VOBISCUM (PEACE BE WITH YOU)

Professional golfer Julius Boros withstood the pressure of the tour with fewer signs of stress than anyone else in his day. When asked how he could remain so calm when so much money depended on every stroke, he replied, "It's not your life and it's not your wife; it's just a game."

Throughout this book I have referred to the varying tastes we in this country have in birddogs. Those varying tastes explain, for the most part, why we have more pointing breeds than anyone can name and why we import more regularly. Those varying tastes explain why we have so many different dog-game formats.

However, those varying tastes do not explain why our discussions about birddogs become so hostile and shrill so quickly. Retriever folks disagree on performance standards, but they do it rather off-handedly. Spaniel folks tend to live in breed-tight compartments, with each group not giving a hoot what the others think. But birddog fanciers take their disagreements quite seriously, and they tend to pick at them whenever the occasion arises (namely, whenever an enemy approaches). Each side seems desperate to convince all other sides of their errors in judgment, or at least to verbally pound them into sullen submission. I have referred to this phenomenon several times as the Great American Range War because range is so often a major point of disagreement.

Why the hostility? Although I have no way of proving it, my longtime observations of many skirmishes in this war incline me to believe that most of the soldiers on every side entertain nagging but secret doubts about the rectitude of their own positions, so seek confirmation through verbal victories over opponents. Perhaps I'm wrong, but if I'm right, I can do a lot in these last few pages to bring you peace of mind. Here goes.

If you prefer a big-running Pointer that you can only stay in sight of if you ride a horse, congratulations, you are right! *Pax vobiscum.*

If you prefer a gorgeous English Setter that hunts at a nice horseback shooting-dog range, congratulations, you are right! *Pax vobiscum.*

If you prefer a close-working Gordon Setter that hunts grouse within spitting distance ahead of you, congratulations, you are right! *Pax vobiscum.*

If you prefer a broken-field-running German Shorthair that quarters ahead of you but seldom moves out beyond 100 yards, congratulations, you are right! *Pax vobiscum.*

If you prefer a fullback-like cover-busting German Wirehair that hunts close and also retrieves ducks for you, congratulations, you are right! *Pax vobiscum.*

If you prefer an all-purpose Wirehaired Pointing Griffon that hunts upland birds, trails fur, and fetches up ducks, congratulations, you are right! *Pax vobiscum.*

And so on. Whatever your tastes in breed, range, and function happen to be, congratulations, you are right! *Pax vobiscum.*

And if your tastes change over the years—as often happens among birddog fanciers—congratulations, you will still be right! *Pax vobiscum.*

If you win every skirmish you enter in the Great American Range War, congratulations! *Pax vobiscum.* If you lose every skirmish, but retain your own opinion, congratulations! *Pax vobiscum.* If you avoid every skirmish, content in your own opinions, unconcerned about who agrees or disagrees with you, congratulations! *Pax vobiscum*—although you don't need my wish of peace, for you're already at peace.

Whenever you doubt your preferences, relax and remember that at least one other person agrees with you completely. I do. Whatever your tastes in birddog breeds and/or performance standards, I concur. You are right—*for you.* And that should be all the rightness (righteousness?) you need.

When you feel pressure to prove something about birddogs to someone, remember Julius Boros' saying: *It's not your life and it's not your wife; it's just a game.* Perhaps, to be politically correct here, I should offer this alternative wording: *It's not your house and it's not your spouse; it's just a game.* I think it loses something there, but take your pick.

QUO VADIS? (WHERE ARE YOU GOING?)

Now that you are comfortable with your preferences in birddogs (with my help or in spite of it) you should give some thought to where you want your birddog hobbies to fit within the framework of your overall lifestyle.

Like most areas of human concern, hobbies have a *real* purpose and an *intended* purpose. The two are seldom the same. For example, the real purpose of food is to nourish the body. But when I tear into a hunk of medium-rare sirloin, I have no thought for my body's need for protein. No, I focus on its *intended* purpose, namely to delight my sense of taste. I eat it because it tastes good.

Over the years, I have known two people who have temporarily lost their sense of taste. Both of them lost large amounts of weight. Their doctors put both on regimens in which they had to eat so much per day whether they wanted to or not—and neither of them followed the regimen very closely. Both told me they hated to eat, that it was work, all that cutting, chewing, and swallowing. Fortunately, both regained their sense of taste before suffering any permanent damage from malnutrition. I have often thought that, if medical science ever gets serious about helping people with health-threatening weight problems, they will stop messing with appetite suppressants and find a taste suppressant. Folks don't overeat because they are hungry. They do it because food tastes so good.

Dulling (but not eliminating) the sense of taste would help much more than dulling the appetite.

The *real* purpose of any hobby or recreational pursuit is to refresh the human psyche so the person can persevere more effectively in his life's work, whatever that may be. But just as in the case of the steak mentioned above, when I take my dogs out into the field, I do not think of that real purpose. No, I think only of the *intended* purpose, namely how much fun I'm having.

I have often said that if someone were to interrupt me while I'm training dogs and convince me that the world would end the next day, I would be unable to worry about it until after the training session. I might panic then, but while working with my dogs, I couldn't focus on anything else.

That's how a hobby should affect a person, and I hope each of you finds one that does it for you as completely as working with dogs does it for me. Since you are this far into this book, I assume that your most effective hobby—the one that best refreshes your psyche, the one that best entertains you—must lie somewhere in the world of birddogs.

But that is a large world, with many roads leading in many directions: many kinds of hunting, many types of field trials, hunting tests, working certificate tests, dog shows, obedience competition, and breeding. Stay on the right roads (for you) and you will enjoy your birddogs the rest of your life. Take a wrong turn, and the trip will become a trudging drudgery that leaves you depressed rather than refreshed.

Most of us take a wrong turn periodically, mostly when we follow the crowd rather than make our own decisions. For example, everyone in the club wants to own a field champion, so you begin to see that as a big deal, the mark of a real dog person, the thing to do. If it works out for you, great! Go for it! But if training and competing at that level puts you under so much stress, so much pressure, that you find yourself working late to stay away from your hobby, look in the mirror and ask yourself—seriously—*Quo vadis?*

Another common wrong turn: breeding. You own one, or several, good birddogs. You enjoy working with them. You earn whatever titles you seek. You're a happy person. Then, you get a bright idea: Why not breed some dogs yourself? This might be a great idea—if you are willing to study genetics, familiarize yourself with the hereditary problems within your breed, and select both dams and sires with your head more than your heart; if you are willing to take a financial bath for years and years to make a contribution to the betterment of your breed; and if you are willing to bear up through disappointment after disappointment before seeing significant positive results. But if your interest isn't quite so serious, your altruism (or your pockets) not so deep, and your disposition not so long-suffering, you will bog down. You will lose significant amounts of money on every litter—"No one told me about all those unexpected expenses!" You won't sell all the puppies before you are as sick of them as their mother is. You will find yourself giving a few away. To make matters worse, few of your pups will get the opportunity to amount to much. Most buyers won't persevere in training. The few who do won't do it right, or won't enter trials or tests where your stock can be publicly displayed and evaluated. Results? You will find yourself working overtime at your job to avoid your hobby. Look in the mirror, friend, and ask, *Quo vadis?*

I could go on with these examples, which (as you surely suspect) reflect my own misdirected detours through the years. Fortunately, dogdom's roads run both ways. If you take the wrong one, just turn around and go back. I've done it many times. How do you know when you are on the wrong road? Easy. When your hobby stops fulfilling its *real* purpose of refreshing you. Of course, by that time, it will have long since stopped fulfilling its *intended* purpose of entertaining you.

In short, anytime you feel the need to ask yourself, *Quo vadis?*, you are probably struggling down the wrong road. Turn around, go back, and find another road, one on which you can again enjoy your birddogs. That's their *real* purpose *and* their *intended* purpose, the purpose they most want to fulfill in your life.

Enjoy! Enjoy! Enjoy!

APPENDIX

I

Glossary

Titles found in pedigrees are listed in Appendix II, "Reading Birddog Pedigrees."

Aggressive: In the language of dog folks, this is a euphemism that means *bites*. An aggressive dog has a serious temperament problem. The dog may bite people, other dogs, or both. Unfortunately, many newcomers misunderstand this term, thinking it means a hard-working dog. It doesn't, unless attacking people and other dogs happens to be its life's work.

All Age Stakes: All age field trial stakes—open all age, amateur all age, limited amateur all age, and so on—are the highest level of competition. Dogs are not restricted by age, as they are in the puppy and derby stakes. Further, all age stake judging standards require the widest-ranging dogs. In FDSB trials, all age dogs run much wider than shooting-dog stake dogs. In AKC trials, all age range approximates that of the FDSB shooting dog stake, but is much wider than the AKC gun dog stake. See Chapter 22, "Field Trials," for details.

Amateur Stakes: Amateur field trial stakes—amateur derby, amateur all age, and so forth—are only for handlers considered amateurs by the sponsoring organization (the AKC or the FDSB). See Chapter 22, "Field Trials," for details.

American Kennel Club (AKC): The largest all-breed registry in the country. Headquartered in New York, it regulates AKC dog shows, obedience trials, and field trials, as well as maintains its all-breed registry. AKC field trials for pointing breeds are second in popularity to those conducted by the Field Dog Stud Book (FDSB) in Chicago.

Back: In bracework, when one dog sees the other on point, it should stop immediately. The dog that does this is said to *back* the other dog's point. This is a synonym for *honor.*

Back Cast: A dog back-casts when it makes a cast that takes him behind his handler. This is a fault in field trials, where dogs are expected to hunt in a forward pattern.

Back Course: In a field trial or hunting test that uses the single-course-with-birdfield option, the part of the course that is outside the birdfield is called the back course. The back course may or may not be planted with birds. Its purpose is to allow the dogs to show the judges their range, ground pattern, and class.

Back-to-Back: Two successive AKC hunting tests, usually one on Saturday and the other on Sunday of the same weekend.

Bench: A synonym for *dog show, conformation,* or *breed.* All refer to dog-show competition. The term *bench* derives from the fact that it was once the custom at dog shows to keep all entered dogs on public display throughout the show on benches.

Birddog: A generic term for all dogs of the various pointing breeds. Although spaniels and retrievers also hunt birds, in America at least, only pointing breed dogs are called birddogs, probably because they have been in wide use here much longer than have spaniels and retrievers.

Birdfield: In a field trial or hunting test with the single-course-with-birdfield format, the birdfield is located at the end of the back course. Before every brace, several birds are planted in the birdfield. The purpose of the birdfield is to allow the dogs to show the judges their bird-finding abilities, their pointing style, their staunchness, their steadiness, and in some trials and tests, their retrieving abilities.

Birdless: When a dog finishes its stake in a field trial, hunting test, or working certificate test without finding a bird, it is said to have gone birdless.

Blink: A dog *blinks* when it locates a bird by scent but then, instead of pointing it, avoids it, usually by taking a circular route around it. This is almost always a man-made fault. The dog has had seriously unpleasant results when it pointed birds—like too much gunfire or too severe corrections for bumping birds—so it decides to avoid birds.

Bolt: A dog *bolts* when it runs off to hunt for itself, ignoring the handler's commands. This is serious fault in birddogs.

Bolter: A dog that habitually bolts.

Break: This term has two almost opposite meanings in birddog parlance. Most often, it is used as a synonym for *train.* A birddog trainer "breaks" his dogs, in the same sense that a horse trainer breaks his horses. In fact, the birddog world took the term directly from the world of horse training. When a birddog trainer trains a dog in obedience, he is said to *yard-break* the dog. When he teaches it to retrieve, he *force-breaks* it. When he steadies it to wing and shot, he *breaks* it.

However, *break* can also mean the mistake a supposedly steady (or *broke*) dog makes when it chases after a bird as it flushes or is shot. Thus, you could say a broke dog makes a serious error when it breaks. Oh, well.

Break-Away: The initial departure for each brace in a field trial or hunting test. A fast, classy break-away certainly impresses the judges.

Breed: Another word with multiple meanings. As a verb, it means to mate two dogs with the hope of producing puppies. As a noun, it has two related meanings. First, and most obvious, it means a specific family of dogs exhibiting similar physical, temperamental, and instinctive patterns: a breed of dogs. Second, it refers to dog-show competition. In this latter sense, it is a synonym for *conformation* and *bench.* People speak of showing in *breed* just as they do of showing in *conformation.* The term here derives from the fact that each breed competes separately at the initial level of each dog show.

Breed Split: The unfortunate situation in many breeds today, in which two distinct types have emerged, one for dog-show competition, and the other for field trials, hunting tests, and hunting.

Broke: Steady to wing and shot. A broke dog remains in its pointing position even after the bird is flushed and shot. It moves only on command (to retrieve or continue hunting).

Buck: A wooden force-breaking prop. A typical buck is made of dowelling. The cross-piece, which goes in the dog's mouth during force-breaking is about nine or ten inches long and an inch to an inch-and-a-half in diameter. The legs at each end, which hold the cross-piece up off the ground, are about an inch long and half-inch in diameter. See Chapter 16, "Force-Breaking—Gently" for details.

Bump: A birddog *bumps* a bird when it deliberately flushes it. This is a serious fault, for if the dog is out of gun range, the bird cannot be shot. This is a synonym for *knock.*

Bye Dog: In a field trial, hunting test, or working certificate test, the entered dogs run in braces. If an uneven number of dogs are entered, the odd dog runs with a dog that is not in contention, maybe not even entered. The not-in-contention dog is called a *bye dog.*

Call-back: If a second (or third, etc.) series is run in a field trial or hunting test, the dogs required to run are called back, or given a call-back.

Call-back Pen: A framed wire pen that holds quail out in a training field. It usually has two compartments. In one, birds are confined permanently so they can call the released birds back to the pen at night. The other compartment has birds that are released and flushed for training. They can reenter the pen through a funnel entry.

Cast: When a dog runs toward a birdy objective, it is said to be making a cast.

CERF: The Canine Eye Registration Foundation, located at Purdue University in West Lafayette, Indiana. This organization reviews written reports by board-certified canine ophthalmologists about the condition found in dogs' eyes. If they find the eyes normal in a dog one year of age or older, CERF issues a clearance number. See Appendix II, "Reading Birddog Pedigrees," for more information. CERF clearance numbers indicate healthy eyes in breeding stock.

Chain Training Collar: The obedience trainer's chain slip collar, specially designed to teach heeling. With it the trainer can deliver a series of quick jerk-and-release corrections that induce the dog to return to its proper place by the handler's side—but which do not drag the dog, and which certainly do not choke the animal.

Chase: An unsteadied birddog runs after a flushed bird as it flies away. This can happen whether or not the dog pointed the bird. See also *Delayed Chase,* below.

Checkcord: A length of one-half to three-quarter-inch hemp or nylon rope, usually 20 to 50 feet long. One end typically has a bolt snap for attaching to the dog's collar. The other end may be looped or left plain, depending on the preferences of the trainer. A checkcord is a basic training tool for birddogs, although some of its functions can be better done with the new Flexi-Lead.

Choke Collar: A misnomer for the chain training collar used in obedience training (a.k.a. yard-breaking). Although this collar does tighten up when pulled, it was never intended as a choking device. Properly used, it is the best collar ever invented for delivering a series of jerk-and-release corrections to an errant dog during heeling work.

Class: A dog's manner of doing things. Synonyms: style, animation, enthusiasm. A dog with lots of class is a pleasure to watch.

Collar: In some field trials, handlers are allowed to *collar* their dogs after a flush. They grasp the dog's collar and heel it away before releasing it to hunt again. The intent is to prevent a delayed chase. In some trials, collaring is not allowed. In these, the handler may prevent a delayed chase only by heeling the dog without touching it.

Come-In: An obedience command telling the dog to come to the trainer immediately. Some use *Here, Heel,* or some other variation. Many trainers rely on a whistle signal rather than a verbal command to call their dogs.

Commies: Since the end of the Cold War, this term has been used almost exclusively for "common pigeons," the kind that fly around the courthouse in every city and hamlet in the country; also the kind sought after by most trainers of sporting-breed dogs.

Conformation: A synonym for *dog show, bench,* and *breed.* All refer to dog-show competition. The term *conformation* derives from the fact that in dog shows, dogs are judged on how well they conform to the written breed standard.

Controlled Break: When a supposedly steady (broke) dog breaks to chase or retrieve but is stopped quickly and brought back by a command from its handler, the dog is guilty of a controlled break, which is a less serious fault than a full break.

Course: The area in which birddogs run in field trials, hunting tests, and working certificate tests. The course may have any of several configurations: single course with birdfield, single course without birdfield, multiple course with birdfields, multiple course without birdfields, or continuous course. See Chapter 22, "Field Trials," for details.

Delayed Chase: A dog commits a delayed chase when, ordered to continue hunting after remaining steady through a flush, it runs after the flushed bird. This is a fault most often committed by *green-broke* dogs.

Derby Stakes: Field trial derby stakes are for dogs under a certain age. In AKC trials, the derby stake is for dogs between six and 24 months. FDSB derby stakes held between July 1 and December 31 are for dogs whelped on or after January 1 of the previous year. FDSB derby stakes held between January 1 and June 30 are for dogs whelped after January 1 of the second previous year. See Chapter 22, "Field Trials," for details.

Divided Find: When two or more dogs point the same bird(s) independently, they share a divided find. This sometimes happens when the dogs hit the scent simultaneously. It also happens when one dog points and another cannot see him, so approaches close enough to scent the birds before realizing the other dog is on point. In other words, divided finds happen through no fault of either dog. However, it is not a divided find if one dog sees the other on point and, refusing to back, approaches close enough to wind the birds. There the second dog is guilty of stealing a point, which is a serious fault.

Dog Game: Any type of organized off-season dog activity, including dog shows, obedience trials, field trials, hunting tests, and working certificate tests.

Dog Show: A formal competition in which dogs are judged on how well they conform to the written standard of physical perfection for their respective breeds. Points are awarded toward the AKC show title Champion (CH) based on the location of the show and the number of dogs in competition in each breed.

Down: An obedience command telling the dog to lie down. Many birddog trainers prefer not to teach this command, lest the dog lie down on point or while remaining steady to wing and shot.

Fetch: A command used in force-breaking to tell the dog to reach for, pick up, and carry the buck or bird. Some also use it as a command to retrieve.

Field Dog Stud Book (FDSB): The major birddog registry in this country. Although it registers all sporting breeds, this is primarily a birddog registry. Located in Chicago, Illinois, it is associated with the American Field Publishing Company, which also puts out the weekly birddog tabloid, *The American Field.* Most birddog field trials in this country are conducted under FDSB rules.

Field Trial: A competitive field event, conducted under the rules of either the FDSB or the AKC, to determine which dogs are superior performers in simulated hunting situations. See Chapter 22, "Field Trials," for details.

Field Trial Club: A local or regional organization formed to conduct field trials under the rules of either the FDSB or the AKC. Many AKC field trial clubs also conduct AKC hunting tests.

Find: When a dog locates and points a bird, he *makes a find.*

Flagging: The birddog that waves or wags its tail on point is said to flag. This is a fault in a pointing dog because it indicates a lack of intensity on point.

Flexi-Lead: A mechanical lead device that allows a person to control the distance his dog can go away from him. The lead is coiled up in a spring-loaded housing held by the handler. When the dog moves away, the lead unwinds. When the dog returns, the lead winds back up automatically. The handler can stop the lead at any time with a thumb-button on the housing.

Flush and Stop: Instead of pointing, the dog deliberately flushes a bird, then stops as if it were a wild flush, hoping the boss will be fooled and shoot the bird. This is a serious fault in a birddog. It is also a serious mistake for the handler to shoot the bird, for it encourages repetitions.

Force-Breaking: A structured training procedure by which the trainer teaches a dog to retrieve mechanically. It is useful for dogs with little or no retrieving instinct, natural retrievers that become unreliable, and as a framework for curing such nasty mouth problems as hardmouth and stickiness. See Chapter 16, "Force-Breaking—Gently," for details.

Front-Trailing: When a birddog follows its bracemate, but stays ahead of it, it is said to *front-trail* the other dog. This is a fault because the dog shows a lack of independence.

Game Bird: Any bird that can be hunted. In field trials, hunting tests, and working certificate tests, the term *game bird* means quail, pheasants, or chukkars, since those are the only such birds raised commercially. Most trials and tests are run on planted rather than wild birds, so clubs are limited to those they can buy from commercial growers.

Green-Broke: A dog that has recently been steadied to wing and shot.

Ground Pattern: A birddog's manner of covering ground while hunting. In general, the dog should go from objective to objective, always hunting in a forward direction. In some situations, however, a quartering pattern is best suited to the cover.

Group: The AKC has divided the breeds it recognizes into seven Groups based on similarities of function: Sporting, Hound, Working, Herding, Terrier, Toy, and Non-Sporting (this latter a catchall for breeds that don't fit into any of the other six groups). All birddog breeds are classified as Sporting Group breeds. In dog show competition, the Best of Breed winners from each breed within a Group compete in Group for four placements there. Then the seven Group winners compete for Best in Show, the top award at a dog show.

Gun Dog Stakes: AKC field trial gun dog stakes—amateur gun dog, open gun dog, limited gun dog—have no upper age limit, but are for dogs with more restricted range than those designated as all age stakes. See Chapter 22, "Field Trials," for details.

Gunner: The person assigned to shoot the birds in a field trial, hunting test, or working certificate test in which retrieving is a requirement.

Gun-shy: A gun-shy dog reacts negatively to the sound of gunfire. The reaction may be anything from a little cowering to bolting (running off). This is usually—almost always—a trainer-induced fault. In most cases it is curable, at least by a competent pro.

Hack, Hacking: Over-handling a dog, especially with too much yelling and arm waving. A serious handler error that distracts the dog unnecessarily from its primary job of finding birds.

Handler: The person who handles a dog in a field trial, hunting test, or working certificate test.

Hardmouth, Hardmouthed: A hardmouthed dog, when retrieving, damages a bird so that it is not fit for the table. This is a serious fault, and one that can quickly become incurable.

Heel: An obedience command telling the dog to walk beside the handler, usually on the handler's left side (but some prefer to have their dogs on their right). When the handler stops, the dog may (at the handler's option) sit or stand. Many birddog trainers prefer that their dog stand, fearing that if they teach them to sit when they stop, their dogs may sit on point.

Hie-On: A command some trainers use to tell the dog to go out farther ahead, especially if said dog appears to be pottering around.

Honor: In bracework, one dog honors the other's points by stopping and remaining immobile when it sees the other dog on point. A synonym for *back.*

Hunting Test: A noncompetitive dog game conducted under AKC rules. Hunting tests have three levels of tests, each leading to its own after-the-name title. See Chapter 23, "Hunting Tests," for details.

Interference: In a field trial, hunting test, or working certificate test, when one bracemate pays undue attention to the other bracemate, he is said to interfere. The judges may ask the handler to pick up the interfering dog.

Junior Testing Level: The lowest level in AKC hunting tests. See Chapter 23, "Hunting Tests," for details.

Kennel: A word with two meanings: 1) An obedience command telling the dog to enter the kennel run, a crate, a dog box, or whatever; 2) A synonym for *kennel run.*

Kennel Club: Usually a local or regional organization formed to conduct AKC dog shows. The full club name includes an indication of the club's location, such as "Wichita Kennel Club."

Kennel Runs: Enclosed, outdoor canine living quarters of many types (but I hope that when you speak of your kennel runs you will speak only of the finest concrete and chainlink canine castles—which is no more than your hunting dogs deserve, right?).

Knock: A birddog *knocks* a bird when he deliberately flushes it. A fault. Synonym: *bump.*

Limited Stakes: In AKC field trials, when a club wishes to limit the entry in its all age or gun dog stake, it specifies the stake as "limited"—limited open all age, limited amateur all age, limited open gun dog, limited amateur gun dog—which means that only those dogs that have previously placed in a similar stake (or won a similar derby stake) may be entered. See Chapter 22, "Field Trials," for details.

Line-Steady: In non-slip retrieving, a line-steady dog remains quietly at heel (or beside the blind) until sent to retrieve.

Make a Stand: This is a synonym for *point.* When a dog points, some say he is making a stand.

Mark: When a dog watches a shot bird fall before being sent to retrieve it, he is said to *mark* its fall. Sometimes a shot bird is called a mark, because the dog marked it (or should have).

Marshal: At a field trial or hunting test, the marshal is the person who assists the judges in whatever way they need. He also controls the gallery, calls the competing dogs to the line when their turns come up, and coordinates between the judges and the other officials at the trial or test.

Master Testing Level: The highest level in AKC hunting tests. See Chapter 23, "Hunting Tests," for details.

National Breed Club: A nationwide organization of serious fanciers of one breed. Most of these are affiliated with the AKC and maintain the AKC-approved written standard of physical perfection for the breed. Some national breed clubs are affiliated with the FDSB and conduct field trials under FDSB rules. A few national breed clubs are totally independent, maintain their own registry, and conduct field trials or tests according to their own rules.

Obedience Club: A club devoted to formal obedience training and AKC or UKC obedience trial competition.

Obedience Training: A synonym for *yard breaking,* the process by which a trainer teaches his birddog to *Whoa, Heel,* and *Come-In.* See Chapter 14, "Obedience Training," for details.

Obedience Trial: A dog game for those seriously involved in obedience training. The AKC and the UKC sponsor very similar programs. Both offer three levels of noncompetitive titles. The AKC also offers a competitive title for dogs having all three noncompetitive titles.

Objective: Any birdy-looking place where the dog should seek birds.

OFA: The Orthopedic Foundation for Animals, located at the University of Missouri in Columbia, Missouri, reviews hip and elbow x-rays submitted by veterinarians. If they find the hips and elbows of a dog two years old or older to be normal and free of dysplasia, they issue appropriate clearance numbers. See Appendix II, "Reading Birddog Pedigrees," for details.

Open Stakes: Open field trial stakes—open puppy, open derby, open gun dog, open all age—are open to all handlers, both amateur and professional. These stakes typically offer a higher level of competition than do the corresponding amateur stakes. See Chapter 22, "Field Trials," for details.

Planter: A person who plants birds at a field trial, hunting test, or working certificate test. This is not as easy as it looks. It is necessary to dizzy (or otherwise relax) a bird before planting it to prevent an immediate flush. Dizzied too much, a bird won't flush readily for the handler. A good planter puts the birds down so they stay put but flush readily.

Point: When a birddog scents a bird, he should freeze in place and remain there until the owner arrives to shoot the bird. This is a trained extension of the basic canine instinct to pause and gather all its resources before pouncing on its prey.

Point Dead: Some dogs, instead of retrieving shot birds, point them. The hunter then walks out and picks the bird up.

Point-Stealing: In bracework, when one dog refuses to honor (back) the other's point but instead moves forward until it, too, smells the bird, it is said to be stealing the other dog's point. This is a serious fault.

Puppy Stakes: Field trial puppy stakes—amateur puppy, open puppy—have age limitations for the dogs entered. In AKC trials, the dogs must be between six and 12 months old. FDSB puppy stakes run between January 1 and June 30 are for dogs born on or after January 1 of the previous year. FDSB puppy stakes run between July 1 and December 31 are for dogs born on or after June 1 of the previous year. See Chapter 22, "Field Trials," for details.

Release: An obedience command telling the dog he is no longer required to obey the last command given. It frees the dog from control. Many use such synonyms as *Okay, Free,* and *School's Out.*

Release Trap: A training device that holds a bird and springs it into flight when triggered by the trainer. Some are triggered mechanically, others electronically. These are excellent training tools for those who do not have permanent grounds on which they can locate callback pens with quail.

Relocate: When birds run ahead of a pointing dog, the dog should move forward to relocate them.

Retrieve: The birddog that runs out, picks up a shot bird, and returns it to his handler is said to retrieve the bird.

Retrieving Instinct: The natural inclination many birddogs have to retrieve. This is, technically, a misnomer, for the dog's instinct is really to carry a kill back to its lair, not to deliver it to the trainer. The trainer turns this instinct into retrieving by becoming a secondary lair for the dog.

Roading: This word has two meanings: 1) A birddog relocating running birds; 2) Any method of running dogs on lead for conditioning.

Self-Hunt: A dog that *self-hunts* runs off (bolts) to hunt for itself instead of for the gun. This is a serious fault.

Senior Testing Level: The middle testing level at AKC hunting tests. See Chapter 23, "Hunting Tests," for details.

Series: The running of the dogs in a given field trial stake, hunting test level, or working certificate test. All dogs entered run the first series. In any subsequent series, the judges choose which dogs they want to see run. See Chapters 22 ("Field Trials"), 23 ("Hunting Tests"), and 24 ("Working Certificate Tests") for details.

Shooting Dog Stakes: FDSB field trial shooting dog stakes are for dogs of all ages, but generally require a more moderate range than stakes designated as all age. See Chapter 22, "Field Trials," for details.

Sit: An obedience command telling the dog to sit on his haunches. Many birddog trainers do not teach their dog to sit, lest they sit on point.

Soft Mouth: The opposite of hardmouth. A dog with a soft mouth retrieves birds without damaging them. This is a very desirable trait in any birddog that retrieves.

Soft on Point: A birddog that lacks intensity on point is said to be soft on point. This is a fault in pointing style because it indicates a lack of desire.

Stake: In a field trial, each stake is a separate competition between the dogs entered only in that stake. See Chapter 22, "Field Trials," for details.

Stand Game: A synonym for *point.* When a dog points, some say he is standing his game.

Staunch: A staunch birddog, after pointing, remains in place until the handler arrives and flushes the bird(s). It may or may not also be steady (see below). Staunchness is a minimum requirement for a usable birddog, for a dog that is not staunch will flush too many birds out of gun range.

Stay: An obedience command telling the dog to remain in place. Most birddog trainers do not use this command, relying instead on *Whoa.*

Steady: A steady birddog, after pointing, remains in place through the flush and shot. It remains in place until commanded to retrieve or is sent on by the handler. This is often called *steady to wing and shot.* It is a synonym for *broke.* This is the ultimate in a fully trained birddog.

Stickiness: The inclination some dogs have to refuse to release retrieved birds. This is a different fault from hardmouth. Most sticky dogs don't harm birds, they just won't let go of them.

Sticky: A sticky dog won't release a retrieved bird to its owner.

Stop to Flush: When a bird flushes wild, without being deliberately flushed by the dog, the birddog should stop immediately and remain in place until ordered on. This allows the handler to shoot the bird.

Since the dog did not cause the flush, this is not a fault. In fact, it is a hunting nicety. More than that, it is the cornerstone for all advanced bird-handling training, such as steadying and honoring.

Style: Most often, this term refers to a birddog's physical attitude and intensity while pointing. Sometimes it also refers to its overall animation and manner of hunting. In this latter sense it is a synonym for *class.*

Trailing: When a birddog follows its bracemate rather than hunting independently, it is said to trail. This is a fault, because it indicates a lack of independence and desire.

Training by Association: Giving a command when the dog is already doing the desired action, such as saying *Kennel* as the dog voluntarily enters its kennel run. This is an excellent way to introduce a new command. The dog associates the word with what he is already doing. Repeated often enough, the dog will tend to perform the action when he hears the word. The dog still requires more formal training to reinforce the command, but this is an easy way to start.

Versatile, or Versatile Hunting Dog: Those continental pointing breeds that participate in testing programs (such as NAVHDA) that require a variety of skills in addition to basic pointing/retrieving of upland birds. They retrieve waterfowl, trail fur, even trail ducks across water.

Whoa: The basic stop command, the single most important command in every birddog's vocabulary. Handlers use it to stop their dogs anywhere, and also as a caution when their dogs point or honor.

Working Certificate Test: Any of the field-performance testing programs sponsored and conducted by the various national breed clubs. Different clubs have different requirements, different testing levels, and different titles, but they are all noncompetitive. Birddog national breed clubs have designed some imaginative and diversified programs. See Chapter 24, "Working Certificate Tests," for details.

Yard Breaking: A synonym for *obedience training.* In yard breaking, the trainer teaches the dog to *Whoa, Heel, Come-In,* and so forth.

APPENDIX

II

Reading Birddog Pedigrees

A pedigree lists the dog's ancestors, usually for four to six generations back, in a schematic form. For each listed dog, the pedigree should give the registered name, abbreviations for all titles won, and any health-clearance numbers received from OFA and CERF. Health clearance numbers are as important to anyone interested in a sound birddog as are the various field-related titles. A dog with unsound hips, unsound elbows, or unhealthy eyes can be a disappointment afield—and an expensive burden at home.

If you understand the meanings of the title abbreviations and health clearance numbers, you can evaluate the dogs in a pedigree reasonably well. You should pay little attention to the merits of dogs more than three generations back, for they contributed little to the dog in question. However, parents, grandparents, and great-grandparents (in order of decreasing importance) contributed substantially. Study those fourteen dogs closely.

Trouble is, all the titles and health clearances in which you are interested are abbreviated, which makes them like hieroglyphics to the typical novice. In this appendix, I will help you break the code so you can better evaluate the pedigrees you see when seeking a birddog, whether puppy or older dog.

Pointing breed pedigrees can contain several confusing factors not encountered in pedigrees of other sporting breeds. Birddogs have two major registries, the FDSB and the AKC, and each has its own array of titles. Spaniels and retrievers have only one (the AKC). (Granted, the UKC has grown in popularity among retrieverites, but it still lags significantly behind the AKC). Further, birddogs have attracted a myriad of other organizations that conduct sundry trials and tests, with associated (and esoteric) titles: NSTRA, ABHA, NBHA, NAVHDA, national breed clubs, and so on.

Quite frankly, it would take a complete book like this to cover *comprehensively* every title you could find in a birddog pedigree. And such a book would be out of date by the time it hit the stores, because new organizations start up new programs with new titles fairly often, and old ones wither and die. In other words, gleaning significant information from some birddog pedigrees can be like trying to get a drink of water from a fire hydrant.

Here I will explain only AKC and FDSB titles. If you find other titles in a pedigree you are studying, get the name and address of the organization that awarded each such title from the seller. Then contact each organization and request the following information: the full name of the title, which is abbreviated on the pedigree; the requirements for earning it; and the date on which this dog received the title.

AMERICAN KENNEL CLUB (AKC) TITLES

The AKC follows this convention in placing titles in a pedigree: Competitive titles precede the dog's name; noncompetitive titles follow the dog's name; health clearances go below the dog's name. AKC has only recently worked out arrangements with OFA and CERF to include their health clearance numbers in AKC certified pedigrees. This can only be seen as a giant step forward.

An AKC certified pedigree carries only AKC titles and OFA and CERF health clearance numbers. Few breeders show prospective buyers AKC certified pedigrees, both because of their cost and because they do not contain non-AKC titles, which breeders consider important. If you know and trust a breeder, accept his non-AKC pedigree as reliable. If you don't know him well enough to trust or distrust him, request an AKC certified pedigree before you buy. If you know and *distrust* him, use common sense: Don't do business with him regardless.

AKC Competitive Titles

AFC (also AFTC, Am.Fld.Ch.): Amateur Field Champion, the title won in the amateur all age and amateur gun dog stakes in AKC field trials. This title indicates outstanding field ability. In four breeds (GSP, GWP, Weimaraner, Vizsla), it indicates retrieving ability. In two breeds (GWP, Weimaraner), it indicates water retrieving ability.

CH: Champion, the conformation title won in AKC dog shows. This title indicates that the dog is a good physical specimen of its breed, but says nothing (one way or the other) about its field ability.

DC (also Dual Ch.): Dual champion, the title indicating that the dog has won both the FC and the CH titles. This title indicates that the dog is both a good physical specimen of its breed and an outstanding worker afield.

FC (also FTC, Fld.Ch.): Field Champion, the title won in the open all age and open gun dog stakes at AKC field trials. This title indicates outstanding field ability. In four breeds (GSP, GWP, Weimaraner, Vizsla), it indicates retrieving ability. In two breeds (GWP, Weimaraner), it indicates water retrieving ability.

NAFC (also NAFTC, Nat.Am.Fld.Ch.): National Amateur Field Champion, the title won in the annual AKC national amateur field trial conducted by each of several pointing breeds. This title indicates outstanding field ability. In four breeds (GSP, GWP, Weimaraner, Vizsla), it indicates retrieving ability. In two breeds (GWP, Weimaraner), it indicates water retrieving ability.

NFC (also NFTC, Nat.Fld.Ch.): National Field Champion, the title won in the annual AKC national amateur field trial conducted by each of several pointing breeds. This title indicates outstanding field ability. In four breeds (GSP, GWP, Weimaraner, Vizsla), it indicates retrieving ability. In two breeds (GWP, Weimaraner), it indicates water retrieving ability. Starting in 1994 AKC also sponsors an annual all pointing breed national championship field trial. The winner receives the NFC Title.

OTCH: Obedience Trial Champion, the competitive title won in AKC obedience trials. This title indicates outstanding trainability but says nothing (one way or the other) about its field ability.

TRI-CH: Triple Champion, the title that indicates that the dog has earned the following three titles: CH, FC, OTCH. This title indicates that the dog is an outstanding all-around dog—a good physical specimen, an outstanding worker afield, and a highly trainable animal.

AKC Noncompetitive Titles

CD: Companion Dog, the lowest level title earned in AKC obedience trials. This title indicates basic trainability but says nothing (one way or the other) about field ability.

CDX: Companion Dog Excellent, the middle level title earned in AKC obedience trials. This title indicates significant trainability but says nothing (one way or the other) about field ability.

JH: Junior Hunter, the lowest level title earned in AKC hunting tests. This title indicates basic field ability.

MH: Master Hunter, the highest level title earned in AKC hunting tests. This title indicates very significant field ability, including retrieving ability.

SH: Senior Hunter, the middle level title earned in AKC hunting tests. This title indicates significant field ability, including retrieving ability.

TD: Tracking Dog, the lower level title earned in AKC tracking tests. This title indicates significant ability to trail human scent but says nothing (one way or the other) about field ability.

TDX: Tracking Dog Excellent, the higher level title earned in AKC tracking tests. This title indicates very significant ability to trail human scent but says nothing (one way or the other) about field ability.

UD: Utility Dog, the highest level title earned in AKC obedience trials. This title indicates outstanding trainability but says nothing (one way or the other) about field ability.

UDT: Utility Dog Tracker, a title given a dog that has earned both the UD and the TD titles.

UDTX: Utility Dog Tracker Excellent, a title given a dog that has earned both the UD and the TDX titles.

Health Clearances

OFA-BR-1234E25M-T: This is an Orthopedic Foundation for Animals (OFA) hip clearance number indicating the dog has normal hips. The BR is a breed code, in this case indicating a Brittany. IS is for Irish Setter, GSP for German Shorthaired Pointer, and so on. The next part, 1234 here, is a sequential number assigned by breed. This number would indicate that this dog was the 1,234th Brittany to receive an OFA clearance number. The E is a code indicating the level of clearance (E = Excellent; G = Good; F = Fair). The 25 indicates the dog's age (in months) at the time of the clearance. The M indicates a male (an F would indicate a female). The -T indicates that the dog has been tattooed. This last code is omitted for dogs that have not been tattooed. OFA numbers are permanent and need not be periodically renewed (as must CERF numbers, below).

OFA-GSPEL-123-T: This is an OFA elbow clearance number indicating that the dog has normal elbows. The GSP indicates a German Shorthaired Pointer. The EL indicates elbow clearance. The 123 is a sequential number assigned by breed. The -T indicates that the dog has been tattooed. OFA numbers are permanent and need not be periodically renewed (as must CERF numbers, below).

CERF-ES123/95-18: This is a Canine Eye Registry Foundation (CERF) eye clearance number indicating that the dog has normal eyes. The ES indicates English Setter. The 123 is a sequential number assigned by breed. The 95 indicates the year in which the clearance was issued, and the -18 gives the age of the dog (in months) at which the clearance was received. CERF numbers are valid only for one year, so an old one on a pedigree should be viewed with suspicion.

FIELD DOG STUD BOOK (FDSB) PEDIGREES

The FDSB sponsors only field trials. They have no conformation or obedience competitions. Thus, any information you may find on an FDSB-certified pedigree refers to accomplishments in their field trials. As with AKC pedigrees, you should insist on seeing an FDSB-certified pedigree before you buy unless you know and trust the breeder.

The FDSB places on its certified pedigrees only one title, CH (which stands for Champion). This title goes immediately before the dog's name. The pedigree carries no indication of what titular event(s) the dog won to earn the title. However, whatever it was (or they were), it indicates outstanding field ability. If you wonder about the specific accomplishments of a certain dog, contact FDSB (see Appendix III, "Important Contacts"), and they will provide you with that information.

The only possible confusion here is with the AKC CH title, which means a conformation champion but not necessarily a good field dog. If you study only certified pedigrees (whether AKC or FDSB), you should suffer no confusion over the differing meanings of the two CH titles. If you accept a breeder-produced pedigree, especially for a dual-registered puppy (or dog), you should do whatever research you need to do to distinguish the AKC from the FDSB CH titles. I recommend that you insist on seeing both an AKC and an FDSB-certified pedigree for any dual-registered pup or dog you are considering.

On its deluxe certified pedigrees, FDSB also places a set of three numbers under each dog's name. The first number gives the total number of placements the dog won in FDSB field trials. The second number gives the number of winning progeny the dog produced. The third number gives the total number of wins the progeny of this dog earned. These last two numbers are especially valuable in evaluating a dog as breeding stock.

APPENDIX

III

Important Contacts

REGISTRIES

American Kennel Club (AKC)
51 Madison Avenue
New York, NY 10010
(212) 696-8200

Field Dog Stud Book (FDSB)
542 South Dearborn Street
Chicago, IL 60605
(312) 663-9797

United Kennel Club (UKC)
100 East Kilgore Road
Kalamazoo, MI 49001-5598
(616) 343-9020

FIELD TRIAL & TEST SPONSORS

The addresses of many of these organizations change periodically. For the latest information, contact the AKC or the FDSB.

American Kennel Club (AKC)
51 Madison Avenue
New York, NY 10010

Field Dog Stud Book (FDSB)
542 South Dearborn Street
Chicago, IL 60605

Amateur Field Trial Clubs of America (AFTCA)
Linda Hunt, Secretary
360 Winchester Lane
Stanton, TN 38069

American Bird Hunters Association (ABHA)
Charles Adams, Secretary
510 East Davis Field Road
Muskogee, OK 74401

National Bird Hunters Association (NBHA)
Jeff Hardy, Secretary
P.O. Box 1106
Van, TX 75790

National Shoot-To-Retrieve Association (NSTRA)
Lyle Jordon, President
226 North Mill Street, #2
Plainfield, IN 46168

U.S. Complete Shooting Dog Association
Jan M. Shaw, President
2501 Marguerite Drive
Greensboro, NC 27406

North American Versatile Hunting Dog Association (NAVHDA)
P.O. Box 520
Arlington Heights, IL 60006

NATIONAL BREED CLUBS

The secretaries of these clubs change periodically. For more information, contact the AKC or the FDSB.

AKC Affiliated

American Brittany Club, Inc.
Ms. Joy Watkins
Route 1, Box 114BB
Aledo, TX 76008

American Pointer Club, Inc.
Ms. Karen E. Breeden
P.O. Box 118
Beaver, WV 25813

German Shorthaired Pointer Club of America
Ms. Geraldine A. Irwin
1101 West Quincy
Englewood, CO 80110

German Wirehaired Pointer Club of America
Ms. Barbara Hein
3838 Davison Lake Road
Ortonville, MI 48462

English Setter Association of America
Mrs. Dawn S. Ronyak
114 South Burlington Oval Drive
Chardon, OH 44024

Gordon Setter Club of America, Inc.
Ms. Cathie M. Rzepka
6380 North Territorial Road
Plymouth, MI 48170

Irish Setter Club of America, Inc.
Mrs. Marion J. Pahy
16717 Ledge Falls
San Antonio, TX 78232

Vizsla Club of America, Inc.
Ms. Jan Bouman
15744 Hampshire Avenue South
Prior Lake, MN 55372

Weimaraner Club of America
Mrs. Dorothy Derr
P.O. Box 110708
Nashville, TN 37222-0708

American Wirehaired Pointing Griffon Association
Denny Smith
90566 Coburg Road
Eugene, OR 97401

FDSB Affiliated

National German Shorthaired Pointer Association
Linda Nickerson
P.O. Box 12263
Overland Park, KS 66212

National Red Setter Field Trial Club
Conrad Plevnic
Route 2, Box 748
Terrell, TX 75160

Independent

Wirehaired Pointing Griffon Club of America
Joan Bailey
2373 NW 185th Street, #417
Hilsboro, OR 97124

NATIONAL CONSERVATION ORGANIZATIONS

These organizations promote conservation, especially through habitat improvement and management. Open to private membership, they publish magazines (for members) of interest to birddog owners.

Pheasants Forever
P.O. Box 75473
St. Paul, MN 55175
(612) 481-7142

Ruffed Grouse Society
1400 Lee Drive
Corapolis, PA 15108
(412) 262-4044

Quail Unlimited
P.O. Box 10041
Augusta, GA 30903
(803) 637-5731

Ducks Unlimited
One Waterfowl Way
Long Grove, IL 60047
(901) 758-3825

BIRDDOG-RELATED MAGAZINES

Gun Dog
Stover Publications, Inc.
1901 Bell Avenue, Suite 4
Des Moines, IA 50315
(515) 243-2472

Pointing Breed Field Trial News
American Kennel Club
51 Madison Avenue
New York, NY 10010
(212) 696-8250

Wing & Shot
Stover Publications, Inc.
1901 Bell Avenue, Suite 4
Des Moines, IA 50315
(515) 243-2472

The American Field
Field Dog Stud Book
542 South Dearborn Street
Chicago, IL 60605
(312) 663-9797

Hunting Test Herald
American Kennel Club
51 Madison Avenue
New York, NY 10010
(212) 696-8250

Pointing Dog Journal
P.O. Box 936
Manitowoc, WI 54221-0936
(414) 682-0000

CANINE TATTOO REGISTRIES

National Dog Registry
Box 116
Woodstock, NY 12498-0116
(800) NDR-DOGS

Tattoo-A-Pet
1625 Emmons Avenue
Brooklyn, NY 11235
(800) 246-1216

CANINE HEALTH CLEARANCE ORGANIZATIONS

CERF (Canine Eye Registry Foundation)
Purdue University
1235 South Campus Courts, Bldg. A
West Lafayette, IN 47907-1235
(317) 494-8179

OFA (Orthopedic Foundation for Animals)
University of Missouri
2300 Nifong Boulevard
Columbia, MO 65201
(314) 442-0418

INDEX